Gospel Advocate Biography Library

Biography of H. Leo Boles

I'll Stand on the Rock

Leo Lipscomb Boles
and J.E. Choate

GOSPEL
ADVOCATE
A TRUSTED NAME SINCE 1855

Gospel Advocate Company
P.O. Box 150
Nashville, Tennessee 37202

Biography of H. Leo Boles: I'll Stand on the Rock
Gospel Advocate Biography Library, 2001

© 1965, Gospel Advocate Company

Published by Gospel Advocate Co.
P.O. Box 150, Nashville, TN 37202
www.gospeladvocate.com

ISBN: 0-89225-475-0

DEDICATION

This book is dedicated to the loyal members of the churches of Christ throughout the world, who each Lord's day worship in the manner ordained by the New Testament.

Most especially is this dedication to that great host of faithful Christians who are firmly standing on the "Rock," and who are honored to be counted among Boles' "children" in the gospel.

Finally, this effort is dedicated to H. Leo Boles' disciple and staunch friend, Benton Cordell Goodpasture, who for a quarter of a century as Editor of the *Gospel Advocate* has also traveled in the main stream of Restoration History.

CONTENTS

FOREWORD

The Restoration Movement on the American frontier is the most significant single event that has occurred in church history within the last one hundred fifty years. Upon the western slopes of the Appalachians, and in the fertile valleys of the Ohio, Tennessee and Cumberland rivers, as well as the not so fertile soil of these rivers' smaller tributaries, a New Testament Christianity was planted and flourished. The Restoration Movement has now grown until it has spread throughout this nation, and its seeds now have been planted in the uttermost corners of the earth.

Most of the major religious groups in America today are transplants from Europe. The Restoration Movement is indigenous to this country and is unique in its avowed purpose. Free from the pomp and ceremony that marked the churches of the Medieval Ages, and free from the trappings and embellishments of the magnificent cathedrals of Europe, the roughhewn churches of the American frontier were also free of the religious hierarchy, associations, conventions, and synods of the Old World. The people living on the frontier were used to hardship and privation, and they took their comfort mainly from their Bibles. They envisioned a humble Savior who tread the arid paths of Galilee preaching a gospel so plain and simple that all who heard could understand.

The names of Alexander Campbell and Barton W. Stone are immortalized for the roles they played in the early years of the Restoration. The lives of Tolbert Fanning and David Lipscomb must also be associated forever with the efforts to return New Testament Christianity to its original character. H. Leo Boles, by virtue of hard facts must now occupy a major place in the history of the New Testament Church in modern times.

In many respects Boles may be called the "last of the pioneer preachers" inasmuch as he not only reaffirmed most of the positions taken by the early leaders of the Restoration Movement in his hundreds of articles published in the *Gospel Advocate*, but he also met many departures from the scriptural pattern of the New Testament Church with uncompromising vigor and zeal. H. Leo Boles was a direct descendant of the pioneer preacher, "Raccoon" John Smith, and Boles was just as resolute in his "stand on the Rock" as his famous forefather. But because of his splendid, although hard-won education, the defense of the Gospel by Boles was superior to that of his forebear. He was a scholar and the far-reaching power of his printed words made the name of Boles familiar to thousands of Christians throughout the land. These facts coupled with the hundreds of students whom Boles taught made his place in the later days of the Restoration secure.

David Lipscomb in 1913 personally placed his mantle upon the younger Boles when he selected him to direct the activities of the Nashville Bible School. David Lipscomb at first supported, then subsequently depended upon Boles until the day of his death. The intervening years bear eloquent testimony to the judgment of Lipscomb in his decision.

The members of the churches of Christ wishing to honor David Lipscomb have often done so, but only in recent years has the unparalleled significance of David Lipscomb to church history come into such sharp focus. Many people who should also have honored H. Leo Boles for cherishing and defending the ideals of Lipscomb and his associates have often neglected to do so. The irony of this, in some measure, may be attributed to Boles himself because of the direct and abrupt manner in which he went about practically everything that he did.

H. Leo Boles needs no introduction to the tens of thousands who knew him in his lifetime. To those who did not, Boles distinguished himself as a preacher, writer, debater, and a Christian educator. In these respects he had no superior among his brethren. Lest the memory of this singular man fade into oblivion this biography is erected as a lasting monument to his words and deeds, and only eternity can record the full measure of his life. Boles' supreme mission in life was to restore New Testament Christianity in this century to its Scriptural purity. He travelled in the main stream of the Restoration Movement in its later years. Few, indeed, could be found who would say that Boles did not do his part, and now he too belongs to the ages.

The composition of this biography is suited to its subject. H. Leo Boles was a man of directness and simplicity. There was in his character an austerity and severity that shunned compromise. This biography does not attempt to portray him as a perfect man, nor would Boles have wished it. He was both a good and a great man, and he knew better than anyone else his self-contradictions and inconsistencies.

Many of Boles' former students and other associates have contributed to this work. It would be impossible to list them all. This biography grew out of the desire his friends had to honor him and to give him his proper place in history; the place he already holds in the hearts of his brethren. To all those who have helped, researched, written, or otherwise given their sympathy, the co-authors wish to express their warmest heartfelt thanks. Without the help of many hands this book simply could not have reached publication.

Chapter I

SCION OF IRELAND

The story of the life of H. Leo Boles may well be a part of the life and legends of "Old Ireland"; to say the least, the Boles family have always regarded it so. The paths of the ancient Celts and Anglo-Saxons have so often merged and crossed it would be of little profit to tarry long in this place. The history of no other country is interwoven with mystery and legend as is that of Ireland. This island of mists and shadows has been shrouded in antiquity for so long that today it is difficult to trace the history of the tribes and races of people who have invaded the country at different remote periods.

The derivation, therefore, of the origin and meaning of a surname such as "Boles" must remain a subject of considerable uncertainty. One theory holds that the name is of Saxon origin, coming from the occupation of a "Bollman," or steward. Another theory has it that the name is derived from the Norse word "Bauli," meaning "bull." Still another belief postulates that the name has descended from the Viking "Bolla," who according to tradition, was one of the Norse conquerors in the ninth century. Finally a fourth view has it that the name originated in Normandy, possibly having been taken from the Norman town of Boulles, and transplanted to Ireland by an individual known as Bole, or Bolle, following the invasion of William the Conqueror in 1066.

Which of the above assumptions, if indeed any, is true probably will never be proven. One thing, however, seems positive; the name of O'Bolles was fairly well established in Cork County, Ireland, by the turn of the sixteenth century, which gave ample time to stamp the family as Irish. The surname was pronounced in three syllables with the accent on the second or middle syllable as "O—Bol'—les".

When the world was less crowded with people, only one name was necessary to identify a man or woman. As

1

the earth became more densely populated it became necessary to show both family relations and individual personalities. For that reason both Christian or given names, and surnames were needed. Surnames, in the sense of hereditary designations, are only about nine hundred years old. Some surnames were modified to denote the relationship of a son by simply adding a prefix or suffix. English names show "son of" by ending in *son, ing and kin,* or by names prefixed with the Gaelic *Mac,* the Norman *Fitz* and the Irish *O'*. Thus William's son became Williamson; Donald's son, Donaldson; Dougall's son, MacDougall; Patrick's son, FitzPatrick and Brien's son, O'Brien.

It has been ascertained that two unmarried brothers name of O'Bolles sailed from Plymouth, England, bound for Jamestown in the colony of Virginia in the spring of 1710. Upon landing in the New World, they rightly left the "O'" off their name, using the two syllable word "Bol'-les." The Boles progenitors moved through the crowded and mosquito infested tidewater region of Virginia, stopping for a while in the "back country" of that colony, and thence moving on to eventually settle on the frontier. The inhabitants of the wilderness soon took care of the two-syllable surname and contracted it into the monosyllable "Boles."

The bearers of the name Boles liked the contraction. It was a short, distinctive name, easy to pronounce. It was a new name in a new free land. It was to become the badge of family honor. It was to be a "good" name of which its descendants could be proud; a name to wear and protect, and should the occasion demand, for which to fight. The marching generations were to give the name character and dignity. The name "Boles" has become the most treasured possession of those who bear it.

Names become changed through either accident, ignorance or preference. Most of the corruption of family surnames seems to have resulted from errors in spelling or variations in pronunciation. The most common deviation of the name "Boles" appears to be doubling the "l" or placing a "w" in the word. The surname is found in the various records as Bolls, Bolles, Bowles, Bows, Bowls and even Booles. After all, there were very few people who could read and write on the American frontier of 1750!

It seems fairly well established that the progentry of the subject of this biography were literate and thus spelled their name the way they preferred. The Boles were a religious family and they reasoned that their children should be taught to read and understand the Holy Bible if they were to be saved. Thus the bearers of the name Boles, though often physically frail, bequeathed to their offspring a birthright much more valuable on the frontier than gold—they taught their children to read and interpret the Bible for themselves!

Progenitors must be considered in this biography other than those who came from across the Irish Sea. Even though obvious, it seems worthy to note here that every child has two parents, four grandparents, eight great-grandparents, sixteen great-great-grandparents, and so on, *ad infinitum*. It was only three generations from the American War of Independence to the War Between the States. A child born in 1874 would be in the fourth generation after the American colonies rebuked the mother country. Thus there sixteen ancestors who contributed more or less equally to the hereditary characteristics of a fourth generation offspring.

Ordinarily it is much simpler to trace the paternal surname line than it is to pierce the shadowy darkness that veils the ancestry of the maternal names. This is especially true of the frontier ancestry where first hand records may have been a family Bible that has long since been lost, moth-eaten or otherwise destroyed. If indeed only the great-great-grandfather's surname is known, then it follows by simple arithmetic that fifteen-sixteenth of the heredity from the fourth generation has been lost.

Happily, tracing the lines of inheritance of H. Leo Boles in this biography is by no means hopeless or obscured. Enough of his ancestors and their characteristics are known so that it is fairly easy to ascertain the inheritance of this individual. The environment of all of these ancestors is known. The historical geography of the Tennessee and Kentucky mountains had a way of stamping its own, and the indelible marks of the wilderness left its imprint upon all who inhabited this region.

A progenitor of H. Leo Boles on the maternal side who came into the wilderness about 1775 was Johann Schmidt. He had tired of the religious upheaval in his native German state and had come westward to seek his way in the New World. The frontier soon made Johann Schmidt just plain John Smith. He migrated to the western slopes of the Carolina Appalachians, where he settled in a small V-shaped valley, cleared up a little land, married and raised a family of eleven children, six boys and five girls.

The oldest son of John Smith (Johann Schmidt) was named George Smith. George married the daughter of an Irish immigrant named Bowen, who lived in a nearby valley, and the two of them set out to settle and clear themselves a small farm of their own. There was so much land to the west and it was theirs for the taking!

George and Rebecca Bowen Smith cleared the primeval forest to build their cabin in Sullivan County, Charter Colony of North Carolina. This location is now in East Tennessee, but since that state was not admitted to the Union until 1796, the area yet belonged to North Carolina.

George Smith volunteered for service in the Continental Army. He fought valiantly at King's Mountain; rendered distinguished service at Yorktown and did not return home until after the British had finally surrendered to Washington in 1780.

Rebecca Bowen Smith was a remarkable woman. During the Revolutionary War while George was away, this woman was winning the economic battle by providing a living for herself and her eight children by working their small farm. It was a precarious existence, but Rebecca managed "to do," and at the end of the war George Smith returned home to find his family well and his farm intact. George and Rebecca no doubt had been impressed with the strength of the combined mutual assistance of the thirteen colonies, and upon his return home the family was expanded to include thirteen children.

The ninth child was born October 15, 1784. This boy was named John, possibly in honor of his grandfather, Johann, from Germany, but the child was to become one of the most prominent and beloved men on the frontier under the appellation "Raccoon" John Smith.

George Smith was a devout follower of John Calvin, and his children were reared in the strict obedience demanded by the Baptist Church. His son John accepted the family's beliefs. Very early in life he developed a strong desire to become a preacher. According to the Calvinistic theory, before a person could preach, he first had to "get religion" and "join the church." Then in order to preach, he had to "be called." John Smith tried in vain to "get religion," but each time he seemed to fail miserably. In his disappointment John turned to reading the Bible, in the hope that he might find comfort for his distressed condition. Finally, the "elect" told him that he had been converted, and eventually his Baptist brethren thought that he had received the "call" to preach the Gospel. John accepted the word of the Baptist Association which had ordained him to preach, even though he still had grave doubt in his own mind on the matter.

John Smith continued to read the New Testament. He memorized great portions of the scriptures, and in his sermons he freely quoted from the Bible. It was a rare thing in those days for a frontier preacher to quote from the Bible and some of his brethren reprimanded him for it. When he was called before the Baptist Association to explain himself, Smith was plainly confused. He simply said, "Brethren, what shall I do? I must preach! I cannot preach if I do not study the New Testament." He was told that the Lord would put the words into his mouth; all he had to do was to "open his mouth and let the Spirit of the Lord pour forth!" John Smith knew that this was not so. He had to work hard to prepare his sermons.

It was inevitable that John Smith should run afoul of the dictates of the Baptist Association. He preached the New Testament Church as he read and interpreted it from the Scriptures. Whenever the teaching of the Bible crossed with the doctrine of the Baptist Church, John

Smith unhesitatingly preached the Bible. This kept him in constant turmoil with the Association. The latter was loath to press its charges against Smith, however, for he was becoming by far the most powerful and effective Baptist preacher on the frontier. Smith drifted farther and farther away from the erroneous teachings of the Calvinists, until when the break finally came, it was John Smith who withdrew from the Baptist Association, not the Association that withdrew from him.

John Smith received his unusual nickname rather early in his preaching career. He had been invited to make an address at the meeting of the Tate's Creek Baptist Association at Crab Orchard, Kentucky, in 1815. A vast audience had assembled but seeing Smith's striped coat and general unkempt appearance, started to leave when he got up to speak. John Smith's eloquence however, soon had the crowd leaning forward in their seats. He said, "I am John Smith from Stockton's Valley. In more recent years, I have lived in Wayne, among the rocks and hills of the Cumberland. Down there, saltpeter caves abound and raccoons make their homes." Forever after the nickname, "Raccoon," was attached to his name.

John Smith was a man with very little formal education. He attended school four months in a log school house when he was but a lad. A little later he enrolled as a student in a private school. This school was so crude that it accomplished very little. The teacher was a drunkard, and frequently came to school in an intoxicated condition. Young Smith one day expressed his contempt for such a teacher by pouring a shovel full of hot embers in the teacher's coat pocket while he sat before his pupils in a drunken stupor. This broke up the school and he never again enrolled in a school, consequently he was largely self-educated. He could hold his audiences spellbound with his simple eloquence. He was a product of the wilderness and he understood the nature of his congregations as few men ever did. Consequently, his preaching struck fire in the hearts of the backwoods people who heard him. Alexander Campbell, who in later life became closely associated with him said, "John Smith is the only man that I ever knew who would have been spoiled by a college education."

Many stories are told concerning "Raccoon" John Smith's wit and repartee. He was accustomed to rise early and take a long walk through the woods. This time was spent in solitary prayer and meditation. One morning three boys, wishing to play a practical joke on the old preacher, hid themselves at various points along the path that Elder Smith's walk would take him. The first boy meeting him said very politely, "Good morning, Father Abraham." John Smith replied kindly, "Good morning, son." A few moments later the second boy interrupted John Smith's solitude by stepping out from the tree behind which he had been hiding and said, "Good morning, Father Isaac." "Raccoon" John Smith looked at him sharply, but he answered gently, "Good morning, son" and continued on his walk. After he had taken only a few paces, the third boy appeared in the pathway and cried in a loud voice, "Good morning, Father Jacob." That was more than John Smith could take and he answered tartly, "I am neither Abraham, Isaac, nor Jacob, but I am Saul seeking his father's asses, and lo, I have found three of them already this morning!"

One time when Elder John Smith was making his home in Huntsville, Alabama, a terrible catastrophe befell him. His family at the time consisted of his wife and four small children. While he was away from home on a preaching tour, his house and two of the children were destroyed by fire. Two little girls were rescued from the burning building. One of these was Jane, who grew up to marry Thomas Jefferson Boles, of Kentucky, who was a surprisingly well-read young man for this region.

Thomas Jefferson Boles must have met the rigid requirements of Elder Smith. The marriage with Jane produced only one child; Henry Jefferson Boles. This child was born posthumously, as Thomas had died of a summer disease, probably typhoid fever, a few months before.

Henry Jefferson Boles was born in Caldwell County, Kentucky, on November 19, 1845. As the grandson of "Raccoon" John Smith, "Jeff" Boles was in the company of Elder Smith many times and he often heard him preach. It was only natural that Jeff should have a strong desire to become a preacher of the Gospel like his illustrious grandfather.

The dark clouds of war were gathering ominously after Abraham Lincoln was elected president in November of 1860. He had run for office on an Abolishionist platform and had received less than half the votes cast, as there were five candidates in the race. Lincoln did not carry a single Southern state. The secession movement was already in full flower when President Lincoln took the oath of office. It was quite apparent that the thunder of cannon and the whine of Minie balls were soon to be heard. Hitherto small insignificant places like Bull Run, Shiloh Church House, Seven Pines and Chickamauga would shortly leap into prominence, and would become immortalized forever afterward in the chronicles of American history.

A way of life in the southern valleys and coastal plains was soon to perish. The entire framework of the culture of the "Old South," which was based upon slavery and the production of the export crops of cotton and tobacco was destined soon to pass. As Margaret Mitchell phrased it, a civilization would abruptly be "gone with the wind," and not only Tara, but practically every other plantation mansion would be defiled and destroyed by the armies of Sherman, Sheridan, Thomas and Grant. The Confederate soldiers who survived the war would return to their once-proud Southland only to break the ashen crust, and it was to be moistened with the tears of the mothers, widows and children whose loved ones would never return from the war.

Mountain economy was, of necessity, based upon small farms. The geography of the frontier did not permit the development of large estates. Consequently there were no plantations in the Cumberlands and Negro slaves were practically nonexistent.

The land of the wilderness was not cleared with backbreaking labor in order to grow cotton. The pioneers living in the mountainous regions of Virginia, Kentucky, North Carolina and Tennessee had entirely too much trouble in producing the staplefood crops on which they reared their large families to worry about the problems of slavery, or the growing of export commodities. The entire idea of human bondage was completely contrary to their way of thinking, consequently the mountain people were tremendously anti-slavery in their sentiments as many of their ancestors had come to this country as bonded servants.

The impact of the bloody fratracidal struggle caused serious repercussions even on the people living in the isolated parts of the Cumberlands. Their Virginia kinsmen who inhabited the remote mountainous section of that state found a unique solution. After Virginia had seceded from the United States, the people of the wilderness in turn seceded from Virginia. They applied for admission into the Union during the war, and were admitted as the state of West Virginia in 1863.

The mountain people of Tennessee did not bother to try to secede from anybody. Their menfolk simply "joined up" with the Union army. It is significant that Tennessee was the last Confederate state to leave the Union and the first to be re-admitted after the war was over. It is equally significant that Kentucky never seceded from the Union at all.

It should be noted here that the East Tennessee mountaineer, Andrew Johnson, was not only appointed by President Lincoln to serve as the military governor of Tennessee after it fell before the terrific onslaughts of the Northern armies, but he was also Lincoln's own choice for the office of vice-president of the United States. Upon the assassination of Lincoln in 1865, Johnson succeeded to the presidency itself.

When the volunteer regiment of Glasgow, Kentucky, marched away to join the Union army in 1861, Jeff Boles, a youth of sixteen, was with them. He was wounded three times in battle and received his honorable discharge only after Lee had surrendered to Grant at Appomattox four years later. Jeff Boles was a veteran of the murderous War between the States at the age of twenty! From Jeff's viewpoint the war had delayed the start of his preaching career nine years.

9

George Smith of the thirteen children fame had a brother who had laboriously made his way westward into Kentucky country through the Cumberland Gap in one of the first parties that Daniel Boone had consented to guide. He had a son whose name was Thomas. This Thomas Smith was the father of a girl named Sarah Smith. Thus Sarah was the grandniece of Raccoon John Smith.

Henry Jefferson Boles and Sarah Smith lived in the same rural community not far from the present town of Glasgow, Kentucky. Upon Jeff's return from the war, he began courting Sarah, and in 1870 when Jeff was twenty-five, he married this distant member of his mother's family.

Jeff immediately moved with his young bride to his recently acquired farm in Jackson County, Tennessee. There he and Sarah began on their own and tilled the virgin soil "until death did them part."

The ancestry of H. Leo Boles, the son of Henry Jefferson Boles and Sarah Smith, has been briefly sketched in this chapter. The heredity of the inhabitants of the Cumberland was the birthright of this boy.

The people of the Cumberland country in the latter third of the nineteenth century were almost totally of Scotch, Irish and German descent. The rugged geography of this land that kept both the inhabitants in, and the later immigrants out, led to frequent intermarriage between cousins. The inherited characteristics of the Cumberland people, as well as their civilization, was almost pure Elizabethan. The people of this region became welded together under the general name of "Scotch-Irish." This term was used to include the fused mixture of Welsh, English, German and the few French Huguenots who had drifted up from the Carolinas. The name "Scotch-Irish" became broadened to characterize the distinct people who developed in the isolated valleys and plateaus on the western slopes of the Appalachians. It came about that these people, in time, were almost as different in their culture as the Canadians of today are from the people of Texas.

The son of Henry Jefferson Boles must be classified as Scotch-Irish, but by blood, temperament, appearance, personality and loyalty he was a throw-back to his forebears in County Cork. After almost 200 years in the Cumberland country, during which the Irish blood was freely mingled with the German, Scotch and English, a boy was born, who, although far removed from Erin's green, was nevertheless a scion of old Ireland.

Chapter II

A BOY IS BORN ON FLYNN'S CREEK

The winter of 1874 had been a severe one for the inhabitants of the Upper Cumberland region of Tennessee. Particularly it seemed that the people of the Flynn's community of Jackson County had suffered. But now, on February 22, the winter seemed to have broken. According to the popular superstition there, the ground hog had not seen his shadow as it had been cloudy. Consequently most people were convinced that the spring could not be far away.

The landscape was not very pretty at that time of year. The cold winter had left its imprint upon almost everything out-of-doors. The usual rich green of the indigenous vegetation and the wild flowers with their beauty and fragrance were still at least six weeks away. Instead, the dark brown of the fallen leaves, the full cinnamon color of the fallow fields, and the lighter tawny brown of the dead grass that footed the black skeletons of the leafless trees, were everywhere to be seen. Even the wildlife all seemed to have hibernated for the winter, or had moved away entirely until spring should come. Not even a bird was to be seen. Nature indeed seemed dead on this anniversary of George Washington's birthday. Only a few evergreen trees, mostly red cedars, and the clear waters of Flynn's Creek, swollen by the melting snow and sparkling in the sunlight, seemed alive.

In a log cabin along this stream, however, it was evident that life existed. There were many signs of human activity about the house.

Henry Jefferson Boles, from Allen County, Kentucky, with the help of a few neighbors, had recently felled the logs and constructed this cabin. Only about three months before, Jeff had brought his wife Sarah to live here and rear their growing family.

The activity within and around this cabin in the Cumberlands was climaxed during the mid-afternoon by the sudden cry of a newborn infant. In the midst of these seemingly dead surroundings nature had compensated by the birth of a baby boy. This child who was born on the same day of the year as was the Father of his Country, was a child who was destined to influence the lives of thousands of his fellow Americans during the next seven decades. Many of these people were to owe their soul salvation and their hope for a life after the grave to this child who was that day born on Flynn's Creek.

Flynn's Creek had derived its name from an early Irish immigrant of that name. Buffalo, deer, bear and turkey, as well as other game abounded in the wilderness. Mr. Flynn especially liked to see the deer thrive, so he put salt out around his place for these animals. The deer would come and lick the salt, thus the place, in time, became known as Flynn's Lick.

Henry Jefferson Boles had built his cabin on the south fork of Flynn's Creek in very rugged country. The Boles farm was located a few miles up the "creek" from Flynn's Lick yet several hours were required to make the trip to this intersection with civilization where supplies could be procured. The farm itself consisted of both rich and poor land, but so much more of it was poor than rich. The narrow strip of flood plain on both sides of the branch was fabulously fertile. Corn grown on this part of the farm, even today, may reach a height of from twelve to eighteen feet. A little garden cultivated there could be made to produce enough vegetables to support a small family. The rest of the farm was so precipitous that it could be used only for wood, pasturage for the family cow, or perhaps a small orchard or vineyard.

Flynn's Lick, located in the ancient Indian "Valley of the Graves," consisted of six springs; five limestone and one sulphur. It was significant because it lay directly along the "Old Road" and it was an important stagecoach stop as passengers bound for Gainsborough as well as other points up the river would board the coach there. The traditional "Old Road" was followed by those who traveled from the Watauga settlements in the Tennessee valley around Knoxville, to the "blue grass" region of central Kentucky and middle Tennessee.

Following the "Old Road" west as did so many pioneers, this traffic artery crossed the Clinch River at Low's Ferry and entered the eastern ridges of the Cumberland Mountains through Emory Gap, which is close to the present town of Harriman. On ascending Crab Orchard Mountain, it passed over a large area of uncovered stone called the "Flat Rock," thence it went through Standing Stone, now Monterey. From there the Old Road went to Cookeville and descended the mountain by way of Post Oak Valley into Flynn's Lick, crossing the Cumberland River at Fort Blount. From Fort Blount, the route to Nashville passed through Dixon Springs, Hartsville, Castalian Springs and Gallatin.

The evolution of many of the overland route that people follow today is really quite simple. The buffalo paths through the Wilderness became the Indian trail, and this in turn became the pathway of the white man who traded with the Indian. The trails of the Indian trader became the route of the early settler. These trails or "traces" were widened into crude roads, and the roads eventually became turnpikes. The early railroads followed the turnpikes. It is significant that the Tennessee Central railroad from Knoxville to Nashville today uses practically the same route as that taken by Nashville's early overland settlers who followed the Old Road. Thousands of pioneers, relentlessly flowing westward, followed the Old Road from Virginia and North Carolina to settle in the fertile valleys of the Cumberland, the Mississippi, and beyond.

A majority of the great men that our nation has produced have come from pioneer rural America. People today look back on their ancestors and sometimes wonder how they ever managed to survive the hardships of the wilderness at all. But they should not be amazed at the achievements of these people. There were jobs to be done and they had little time for play. They were fearless God-loving people, and they were founding a nation. Perhaps only a few of them realized it, but they were playing a leading role in steadily building the greatest country that the world has ever known.

Henry Leo Boles was the product of the wilderness

and he was impregnated to his utmost nature with the kind of soul substance that is an essential ingredient in all great men. It was not within the make-up of his being to feel fear from carnal man, but it was inevitable that he should acquire from his environment a fear and respect for his Creator that was to influence and mold his life as a twig is bent before the wind. The winds that were to blow upon the infant of Flynn's Creek were at first rather gentle and mild, then they were fated to increase their force until at times they reached hurricane velocity as the true nature and character of the man was being formed.

The environment into which the Boles' baby was born offered both limited and unlimited opportunities. The pathway that one chose could lead to the White House, or it could lead to an ignominious drunkard's grave. No one in this backwoods country ever questioned the fact that here a man was born free, or that all men were created equal. Even then as today the scope of achievement that a man could attain depended mainly on the zeal and ambition of the individual involved and the amount of brains that he had inherited from his parents.

The native intelligence of the Boles family seems to have been enormous in certain individuals, and in others only average, or even sub-par. When Nature decides to put the germ cells of a human embryo together in such a way that a genius is created, she is no respector of time, place, nation or race. It so happened that the Supreme Being richly endowed the child of Flynn's Creek with a superb intellect. The Omnipotent Power, knowing that this life was soon to be dedicated to the dissemination of His Word, equipped the babe with all the accoutrements both physical and mental that would be needed. Being endowed by his Creator with "ten talents" this boy was destined to go forth into the vineyard and labor unceasingly until the night should fall some seventy-two years later.

The enormity of the harvest for the Cause of Christ that this life was to produce as an evangelist, educational leader, religious writer and theologian was yet to reach fruition.

Chapter III

HERITAGE OF THE CUMBERLANDS

H. Leo Boles loved the high country of the Cumberlands. He thought that no prince could have a richer and nobler heritage, and no scion of noble blood esteemed his heritage and birth right more precious than this "mountain man."

The name Cumberland was introduced into America in honor of the Duke of Cumberland, who commanded the victorious English army at the Battle of Culloden in 1645. The Duke of Cumberland today does not appear to have been particularly important, nor does the Battle of Colloden seem to have must sigificance except that it was the terminating event in the long struggle for civil and religious freedom in England.

The term "Cumberland" proved to be popular on the frontier because it became associated with liberty, and the freedom that the immigrants from Europe so earnestly sought. It symbolized the right of an individual to live his own life and worship his own God in peace. It meant that an individual man, no matter how humble his place in society, should be recognized and honored. Thus it developed that the "Cumberland Gap" became the gateway to the rich promises of endless tracts of wilderness that lay westward in the "Cumberland Country" whose rugged hills and valleys were drained by the tributaries of the "Cumberland River." The settlements in Kentucky and Tennessee were called "Cumberland Settlements" or simply "Cumberlands."

The people who migrated westward through Cumberland Gap came from all strata of society and all walks of life. On the frontier were to be found strong-faithed men and women who wished only to worship God as they interpreted the Bible. In direct contrast to these were the convicted thieves and criminals who had either been pardoned or escaped. Men who had failed in business and had spent years in a debtor's prison were also there on the frontier.

16

Soldiers and sailors who had deserted and runaway, as well as small capitalists who had saved or inherited a little money, and adventurers who had been born with the "wanderlust" were all to be found in the wilderness. Still other groups who had made their way across the mountains consisted of dispossessed farmers, indentured servants and disgruntled noblemen.

The early settlers who passed into the Cumberland Country knew about the perils to be encountered, but whatever the risks, the new land guaranteed freedom, and for that cause alone, they placed their all on the wheel of fortune while they prayed to the Almighty "Thy Will be done." The wheel revolved while the early settlers faced great privations and hardships, but when it ceased spinning, the pioneers found that they had gambled and won! They had hit the jackpot and their wealth was so great that it staggered their imaginations. For the first time in their lives they possessed land of their own, and they were not obliged to say, "Yes Sir," to any man alive!

The children of the original pioneers who settled west of the mountains became the first genuine Americans. For in truth the first immigrants were merely transplanted Englishmen, Frenchmen, or what not, who thought and acted in many ways as they had at home.

The generation born in the trans-mountain country became a westward-facing people. They turned their backs on the Atlanta Seaboard as they continued to carve for themselves a better way of life on the frontier. Without social classes, the poverty of the wilderness spawned a pure democracy that reigned supreme. The people of the wilderness waxed strong in the self-reliance and independence that developed during their never-ending struggle for existence.

Since the laws that governed the people living on the eastern coastal plains could not be enforced in the trans-mountain country, the frontiersmen of necessity framed laws of their own. The pioneers again proved their resourcefulness by evolving a practical method of dealing with both horse thieves and tax collectors in a prompt and effective manner.

Life in the wilderness was stern at best, and it was particularly hard on the frontier women. The rugged existence for them was sheer drudgery from sun up to sun down. Homemaking in the wilds of the Kentucky and Tennessee mountains was a challenge to the ingenuity, resourcefulness, physical strength and raw courage of any woman.

The pioneer family had very little except what the forest and the hunt could provide. Vessels of all kinds were made of wood. Hardware was rare. Houses were fitted together with oak pins. Furs were frequently used as money. Salt was evaporated from the waters of saline springs.

The most valuable possession of any frontier family consisted of their large iron pot that served so many purposes. The wild game that was killed, the food that was grown on the small tract of cleared land, as well as the vegetables to be canned, were cooked in the family pot. The laundry was boiled and washed in this pot with lye soap that was made from oak ashes and lard that had been rendered in this same indispensable vessel.

Besides cooking and keeping house, the pioneer women made practically all of the clothes that the entire family wore. Trading posts were not only few but also far between. Homespun fabrics were made from buffalo wool. Leather and fur furnished many clothing materials on the frontier. "Store bought" clothes were rarely seen.

The main responsibility of the wilderness women seemed to be that of bearing children and rearing large families. A large number of children in a family was almost mandatory on the frontier, as more hands about the place enabled the family to accomplish more work, which in turn meant a greater degree of success to the settlers. Even small hands could tend to the chickens and pigs and do other chores about the place. Soon these hands would be large enough to handle a plow and help their father clear new land. Additional land meant more back-breaking labor, but it also meant wealth. As time went by, the father and mother, if they survived, became old before their time, and were thus more or less dependent upon the help of the strong arms of their growing children.

Women did not, as a rule, live very long on the frontier. The rigors of pregnancy without medical attention, and childbirth often without the help of even a neighbor, took a tremendous toll of the wilderness wives. Consequently a pioneer might take a new wife—a third, or even a fourth, if he could find one. A frontiersman would frequently marry the first woman who would have him, as females were scarce in the west. However, the never ending stream of new immigrants pushing over westward, and the widows of men who had succumbed early to the wilderness, seems to have kept the supply of females on the frontier almost equal to the demand.

The children were taught to do exactly what they were told. Strict discipline was a necessity in the wilderness. The dangers that lurked everywhere in the dark forests made the family conform to the commands of the father almost as if it were a military unit, for in truth, in dealing with the Indians, such was exactly the case.

The children were reared in obedient respect for their elders. There were few children who were spoiled because the rod had been spared. To quote a Cumberland colloquialism, "the fear of God was instilled into their hearts, and the respect of their seniors was emphasized upon the seat of their pants."

The father was a virtual patriarch, and when a child grew so big that he could not, or would not obey the wishes of his father, he simply packed such few belongings as he possessed in a little bundle and struck out to join one of the caravans that seemed to be perpetually heading further westward.

It was inevitable that the flame of democracy should burn brightly in all phases of the life on the frontier. The men of the Tennessee and Kentucky Cumberlands were free-thinking individualists, and their words were absolutely uncensored by any man. In this country a man "spoke his mind." This naturally led to many disputes, arguments, fights and even killings. Everyone had his own opinion regarding many things, especially matters that concerned politics and religion. These people believed with Voltaire "I disapprove of what you are saying, but I will defend to the death your right to say it." In this region, the free worship of a man's individual God was as acceptable as the breathing of the fragrant morning air that was frequently heavily scented by the pleasing odor of the honeysuckle or the wild grape bloom.

The spread of the far-flung British Empire by means of establishing colonies, always created a unique paradox. When a liberty loving nation plants a colony, it cannot be very long until the colonists themselves rise up and demand their freedom from the mother country. The inabitants of the British Isles had wrested their freedom from reluctant kings by the sword, and they stood prepared to perish by the sword to maintain their convictions.

The English had emigrated to Virginia and the Carolinas, and their descendants who migrated westward into the Kentucky and Tennessee Country had exchanged the broad sword for the long rifle, but they guarded their liberty and their beliefs just as zealously as their ancestors who long ago had forced King John to sign the Magna Carta at Runnymede.

The Anglo-Saxon race is great largely because of the character of the people themselves. The Anglo-Saxon has a tremendous sense of personal responsibility to a cause. His deep conviction of right and wrong may cause a man to stand by idly while his only son is being hanged on the gallows, or it may cause a wealthy and socially prominent Lord Astor to voluntarily give his own place in the last lifeboat of the sinking TITANIC to a female, simply because one of the established English mores has it that a gentlemen always defers to a lady.

The Cumberland Mountain folks are a sentimental people whose emotions are easily moved. They are capable of both great love and intense hatred. They are quick to enjoy a joke, but they are almost as easily moved to silent tears. In a fight, these people neither ask nor receive any quarter. If one of them is done a wrong, he is not likely to sue for an indemnity at the local court house. However, sooner or later, that wrong is quite apt to be rectified according to the code of the region. These folks are born without fanfare, live their lives with very little ceremony, and finally are buried in the solitude of a small cemetery that adjoins a rough-hewn community church.

The sentimental ballads that are played so plaintively over the nation's radio stations as "hill-billy" music, are indicative of the emotional character of these people. The same melody will often be played to either a happy or sorrowful beat, but mostly the tune seems to depict the simple haunting expression of a lonesome and despondent soul.

The occurrence of archaic words, idioms and expressions in these ballads symbolizes the virility of the Cumberlands, whose language has been handed down through generations from the days of Shakespeare's England.

From this region where the hooked rug is still woven on primitive looms and native clay is yet turned on homemade potter's wheels, many of the real heroes of the nation have come. Andrew Jackson, Andrew Johnson and James Knox Polk were Presidents. Men like Sam Houston and William Walker founded Republics. The experience of others have ranged from the legends surrounding the life of Davy Crockett to the saving of Fort Nashborough by Charlotte Robertson, wife of James Robertson, who in the absence of the men, loosed the dogs of the fort on the attacking Indians. It was from the Cumberland country that Alvin C. York marched to World War I and Cordell Hull was called to pilot the ship of state for a longer period of time than any other man in American history. A long list of noted legislators, ministers, educators, soldiers, merchants and physicians, as well as great men from other walks of life have come from the Cumberlands. It is to be assumed that this land will continue to furnish such leadership as long as the undiluted blood of the pioneers and the staunch loyalty to conviction earmark their children's children.

One might say that the ancestors of Henry Leo Boles had been indigenous to the soil of the Cumberlands since the early part of the eighteenth century. The Boles family was molded for over two hundred years by the conditions of the Virginia and Kentucky wilderness. If any white man could boast that he was of native stock then Henry Leo Boles was that man. Certainly very few could outrank him in this claim.

21

A man is what he is because of his heredity and environment. The imprint of the Cumberlands was indelibly stamped upon the character of Henry Leo Boles and the historical geography of the region profoundly influenced the destiny of the man. He was quick to acknowledge his debt to his primitive homeland, and occasionally, with reference to himself, he quoted the homely expression, "You can get the boy out of the country, but you can never get the country out of the boy."

True to the tradition of the Cumberland folk, Boles was both sentimental and emotional. He never really got to know his mother as she died when he was four years old. Yet he was a man who respected and hallowed motherhood as few other men. In later life he would listen, with silent tears glistening in his eyes, to the sentimental Irish ballads of "Mother Machree" and "Mother of Mine."

The music he enjoyed was a curious mixture of ballads and opera. He loved the fine Irish tenor voice of John McCormack, but his collection of records also included the instrumental and vocal selections of "Fiddling" John Carson and "Uncle Dave" Macon. Fritz Kriesler's rendition of "The Old Refrain" as well as the Fisk University "Jubilee Singers" contributed many hours to his listening pleasure. The two records that he played most, however, were "Old Folks at Home" and "Listen to the Mockingbird" sung in the high operatic voice of Alma Gluck.

Henry Leo Boles was a man who was proud of his heredity, and he was widely read in Tennessee history. Vicariously he re-lived many times such stirring moments as the trial and hanging of the Southern boy hero, Sam Davis, whose final words were "I would rather die a hundred times than betray a friend." The political exploits of Alfred and Robert Taylor during Tennessee's own "War of the Roses" were most familiar to Boles. He never ceased to be impressed by the flowery flights of oratory in the speeches of Senator Edward Ward Carmack.

The pride that Boles held in his native land was perhaps best evidenced in the homage that he paid to its past. He seldom, if ever, passed through Knoxville without visiting the monument erected to the memory of John Sevier —"Old Nollichucky Jack"—the first governor of Tennessee. The only inscription on the marker simply but impressively reads,

"Thirty-nine battles,
Thirty-nine victories."

Henry Leo Boles, to the writer's certain knowledge, climbed the precipitous mountain on the west side above Cumberland Gap on four different occasions to sit upon the old crumbled cornerstone that marked the site where the boundaries of the states of Virginia, Kentucky and Tennessee come together. Here he perhaps pondered on what circumstance had turned his progenitor northwards into the Kentucky Cumberlands rather than southward into the great valley of the Tennessee. There was not a county seat in Tennessee that Henry Leo Boles did not visit at least once. He drove his car some two hundred fifty miles over mountainous roads just to see his final four counties.

Thomas Fuller once said, "Pride and poverty are ill met, yet often seen together." The isolated valleys of the Cumberland Plateau unquestionably produced conditions of poverty, ignorance, malnutrition, inbreeding and feuding. Yet the regenerating power of the mountain heredity also produced energetic and vigorous individuals, who were unsoftened by easy living, whose nerves were unjaded by tensions of business competition, and whose morals were unsullied with compromise of principle. The Cumberlands have produced men with high ideals and patriotism, and has marked them with the unmistakable words, "Born for Success." In spite of incalculable obstacles, the Cumberlands have produced a noble race of people who walk a poor but proud land.

Chapter IV
GOD MOVES ON THE FRONTIER

The economists say that life, stripped of all extraneous material, consists of adequately meeting the needs of food, clothing and shelter. However, it seems obvious that a fourth essential is mandatory. In order to conquer the wilderness, a great amount of spiritual stamina and an unwavering faith in the God of creation must have been required.

The Savior told Satan that "Man does not live by bread alone," and the poet Longfellow paraphrased it, "Dust thou art to dust returneth was not spoken of the soul." A strong belief in Jesus, the Christ, was a definite factor in the conquest of the West. One thing can be absolutely certain, this great nation was not built by atheists!

From an historical viewpoint, America's separation from England threw all of the young nation's institutions into disorder. After the Revolution, people drew back and took a long look at the heirlooms that they had inherited from the mother country. During the next decade they tried to decide what they wished to keep and what they had better discard. This was an age of both indecision and decision. The years, 1781-1789 have been called "The Critical Period" of American History.

The moral and religious life of eighteenth century America cannot be said to have been of a high order. The churches on the eastern seaboard apparently did not like what their inspection revealed, for they immediately began to reorganize into forms which more nearly fitted the needs of the new national life. In 1784, the Methodist Episcopal Church was organized. In 1785, the first general convention of the Protestant Episcopal Church was held. The first diocese of the Roman Catholic Church was established in 1789. In this same year, the Presbyterian synods united in a general assembly of the Presbyterian Church.

While the established churches on the Atlantic Seaboard were reorganizing, the churches in the Trans-Appalachian country were already simplifying their creeds and doctrines to conform to the needs of the virile people who were slowly but steadily carving their way through the dark recesses of the wilderness.

It has been shown that all human development in the wilderness proceeded along very simple and fundamental lines. Just as the pleats, frills and laces were eliminated from the clothes of the frontiersmen, so were the dogmas, doctrines and catechisms dropped from the worship of God.

Geographically, the settlements in the wilderness were separated from the civilization on the coastal plains by a wide zone of mountainous country. Communication on the frontier was so slow and eratic that very little coordination within a given church organization could be exerted. Particularly was this situation a grave problem in the Cumberlands, where the culture in Virginia was cut off by the very rugged terrain surrounding the Cumberland Tableland. This region even today remains condemned to a somewhat retrogressive civilization due to its geographical isolation.

The historical geography of the region played a great role in modifying and shaping all church government in this area. Religious controls, like political restrictions, had largely been left on the eastern slopes of the Appalachians. Consequently, ministers in the wilderness had acquired much latitude in the doctrines that they taught. It thus developed that they preached not so much to please the associations, conventions and synods by whose dogmas they had been ordained, but they fitted their preaching to the spiritual needs of their particular frontier settlements. Ministers in the wilderness preached less the trappings and embellishments of their particular sect, and more about the simple gospel of the Lamb of God.

Bitter bickerings among the various sects and denominations had kept Protestantism in a very divided state. Finally, one Thomas Campbell, a former Presbyterian preacher, finding that many intelligent and pious people were as dissatisfied with the intolerance of sectarianism as he, began to condemn all creeds. He declared that the Bible was all-sufficient as a basis of union and cooperation for Christians. In 1809, Thomas Campbell announced the famous statement that served as the motto of religious unification in the West. His effective words were, "Where the Scriptures speak, we speak; and where the Scriptures are silent, we are silent."

A great religious movement was set in motion that inevitably led to the establishment, or more accurately, to the re-establishment of the church that was set up on the day of Pentecost, almost two thousand years ago. This is the church that was prophesied in the Old Testament, and is the church that Jesus Christ came to the earth to found. It is, in truth, the "church of Christ."

This simple religion "caught fire" and it spread through the wilderness with all the blistering heat of a mighty conflagration driven before the wind. This movement was known as the "Restoration" or the "Nineteenth Century Reformation." The complete sweep of the Restoration Movement was so momentous that the United States Religious Census of 1850 showed that the "Church of Christ" or "Disciples of Christ" was the fourth largest in the nation!

H. Leo Boles' favorite illustration of the Restoration Movement, upon which he was an established authority, concerns a story of three famous artists and a common canvas.

"According to legend, a famous and masterful artist painted on a linen canvas a portrait of Jesus. Tradition said that the Saviour Himself took time out of His very busy life to pose for this likeness. This painting was a great and inspired masterpiece. People came from far away places to see this matchless work of art; and there were some who were so moved that they fell down and worshipped the Christ of the painting."

As several centuries passed, the dyes and pigments that formed the colors in the masterpiece began to fade, until the painting lost much of its effectiveness. Then a contemporary artist was struck with an idea. He requested and received permission from the curator of the gallery where the masterpiece hung, to paint upon the same canvas his impression of the Christ. This second artist also did a magnificent job, and great was the fame of his work. However, as the throngs viewed the portrait, there were a few who remembered that a previous master had used the same canvas to portray the image of Jesus, and if one looked closely enough, he could follow the dim outline made by the original artist."

"Time is long, fame is fleeting, and all works of man are destined to crumble and decay. As the years rolled into decades, and decades into centuries, the restored Christ faded until again only with great difficulty was one able to trace the outlines of the picture. The present curator of the gallery where the old masterpiece now hung, commissioned the most noted contemporary artist to touch up the canvas and attempt to restore the beautiful magnificence of the ancient masterpiece."

"The third artist, working upon the canvas that was now some eighteen hundred years old, studied the teachings, of Jesus Christ for several years. He visited the museums and galleries of the world to see how other artists through the ages had conceived the physical likeness of the Christ.

After making many sketches, the artist proceeded to paint upon the old blackened canvas, his conception of the Christ. Because his painting of Jesus was undisputedly a work of genius, the same canvas, for the third time, portrayed a great painting. Many people came to view this work of art and hosts of people called it truly magnificent."

"If one looked at the old canvas carefully, however, he could see the outline of the second painting; and if he examined the picture very carefully, he could follow the now very dim lines of the original painting which the first artist had reputedly drawn from life."

H. Leo Boles, telling this story, would here pause, look his audience over, and then say in slow measured tones, "There was a time when the church of Christ that was founded on the day of Pentecost stood out from all other churches in bold relief. The teachings of Christ

27

were so plain and simple that no one who heard him could possibly misunderstand. However, as time passed, various creeds, dogmas and traditions slowly crept into the worship of Christ just as the original painting grew dim and faded."

Boles generally used this analogy in his sermon as an invitation to accept Christ's teachings, however on occasions he related the story while waiting on the Lord's table.

The meaning of this parallelism is easily apparent. The simple teachings of Jesus became embellished by the clergy of the Middle Ages until it became very difficult for the common people to discern what actually was commanded by the New Testament. Then, in 1517, Martin Luther touched off the Protestant Reformation, and dim outlines of the church that was set up by Christ could be seen again. As the years passed, however, unauthorized church practices again crept into the worship as doctrines and dogmas of mortals embellished the truth. Finally, came the "third artist,"—the Restoration of the American frontier—and once again came the rebellion against ritualistic and formalized religious practices. The clouds were rolled back, the sun blazed through, and Christ in all His Glory stood revealed so that every man could feel his presence and touch the hem of his garment.

An interesting feature about the Restoration, aside from the fact that the church of Christ was once again clearly functioning, is that it took place in the North American wilderness. Be it called "God's Plan" or be it called "Historical Geography," the same factors that shaped the conditions of life on the frontier also helped mould the religious practices in the wilderness.

The historical geography of the frontier was such that it was inevitable that a fundamental and simple religion would be practiced by the hardy race of pioneers who were conquering a continent with the help of the Almighty. If the southern Restoration leaders; Thomas Campbell, Alexander Campbell, Barton W. Stone, Walter Scott, John Smith and Jacob Creath had not come along at exactly the time that they did, then most assuredly other frontier clergymen would have risen to the occasion and initiated the Restoration. Furthermore, the movement would have occurred in the only place in the world that was ripe for such an event, namely the nineteenth century frontier of America.

In doing the "spade work" of the Restoration, no tongue was more powerful, no one preached to more people, nor had any preacher greater success in number of conversions, than John Smith of "raccoon" fame. Henry Jefferson Boles, the father of Henry Leo Boles, had been practically raised in the house of his grandfather, "Raccoon" John Smith. Thus it happened that H. Leo Boles was more than a product of the Cumberlands, he was a prodigy of the Restoration movement, whose leaders preached, "there is no creed but Christ, no bishop but God, and no form of church government but the republicanism of democracy."

William Cowper, a long time ago, said,

> "God moves in a mysterious way
> His wonders to perform."

Today, one is prone to ponder why the "Search for the Ancient Order" was destined to end in the poor, humble, unpretentious homes of the frontiersmen. Here, however, one is reminded that the Christ child was born in a manger in a poverty-stricken, almost forgotten province of the mighty Roman Empire. As one reflects upon the Restoration, suddenly and with startling impact, the first beatitude becomes strikingly significant:

> Blessed are the poor in spirit
> for theirs is the Kingdom of Heaven.

29

Chapter V

THREE R'S AND RESPONSIBILITY

"The trouble with you, Henry Jeff Boles, is that you simply don't believe what you are saying—you are just arguing," spoke Andrew P. Davis, a "hardshell" Baptist preacher who lived in the Antioch community of Jackson County, Tennessee.

Jeff Boles answered, "Your trouble is that you are teaching error."

"You say that baptism is necessary for salvation," Preacher Davis continued with a chuckle, and placing both thumbs on his chest and pulling slightly on his suspenders, he delivered his clinching argument in his most convincing pulpit manner, "yet *you yourself* have never been baptized."

With that pronouncement, Preacher Davis walked triumphantly to where his horse was hitched, amid the loud guffaws of the "hangers on" who ranged about the participants in the argument.

As Andy Davis was swinging his right leg over the saddle of the horse he was preparing to ride off, Jeff Boles yelled after him, "The trouble with you, Davis, is that you are avoiding the issue entirely. Whether or not I have been baptized does not alter the fact that when you preach 'What will be will be,' you are guilty of preaching error to your congregation."

Preacher Davis, fully mounted by now, yelled back at Jeff, "Mister Boles, and I say 'Mister' instead of 'Brother,' you have not been baptized, and until you are, you are a hypocrite to even discuss religion with one who has been sanctified like me."

Preacher Davis pulled on his reins so that both he and his horse faced the assembled men, while he delivered his finalé.

"Jeff Boles, if you really believed that baptism is necessary for salvation, you would allow me to baptize you right here and now in Flynn's Creek yonder. What do you say, do I get down and baptize you now?"

With those words sinking in on his impromptu audience, Preacher Davis wheeled his horse and galloped off before Jeff could think of an appropriate answer.

As a matter of fact, the longer Jeff thought about Preacher Davis' argument, the more apparent it became that the preacher "had" him. The argument was unanswerable, and Jeff Boles had heard enough of his illustrious grandfather's preaching to know that faith, repentance and baptism were necessary for salvation.

Jeff Boles slept very little that night, and just before daylight broke, he made a momentous decision. At breakfast Jeff made his announcement to Sarah.

"I'm going to ride over to Andy Davis' house this morning," he announced.

Sarah said, "Jeff, I declare, it does look like you could get your arguing done without taking another full day out of the fields." She continued after a pause, "The bottom corn sure needs choppin' out plenty."

"No, Sarah, no choppin' today." Then Jeff faced her squarely, "I'm riding over to Andy Davis' house right away to be baptized."

Riding over to preacher Davis' house, Jeff Boles did some solid thinking. He had learned the truth from old "Raccoon" John Smith, and he knew that one must be born anew by baptism in order to be saved. He reasoned that a Baptist could perform the function of immersion as well as anyone else, provided he was baptized into the name of God, Christ and the Holy Spirit. After all, he had always meant to be baptized but it was one of the things that he had never quite got around to doing. But by the time that he arrived at Andy Davis' place he was quite pleased about what he was doing.

Andrew P. Davis was surprised to see Jeff again so soon, but he was more surprised when Jeff told him, "I have come to you to be baptized."

As Jeff Boles was coming out of the waters of Flynn's Creek, dripping wet, he suddenly got an idea.

31

"Brother Davis, now that I have salvation according to your "hardshell" Baptist version, how about you and me holding a public discussion on the entire subject of salvation?" Jeff went on, "You can hardly deny me a debate now that I am no longer a hypocrite as you put it yesterday, and have been baptized by you yourself, can you?"

Brother Davis could not, with any degree of dignity fail to accept the challenge, and the debate was held within the month.

Following the debate with Davis, Henry Jefferson Boles began preaching, and his labors in this field were to continue for the next fifty-three years.

Henry Jefferson Boles belonged to that sturdy type of ministers who loved the truth. He had an inquiring mind and he was naturally argumentive in nature. He did not hesitate to compare contemporary religious theories with the teachings of the Scriptures. He named publically the religious bodies that held certain tenets that conflicted with the Bible.

Jeff Boles, during his preaching career, was often drawn into public discussions with preachers of different denominations. He had formal debates with Baptists, Methodists, Presbyterians, Mormons and the Holiness people. He never hesitated one moment when opportunity was presented, to defend the truth as he saw it. Jeff seemingly was never happier than when he was involved in a public discussion with a sectarian. Though not an educated man, he was mighty with the Scriptures. He frequently stated, "I want nothing but the truth, and I have nothing to fear from investigation of what I preach."

The style of preaching that Jeff used was plain and simple. He labored among the common people and he adapted his words to that class. He was a practical man, a preacher with only one book—the Bible. He seldom used an illustration that was not taken from the Bible. In preaching, Jeff would announce his proposition with clearness and then proceed to prove it with a powerful array of Biblical quotations.

Jeff was a successful farmer. He made his living and supported his family from the proceeds of his farm alone.

He expected nothing from his preaching, and in this he was not disappointed, for he received very little for his labors for the Lord.

The home of Jeff Boles became a stopover for itinerate preachers who happened to come into his community. Thus it happened that his son, the boy Henry Leo Boles, grew up in an atmosphere of gospel preachers. The young boy listened with interest to religious discussions and tenets of faith, so that he became thoroughly acquainted with the problems of the church of that time. Hence, very early in life, Leo became interested in spiritual matters. Psychologists now believe that the education of an individual begins immediately after birth. If this be true, then the experiences of the itinerate pioneer preachers visiting in the Boles' home must have had a profound effect on the boy of Flynn's Creek.

In 1879, Jeff Boles traded his farm on Flynn's Creek and moved his family to White County, Tennessee. Jeff, in the course of one of his preaching tours had swapped his Flynn's Creek farm for another on the banks of Cherry Creek. An ever hopeful farmer in White County had decided that he had more acreage than he wanted and traded even for the smaller, but perhaps more orderly farm in Jackson County. The Cherry Creek farm was "creek bottom" land, located about seven miles from Sparta.

Jeff hired three wagons to move his family and their belongings from Flynn's Creek to White County. By direct line the distance was only about sixty miles, but by the primitive roads through the rugged terrain, it was a matter of two good day's travel.

The caravan left the Jackson County farm at daylight on a Tuesday morning. After traveling almost impossible roads all day, they arrived in the town of Cookeville late in the afternoon. It was a slow tedious task to get the heavily loaded wagons over the tortuous mountain road, but it proved to be a great experience for the children. Just as they were getting into Cookeville, Leo, aged five, excitedly yelled to his brother Smith, aged four:

"We are getting into White County now, Smith, look at that white house over there!"

At that, it must have been quite a sight to a child who had never before seen a house that was painted white, or for that matter, any other color. Leo had seen only houses constructed of crude logs!

Henry Leo Boles entered the Cherry Creek School at the age of six. This was the public school nearest Jeff Boles' farm. The school was a one-teacher affair, as were practically all of the public schools in the Cumberland Tableland during the 1880's.

The teacher of the Cherry Creek school at this time was a man named John Cooper. He was a large man being well over six feet tall. The main requisites of teachers in this region were that they be "bigger" than their largest pupil, or at least tough enough to "handle" the boys if they got too rowdy. Mr. Cooper was well qualified to do this and besides that, from meager reports now available, he was, incidentally, a good teacher.

The school house was a large log cabin, consisting of a single room. There were no desks or seats; only crude benches made from slabs of lumber. The children sat on these backless benches from eight o'clock in the morning until five o'clock in the evening. Going to school under these conditions worked a tremendous hardship on all the children, especially the little ones in the lower grades.

There were blackboards all around the inside of the schoolroom. These were literally "black-boards" inasmuch as they were made out of boards that had been painted black so the white chalk marks would show to greater advantage. The children had very little writing paper to use. Instead each child had his own individual gray-black slate, on which he would write his lessons. After the teacher had inspected what the pupil had written, the "slate was wiped clean" with a damp cloth and thus was ready to use again. The use of a slate, of course, had many objectionable features, but it was economical for a slate would last a careful child a long time; it was useful until it became scratched or broken.

The public schools of White County that Leo Boles attended were "ungraded" in that there was no formal classification of pupils. While there were many adverse criticisms to be lodged against that type of school, this system was not without its blessings. Much provision for the individual differences of the pupils was almost automatically accomplished as each child was allowed to work along at his own pace. For example, a pupil who was poor in reading and spelling but good in arithmetic, could very easily be scheduled into a lower reading class but a higher arithmetic group. It was a comparatively simple matter for the instructor of a one-teacher school to classify his students in such a manner that more or less adequate provision for the individual was accomplished.

Another principle of modern pedagogy that characterized the one-teacher school concerns the integration of as many subject matter fields as possible, so that the pupil realized relationships in the topics that he was studying. Whatever else that one might say about the unsound instruction that went on in the old one-teacher schools, it certainly must be admitted that with only one instructor doing the teaching, all subjects were obliged to be integrated into the training, experience, and sagacity of the teacher.

The public schools in White County, as well as many other sections of rural Tennessee during the latter part of the 19th century, were in session only three or four months of the year. School would begin about the middle of July, after the crops were "laid by", and close around the middle of December. There would be a two weeks vacation at harvest time, as all hands, even the children's, were needed in the fields. This was raw, rural life in a strictly farming area. The harvest vacation from school was known as "fodder-pulling" or "pea-picking" time.

The authorities who scheduled the school sessions for late summer and the fall seemed to be acting on sound reasoning since there was no money to continue the schools for more than four months. If there was only to be a short session then these people were undoubtedly logical in selection of the middle of July as the time for opening the schools and early December for their closing. The reasons for running the school during the late summer and early fall are interesting.

The crops having been planted and cultivated, there was very little more for the farmer to do until harvest time. The corn would not be harvested until fall; the wheat had already been reaped and threshed. The hay was in the barns, and the vegetables in the garden required only gathering, cooking and canning. Therefore a school which began in July would require the children's attendance during a time when they were not especially needed at home.

It was sensible for the schools to close about the first of December. Practically all of the children had to walk to school every day, rain or shine. The weather in the Cumberland Mountains during the months of January, February and early March was frequently severe. The roadways in the rural areas were a sea of mud during the rainy seasons, which often made them virtually impassable. Hard freezes on top of the mud added other hazards, while deep snows made long walks to school impossible for many of the children. The roads were so bad during the winter that the children would frequently climb over fences along the road in order to take a less difficult route through the fields, pastures and woodland. It was imperative that schools be "let out" before the really bad winter weather began.

Schools that started in July and ended in December left the young people free to help at home during the busy spring planting season. They also helped to cultivate the crops in the summer until they were "laid by," after which they were not sorely needed on the farm until harvest time.

With the ending of the school term just before Christmas, the teachers were given a chance to attend one of the "colleges" that were scattered around the Cumberlands in a rather liberal manner. Those teachers who did not wish to further their own education were at liberty to put in a crop of their own, and thus supplement the meager salary paid teachers by the counties.

Unquestionably, the fact that the schools did not continue in session longer than three or four months limited the opportunities of a child to acquire a good basic education. The poor equipment of the schools, paucity of textbooks and poorly prepared teachers also mitigated tremendously against a child's obtaining very much formal education in the public schools of the region.

Six children were born to Jeff and Sarah, but infant diseases took the life of Ed, the firstborn. Henry Leo was the third child. Laura, a year older than Leo, was the eldest in a family of five children. After Laura and Leo, in order, came Smith, Roscoe and Nettie.

Leo's mother, Sarah Smith Boles, had died when he was not quite five years old. While living at Flynn's Creek, Smith Boles later recalled how he and his brother Leo slipped away from the house and crawled under the wire fence that surrounded the cemetery and witnessed their mother's funeral. Leo never forgot the weeping willow tree that still stands at the head of his mother's grave in Jackson County.

Jeff Boles had re-married in Jackson County shortly before he moved to White County. This time, a widow by the name of Mrs. Alcie Brown became his wife. "Miss Alcie" made a good step-mother for the children. She was kind and gentle by nature and breeding. She was the daughter of another Upper Cumberland preacher of the gospel, one Dudley Haile. Jeff had three children by Alcie; Maggie, Gertie and Ozro. Alcie was not strong physically; farm life was hard, living was primitive and the winters in the poorly equipped houses were cruel. Alice contracted a cold during the winter of 1885 and soon this developed into pneumonia. She died after a short illness, leaving Jeff with eight children to rear.

On April 27, 1887, Jeff Boles married a third time. Miss Adina Golden of Sparta was the bride. Adina did not object to children—as a matter of fact, she loved them. It was a good thing that she did have an affection for children because she was destined to bear for Jeff nine children of her own, making a total of seventeen children that Jeff and Adina reared.

To the union of Jeff and Adina, the following children

37

were born: Oscar (died in infancy), Otto, Ulzo Louise, Avo Margaret, Elmo Christine, Larrimore (died in infancy), Howard Sutton, Oleta Ann, and Lloyd White.

Adina Golden Boles was a sturdy whole-souled woman. Where Sarah Smith and Alcie Brown had been physically weak, Adina was strong. She was endowed with a good mind and a sound body. Jeff and Adina spent their next thirty-six years together, before death separated them. These were to be busy years for them both. Jeff was away from home much of the time doing evangelistic work in the surrounding area. He labored much in Jackson, White, DeKalb, Warren, Overton, Clay and Pickett counties in Tennessee and several of the border counties in Kentucky.

While Jeff was away from home preaching and holding revivals, the management of the farm fell upon Adina and the two oldest boys, Leo and Smith. This strong-willed woman assumed her additional duty in stride, and she saw to it that the work was carried on in a highly efficient manner. With the aid of the strong backs of the boys, sufficient crops were produced to support the large family. Leo, practically acted as a father during Jeff's absence from home. In later life, when H. Leo Boles was rearing a family of his own, it was especially noticed by his younger son, who developed into something of an athlete, that his father was not the world's best at games which involved swift physical coordination between eye and muscle, such as baseball, and tennis. When questioned about this lack of adeptness, H. Leo Boles would quietly explain that as a boy he never had any time for play.

Young Boles and his brothers and sisters were taught to do the farm chores at a very early age. They were taught the meaning of "strict economy and insistent industry." All members of the family learned to earn a living and to "make their own way," but the responsibilities placed upon the oldest son due to his father's absence were most weighty.

When Leo was fifteen years old, Jeff Boles sold his farm on Cherry Creek and bought a much larger tract of land on Sink Creek in DeKalb County. DeKalb County adjoined White County, so that this time the wagons moving the household belongings of Jeff's ever-expanding family had only about forty miles over much better roads than had been the previous trip when the Boles' moved from Flynn's Creek.

It is noteworthy that each of the four farms Jeff Boles owned were located in "bottom land." The Boles' family farmed rich alluvial flood plains along small mountain streams that never ran dry. Jeff in succession operated farms on the banks of Flynn's Creek in Jackson County, Cherry Creek in White County, Sink Creek in DeKalb County and finally Mountain Creek in Warren County.

Hard labor by all the family on these bottom lands produced crops that were plentiful and harvests that were bountiful. This was indeed a blessing considering the very large family that Jeff and Adina were rearing.

The boy Leo attended the White County public schools for nine years. When the family moved to DeKalb County it is indicative of the importance Jeff Boles placed upon the education of his children when he emphatically refused to leave the Cherry Creek school until it closed its term in December of 1888. Leo attended the local DeKalb County school two years. This gave young Boles a total of eleven years in the three to four months school year prevalent in the Cumberlands. Simple arithmetic will show that these years add to something less than four years of formal education! —a very sad comparison to the public school term now being offered.

When H. Leo Boles was seventeen, a misfortune happened to his father which caused Jeff to temporarily lose his sight for about two years. He selected his son Leo to read to him. The other boys were sent to the fields, but this son was kept at the house to read to his father. In this way Leo developed into an excellent reader. This event also engendered in him a strong desire for more knowledge. Leo's intellectual powers were awakened by the thought and reflection of the subject matter that he read to his father and the more he would read, the more thirsty Leo became for a better education. His was a naturally inquisitive mind and his thirst for information was never to be quenched as long as breath remained in his body. Even though this boy was eventually to hold four college degrees, and was to gain the academic respect of many educated people, his intellectual curiosity was never satisfied. He literally died "a learning."

Chapter VI
COLLEGES IN THE CUMBERLANDS

Most of the public schools in the Cumberlands during the latter part of the nineteenth century terminated at the eighth grade level. If one desired to pursue his education further, it was necessary that he attend one of the private schools that were scattered rather liberally around the region. Although these private schools did most of their work on a secondary or high school level, many of these institutions attached the more ambitious term of "college" onto the name by which they identified themselves.

In the late summer of 1892, Leo and Smith Boles, aged eighteen and seventeen respectively, entered Center College located at the base of Shirt Mountain, in Cannon County. The "college" was only about eighteen miles from the Boles farm on Sink Creek, but the roads in that area, while not precipitous, were very muddy in rainy weather. Even in good weather the round trip took an entire day.

Center College was known to people in that section simply as the "Short Mountain School." It was operated by its president, L. P. Evans, who was a noted educator in the Cumberland Tableland.

The enrollment of Center College in 1892 was about one hundred fifty. The institution was coeducational. Most of the boys lived in the dormitory, while the girls were quartered in private homes within the immediate neighborhood.

The dormitory at "Professor Evan's School" consisted of a row of single story brick buildings. Each house was a large square structure divided into four equal rooms. This arrangement allowed one large chimney in the exact middle of the building to serve all four rooms. Each room was calculated to accommodate four boys.

Leo and Smith shared their rooms with three Allen brothers; Alf, Doak and Lem. In order to crowd five boys into the space that had been originally planned for four, one of the Allen boys had to sleep on a "pallet." This bed-

41

ding was rolled up during the day so that all the floor space could be utilized.

The beds were double-decked affairs. Smith lost the flip of the coin and therefore had to sleep in the upper bunk, with Leo in the lower berth. The Allen boys located themselves on the other side of the room. The dormitory had been arranged and furnished so that light housekeeping in the single room could be accomplished. These five boys did all their eating, sleeping and studying in this one room.

The students living in the dormitory did their own cooking and housekeeping. In short, they kept "bachelor's hall." Foodstuffs were generally brought from home and the boys, aside from an occasional case of homesickness, managed to fare surprisingly well in the dormitory. They ate such things as hickory smoked ham, chicken, eggs, dried beans and fruits, canned vegetables and biscuits with jam and jellies.

About every two weeks, a two-horse wagon would make its way over the mountain road to carry supplies to Leo, Smith and the Allen boys. "Old Man" Allen, a Baptist preacher living in Smithville, the county seat of De-Kalb County, and Jeff Boles would alternate sending a wagon carrying supplies from Smithville to Short Mountain. In spite of the fact that the same wagon brought all their food supplies, there was very little sharing done by the Boles and Allen boys. The Allens prepared and ate the foodstuffs sent to them by their father, while Leo and Smith used the supplies that came to them through Smithville from the Sink Creek farm.

An anecdote that occurred in the dormitory seems worth mentioning. Following the custom that is still preserved by most schools today, Center College had no classes on either Saturday or Sunday. Consequently, the boys and girls who lived nearby generally went home on Friday afternoon and returned Sunday afternoon or evening. Frequently the students who lived near enough to go home for the week-end would invite other not so fortunate students to spend the week-end at their home.

Once during a rainy week-end the dormitory was completely deserted except for the room shared by the Boles and Allen boys. Since they were "holding down the fort" by themselves, Lem Allen, the youngest of the brothers, who was very parsimonious, worked out a scheme and suggested that the five of them prepare and eat a very special dinner in honor of the occasion. Lem's plan called for the Boles brothers to furnish the ham and vegetables, and do all the cooking. His brothers, Alf and Doak, were to wash all dishes and clean up, while he would furnish the honey and butter for the meal. Seeing through the unequal bargain at once, Leo had his mouth open to veto the scheme, when he noticed the sly wink that Smith was giving him.

The plan that Smith had in mind was literally a "honey." He knew that the last supply wagon had brought Lem a whole gallon and half of pure honey. Now when Lem worked out his scheme to fleece the Boles boys out of some hickory smoked ham, he unwittingly made one serious error. He did not know about Smith Boles' tremendous appetite for honey. Jeff Boles had never kept an apiary, so Smith very seldom got to taste this delicacy. His desire for sweets had to be mainly satisfied by sorghum and jellies.

No one paid any particular attention to the large number of biscuits that Smith was baking. The Allen boys were chuckling about how much good ham that they were going to eat, as Leo cut very liberal slices for the skillet.

Lem was congratulating himself again on the clever deal that he was putting over on the older and more advanced Boles boys as they all sat down to their feast. However, when Smith proceeded to make his entire meal on hot biscuits, butter and honey, Lem began to wonder. There was no accounting for the number of biscuits that were consumed but when Smith and Leo finally finished eating, the bucket of honey was empty. Lem looked at the empty bucket and sorrowfully said, "I thought that you would only eat my honey for dessert. Now you boys have eaten all of my honey." With that Lem broke down and actually cried!

On another week-end Leo and Smith decided that they wanted to go home. It was only eleven miles, they had been told, if they took a certain mountainous short-cut. It was explained to them the reason that this short-cut road was not used more often was that people just didn't know about it. Accordingly, Leo and Smith set out at daybreak Saturday morning; destination—home on Sink Creek. It was soon apparent why the short-cut was so seldom traveled. This road was narrow, steep and practically impassable for anything heavier than a man on horseback. However, after an all day's walk, they arrived at the Boles' farm just a little before supper time. The next day they had to walk back to Short Mountain, but this time they elected *not* to take the short-cut. They hiked the eighteen miles around the old road. They were dog-tired when they got back to the dormitory. That was the first and last time that either of them walked home.

Leo and Smith were very busy young men in the Short school. Under capable teachers they made exceptional progress. Like many others in their class, they had much "catching up" to do in order to understand the lessons that were taught them on the high school level.

The scholarship demanded by the teachers at the Short Mountain school was high, as students were made to "toe the mark." The curriculum consisted of reading, penmanship, spelling, geography, grammar, composition, American and Tennessee history. Since Leo and Smith were always in the same classes, they bought only one set of textbooks. Among the texts studied were the classic *McGuffey Readers, Ray's Higher Arithmetic* and the famous *Blue Back Speller.*

The early morning routine for Leo and Smith consisted of getting up before daylight, dressing, preparing their breakfast, eating, washing the dishes, tidying up their half of the room and then studying an hour before going to their first class. The school day lasted from eight in the morning until four o'clock in the afternoon. This left the boys pretty tired. After a little rest and recreation, it was time to cook their evening meal. After supper came the homework for the following day. Practically all of their waking time was spent in "getting" their own meals, "learning" their lessons and "reciting" in the classroom.

Leo was very good in grammar, and he spent much of his time in the study of English. Smith was exceptionally bright in the mathematics classes, but he was very weak in his grammar and English. He simply was not interested in grammar, but there wasn't a problem in the mathematics book that Smith did not solve. Leo, realizing that his brother was the best mathematics student in school, would frequently spend all his time in studying everything but his mathematics lesson. Then after the lights were put out and they had retired, Smith from his upper bunk would explain the problems in the morrow's mathematics lesson, while Leo listened attentively. From sheer memory, Smith would state the problem and then explain the examples, and Leo would remember the explanation well enough the next day to put problems on the blackboard that he had actually never seen before!

It was in Center College that H. Leo Boles made his first public speech. He made his talk in a small debating club that was organized by some of the young men in the school. Little then did he or anyone else realize that this was only the beginning of thousands of addresses that he would deliver during his very active speaking career. There was certainly nothing in the hesitant, stammering speech of this blushing country adolescent that day in the debating club that gave promise of the persuasive orator and polished pulpit preacher that was later to develop.

Leo and Smith had earned the money for their tuition by hard work on the farm, and they went to Center College with the conviction that they were going to get their money's worth out of their schooling. There is frequently a great difference in the scholastic attainments of those who are "sent" to school compared to those who "went" to school. The Boles boys *went* to school at Short Mountain against such financial odds and personal sacrifice that they were able to attend Center College only the single semester.

The winter of 1892 came early. Before school was out at Christmas time, the Cumberlands were blanketed under eighteen inches of snow. It had been an extremely arduous task to get the supply wagon through from Smithville during late November and early December.

45

Conditions at home on Sink Creek were such that Leo and Smith were needed there rather desperately, and as soon as school was out Leo and Smith hastened home. Smith was put to work in the fields and he acted as a "strawboss" in seeing to it that the farm was kept going in a fruitful manner.

Jeff Boles' eyes were troubling him again and Leo once more was given the duty of reading the Bible to him. The farm work was heavy, and Leo could have given much help by joining in the cultivation of the crops, but Jeff was in the habit of studying his Bible for six hours every day. He uncompromisingly considered that the spiritual side of life should not be neglected, so his eldest son was again used as a reader.

The crops raised on the Sink Creek farm were mainly corn, hay and garden vegetables. The corn harvested went mainly into feed for the horses, mules, hogs and poultry. The hay went to the live stock while what remained of the grain was taken to the mill to be ground into meal and flour.

An old-fashioned "grist mill" was located at Keltonburg, about four miles downstream from Jeff Boles's place. There a dam had been built across Sink Creek, causing a mill pond to be formed. The Keltonburg mill pond was a popular picnic and party place for people who lived for miles around.

Viewed from the middle of the twentieth century, there seemed little entertainment and relaxation for rural people in the 1890's. During the growing season, folks on the farm were busy with chores from sun-up to sun-down, leaving little time for play. It was impossible to travel for any distance and get back within a day's time. Consequently, most of the social activities in the Cumberlands centered around the attendance of church services on Sundays. No one in this region ever considered working in the fields on a Sunday! This was set apart as the Lord's day and the good and bad alike respected it as a rest day whether or not they attended church.

There was much practical joking in this area. The people took great delight in jibing one another. Most of the jokes played in this era were rather crude, inasmuch as the victim was almost always embarrassed and humiliated. For example, a particularly wicked man lived about a mile and a half up the creek from the Boles' farm. This man had his own "moonshine still" and sampled his private stock quite liberally at times. He did not have to be drunk to beat his wife and children, but he seemed to put more zest in his swings when he was intoxicated. One cold winter night, with a three inch snow on the ground, Leo and Smith were considering what they could do for excitement after supper. Smith suggested that they might help their neighbor to sober up a bit. In short order they worked out a not too subtle plan to accomplish this feat. Smith and Leo each took a five gallon bucket and walked through the snow to the moonshiner's place. As they crossed the footlog that spanned the creek, they stopped and each filled his bucket with water. Leo called the man out on his front porch. Then he and Smith drenched the drunk man with ten gallons of very cold water as he stood swaying there just outside his doorway.

Playing practical pranks was not restricted to the winter season. One hot August night, Leo and Smith rode the same horse up to a stranger's house in another part of the county, and after "hollering him out" in the dead of night, they told him that they wanted to buy a pound of chewing tobacco. The old fellow pulled his boots on, got his lantern lighted, walked in his long nightshirt out to his barn and climbed up into the loft where he kept his tobacco. Just as he was tying up the tobacco, Leo and Smith galloped away shouting, "Merry Christmas"! The old man was left standing there in his nightshirt holding the tobacco in one hand, the lantern in the other, and his mouth and eyes open in surprise. The true quirk in this incident was that no one in the entire Boles family used tobacco in any form as Jeff believed that the use of this narcotic "defileth the body" and so must be regarded as a sin.

One Fourth of July, when Leo and Smith were in their middle teens, they decided that they wanted some firecrackers and sparklers in order that they might befittingly celebrate the occasion. The boys walked four miles to the nearest country store to make their purchase. When they arrived at this store, they found that the storekeeper had completely sold out of fireworks. Undaunted, Leo and Smith walked four more miles down a side road to another country store where they made their purchase. They paid for the fireworks with a quarter that Leo had been saving for over a year. The twenty-five cent piece had been given him by an itinerate preacher who had stayed a night at the Boles's place, after Jeff had refused pay for the lodging. Leo and Smith walked the eight miles back home with their fireworks. They ran the last two miles home as Jeff was very insistent that all members of the family be together for the evening meal. That night the Boles family were entertained by Jeff reciting the preamble to the Constitution of the United States, followed by Leo and Smith setting off their pyrotechnics.

As may have been assumed, Leo and Smith were not only brothers, but they were also close friends and buddies. They were almost inseparable. They did practically everything together. They fought together and they courted together. Fifty years later Smith smilingly boasted that he and Leo could, and did "lick" every other group of boys in the Sink Creek neighborhood.

Jeff Boles believed that his children should follow Benjamin Franklin's "Early to bed, early to rise" dictum, consequently running around at night or even staying up late was strictly taboo. The boys slept upstairs in the big two-story house where they lived. Whenever they had a date or wished to go somewhere, they would wait until after dark, then Smith would get the ladder from the barn and place it against the house by their bedroom window. After Jeff got to sleep, Leo and Smith would get their "Sunday clothes," climb down the ladder, dress in the barn, saddle up a couple of horses and be on their way. When they finally got home they would simply reverse their exit procedure. Leo would then get up before his father arose, and take the ladder back to the barn before it was discovered. Many times this practice was repeated and Jeff apparently never caught them. However, it did seem a little more than coincidental that after a night in

48

which the boys "had their fling," Jeff would almost always assign them some kind of extra work on the farm.

One night during the spring of 1893, as Smith was undressing for bed, Leo turned to him and asked, "Smith, what are you going to do, now that you have quit school?"

Smith replied, "I just don't know. What are you going to do?"

Leo said, "I believe that I'll teach school."

Much sooner than Leo could have possibly anticipated, he got his chance to teach. The public school nearest to Jeff Boles' farm was located at Bildad, about two miles down the Keltonburg road. The Bildad school, like so many others in the Cumberlands, was a one-teacher affair. The teacher, F. J. Potter, was sorely pressed with the large enrollment at Bildad in the summer of 1893. "Professor" Potter entreated the DeKalb County School Board to give him an assistant teacher to help him with the heavy load that he was carrying. The DeKalb County officials, after making an inspection of the school, decided to comply with Professor Potter's request, and they told him to pick his assistant. He immediately invited his former student, Leo Boles, to be his assistant. Of course, Leo accepted with great excitement, as it was a wonderful opportunity for him to get started on what he wanted to do. For his services, Leo received a salary of $10 per month for the five month school term!

All of the Boles children who were of school age attended the Bildad school, just as Leo and Smith had before they had graduated and gone to Center College. Now that the Boles family had more children in school, Leo would carry a lunch in a large basket to school every day for himself and his brothers to eat, while his sisters would take a similar basket of food for their noonday meal. Considering the early rising hour, getting ready for school, walking the two miles to the school house and the five o'clock closing time, a hearty noonday meal for all was essential. Even though the term was short in months, the school day was certainly long enough in hours. Many of

49

the children did not get home from school until after dark during the short November and December days.

An incident that happened immediately after the Bildad school closed in December revealed Leo's tremendous popularity with the children of the community. A Christmas party was being given the boys and girls down at Keltonburg. There in the Methodist church an enormous Christmas tree had been placed. Back in those days it was a custom in many neighborhoods in the Cumberlands to have a community Christmas tree. Under the tree which was decorated with many lighted candles, much candy, fruit and other presents were placed.

The occasion usually called for a speech, so the Methodist preacher obliged. He told the large crowd that Christ was born on the twenty-fifth day of December, and that following the example set by the Three Wise Men who brought gifts to the young Lord, people throughout the ages had celebrated the birth of Jesus on the proper day by giving presents to one another.

When the preacher had finished his nice little talk, the crowd began hollering for Boles to make a speech. They kept yelling until they finally got Leo to the platform. Leo Boles, though only nineteen, knew the story of the birth of Christ far better than the Methodist preacher. He could not have been Jeff's reader for several years and not have learned a few things about the Bible.

Leo told the people in the crowded church; "I'm sorry to say that what you have just been told concerning the birth of Christ on December twenty-fifth is not true. This preacher thinks that he knows the exact day that Jesus was born. He hasn't learned yet that *nobody* knows the exact day that our Lord was born."

Leo then sat down amidst thunderous applause from his students and about three-fourths of the grown people of the community there assembled; the other fourth being Methodists.

The teaching experience that Leo Boles gained in the Bildad school was an excellent preparation for his life work. He early developed poise and a sense of self-reliance that he never lost. He was acquiring skill in the art of making a favorable impression in public appearances, and he was on his way to becoming quite adept at speech-making.

It was during his teaching at Bildad that Leo felt for the first time that he had become a self-supporting man. He had earned the respect and admiration of his neighbors by much personal effort and sacrifice. Now he thought that he had arrived at manhood!

When the Keltonburg episode was related to Jeff Boles, his blue eyes sparkled and a wide grin that was seldom seen came to his face. He no doubt thought about the many experiences he had had with "sectarians." He must have remembered a certain debate that had been held in Jackson County because of a challenge that had been hurled by a man coming out of Flynn's Creek soaking wet from baptism. Jeff also must have recalled the thundering denunciation of all creeds by his eloquent grandfather. Jeff probably thought of the example that he himself was setting for his children by spending hours every day with God's word. Reflecting on the Christmas tree incident, Jeff must have reviewed it carefully. After much thought, another slow wide grin appeared on his face, for upon his life, he couldn't see how even he with all his experience in dealing with sectarianism, could have improved one iota on the words that his son had uttered on the spur of the moment. He then must have realized that he had an exceptionally brilliant son.

Jeff never commented on the matter to anyone, but all throughout the holidays that Christmas, he seemed in an unusually happy mood.

Chapter VII

TRAGEDY AND DETERMINATION

When Leo Boles went "courting" he did not have very far to go. The prettiest girl in the Sink Creek community was Cynthia Cantrell.

Leo and Cynthia had been going together, off and on, ever since Jeff Boles had moved his family to DeKalb County five years before. The Cantrells had been among the good neighbors who had helped the Boles' get set up in their new place. The Cantrell farm was located about a mile up Sink Creek from the Boles' place.

Since the Boles home was situated in the creek bottom along which ran the Keltonburg road, Cynthia and her brother J. B., must needs pass the Boles house in order to attend the Bildad school. It was only natural that the Boles children should walk to school with the other children going their way. Consequently, Leo found it convenient to spend many delightful hours in Cynthia's company. Frequently in the afternoons Leo would "walk her home" the additional distance to the Cantrell place. It was during this last mile that Leo managed to get in his best courting. It was easy to send young J. B. on ahead of them, and it was so much more romantic after the several smaller Boles children had been left off at home!

Cynthia and Leo had attended Bildad together as students for three years, then Leo had gone to Short Mountain for the single semester. During the summer and fall of 1893 they were in the Bildad school again, this time in a teacher-pupil relationship.

Oldsters who knew Cynthia remember her as being blue-eyed and fair complexioned with light brown hair. She was five feet, three inches tall and was inclined to be a little stout, her weight being about one hundred eighteen pounds. Her features were regular, her face oval and she was very attractive. Cynthia was a lively conversationalist and she seems to have had a pleasant personality in that she was "easy to get along with."

While the Cantrell farm was further from the Bildad school than the Boles place, it was closer to town as it was only a short distance from the main McMinnville-Smithville road. Cynthia's folks were considered to be fairly prosperous middle class people, and they were considered as "good people" in the neighborhood. The Cantrells had only the two children, Cynthia and her brother, who simply went by the initials "J.B." J. B. Cantrell was four years younger than Cynthia.

Cynthia had considered Leo "her fellow" for the past two years, but the tempo of the courtship was stepped up considerably after Leo had returned from Center College. Consequently, when the Cantrells announced that their daughter, Cynthia, was engaged to marry Henry Leo Boles, no one seemed greatly surprised. Cynthia had now passed her nineteenth birthday and soon Leo would be twenty. True they were a little young, judged by standards of today, but in the Cumberlands of the nineteenth century, their ages were about par for marriage.

Early in the morning, February 10, 1894, Leo arose earlier than usual, borrowed Jeff's best horse and buggy and drove with Cynthia to Bildad. There the Justice of the Peace performed the marriage.

After the ceremony, the bride and groom returned to the Cantrell home, where they were honored by a gigantic wedding dinner and reception—Cumberland mountain style.

There were perhaps a hundred people awaiting the young couple. Practically everyone on Sink Creek was there, as both the bride and groom were very popular in the community. The large table in the dining room at the Cantrell's must have groaned under the weight of the feast that was spread upon it. Five kinds of meat, many dishes of vegetables and sixteen different kinds of cakes, instead of the large wedding cake, were served. Being religious people, no alcoholic beverages were present, but ever so often several of the menfolk would slip away to a certain buggy to return later with flushed cheeks and eyes a little more red than usual.

Toward the middle of the afternoon, the crowd began

to break up as darkness came early in February. Many chores at home had to be done by the country folks before sundown.

As their friends began to leave, Leo escorted Cynthia once more to Jeff's buggy. This time he drove some seven miles up a terrible road to the farm on Bear Branch that he had rented on a "share crop" basis.

The house consisted of little more than one bedroom and a kitchen, and it was very sparsely furnished. It was the direct antithesis of the sumptious home that Cynthia had left just a scant two hours before. But she was a bride, it was her wedding day and she was very much in love with her husband. The stars shining in her eyes as she looked from the rude house to her groom told him that she thought that their new home was wonderful.

It forever remains one of God's greatest blessings that mortals are not granted the gift to look down the pathway of their own lives and see what evils and suffering lie in store for them. The cabin on Bear Branch was destined to be Leo and Cynthia's home throughout all of their married life

February was one of the best months of the year for a young farmer to get married. By setting up housekeeping during this month, a man could get his spring plowing done in March, his planting in April and the cultivation of his crops accomplished in May and June.

Unlike the bottom land that both Cynthia's and Leo's fathers owned, the land that they had rented was on a hillside and was not very fertile. They had to scratch hard for everything that was made on that farm, and they didn't make much of any crop they tried to grow. The land up Bear Branch was "top" land consisting of thin and infertile soil.

Leo was offered the position of assistant teacher at Bildad again for the term of 1894, but there was entirely too much work to be done on his rented acres for him to spare the time from his work on the rocky mountainous farm. Even if he could have managed to leave the farm, Bear Branch was too far away from Bildad to permit his making the daily round trip.

Leo and Cynthia had little chance to hear the preaching of the gospel. They went to church every Sunday but they heard preaching only when Jeff Boles preached at the Olive Church, his home congregation. This occurred once a month during the late fall and winter when Jeff was home from his summer meetings. Although early in life Leo had learned the truth, and Cynthia's folks were members of the church, neither obeyed the gospel until September 27, 1894. W. T. Kidwell was holding the annual revival services at the Olive Church of Christ in DeKalb County, when Cynthia and Leo made the good confession and were baptized into Christ on the same day in Vine Creek.

By the time another February (1895) had rolled around, and Leo had celebrated his twenty-first birthday, it was apparent that Cynthia was to have a child sometime in July. Leo and Cynthia had the baby's name selected long before the child was born. Cynthia's full name was Cynthia Cleo Cantrell Boles. The baby would be named Cleo Cynthia Boles if a girl; Cleo Cantrell Boles if a boy. In either case Cynthia's name would be perpetuated.

During the spring of 1895, Leo worked his rented acres with a dogged determination to wrest from that poor soil all that was possible to produce. He reasoned that if his yield per acre was small, he could produce more only by cultivating more land. He therefore requested his landlord to allow him to clear up some adjoining "cut over" land. This permission was gladly granted and Leo dug and pulled out the stumps by brute force. Usually stumps were removed by blasting with dynamite, but Leo had no money to spend in that way. He succeeded in clearing the stumps from the land, but in doing so, he worked both himself and his mule so hard that he made himself sick, while the mule died!

As Cynthia's time came nearer, Leo took her back to the Cantrell home so that she would have better attention when the baby was born. Bear Branch was located in very rugged country, while the Cantrell place was easily accessible to the doctor who lived in Dibrell.

On the anniversary of Bastille Day, July 14, 1895, Cleo Cantrell Boles was born. It was well that Cleo was named for his mother. It seems almost prophetic that Leo and Cynthia had decided to give the child his mother's name. Although they had not even an inkling of the gravity of the situation that would develop, the decision to give the baby Cynthia's name was an event that foreshadowed things yet to come.

Cynthia was in much labor pain before her child was born, and her condition became critical immediately after Cleo's birth. Three days after Cleo was born, his mother died of uremic poisoning.

Jeff Boles preached his daughter-in-law's funeral. He was in a meeting in Cannon County at the time, but he immediately closed it and hurried home when he was notified of the tragedy. After a simple funeral, Cynthia was laid to rest in the Cantrell family lot in the Olive Church Cemetery.

Leo remained with the Cantrell family for a while. He was now a father and his responsibilities had increased many-fold. By far his greatest problem was what could be done to insure the survival of his young son. Fortunately there was a woman in Dibrell who had a baby only two weeks old. Leo managed to persuade this young mother to take Cleo and nurse him along with her own child until he was old enough to be weaned. Leo paid the woman $10 per month to take care of Cleo.

Leo next paid Jeff Boles a visit. The old patriarch was not at all insensitive to the plight of his son. He no doubt thought back to the tragic day on Flynn's Creek when he had buried his beloved Sarah, and he had been left with not one, but five small children. Cleo Boles was Jeff's first grandchild. Jeff liked the name "Cleo." As a matter of fact, Jeff seemed rather preferable to names ending in an "O." But most of all the boy was a Boles, and a fierce pride in the family name had earmarked them through the generations in the wilderness.

Jeff told Leo that he could bring Cleo to the Sink Creek farm and be raised as one of his own children, if Leo could persuade one of his sisters to care for the child. Leo's oldest sister, Laura, agreed to do this and Cleo was brought to Jeff's home as soon as he was able to be taken from his foster mother. As it worked out, not only Laura, but the entire family helped rear the boy.

Now that the problem of caring for Cleo had been solved, Leo Boles turned his attention to two other problems that seemed most serious to him. He returned to Bear Branch where he lived in solitude until after he had harvested the crops in the fall. When Leo finally moved from the "topland" farm, he had the course of his life charted and he knew exactly what action he must take.

First he would reap the result of his labor on his crops. He had done entirely too much work on that place not to procure the profits of his products. After Leo had gotten the harvest into the barn, he called his landlord over and gave him the part that was due him for rent. Then he borrowed Jeff's two-horse wagon and with Smith's help, moved his belongings back to his father's farm. He did not return home empty handed for he took all his belongings, even the hay in the barn, to his father's place where he contributed it all to the common family cause. Leo was in no way "sponging" on his father. He was a grown man and he made an excellent farm hand during the remaining time that he lived at Jeff's place.

The second, and by far the more serious decision that Leo had made in the quiet seclusion of the Bear Branch farm, concerned his future education. After wrestling with Mother Nature by making two crops on the infertile topland he was renting, Leo could see that only poverty and drudgery would reward his efforts on Bear Branch. The natural sharpness of his brilliant mind was becoming blunted by the sheer physical fatigue of his body. Leo could see clearly that he had nothing to look forward to except perhaps an early grave. There was only one way out of the bind that held him. That was to acquire a really good education. But how could a poor mountain boy like himself expect to go to college? Jeff, with his large family to rear, was in no position to see him through. The only glimmer of hope Leo had was to find some way to earn enough money to put himself through school. Leo didn't know *how* he was going to do it, but he *knew what he must* do and furthermore, he knew *how he must start*

Leo felt that without an education a man was a nobody; while the whole world lay at the feet of an educated person. There was no profession that a learned man could not enter. So he determined in his heart that a college education he would have. He would begin by entering Dibrell College when it opened its doors for the winter semester early in January, 1896.

B. C. Goodpasture, who perhaps of all people best understood H. Leo Boles, in writing of the man many years later seems to have expressed it concisely when he said, "He seldom failed to do what he set out to do. His will was inflexible."

Jeff Boles followed the custom of the Cumberlands by giving each of his sons a saddle horse on their twenty-first birthday, and each of his daughters a milk cow when they were married. Jeff was insistent that his boys ride their own horse and not his fine animal that he used to cover so many miles around the Cumberlands while doing his preaching. Once Smith was caught red-handed slipping a saddle on his father's horse. Jeff quietly but very firmly said, "Smith, you can just put that horse back and get yours."

Leo decided that he had no need for a horse as he had made up his mind to go to school in Dibrell. He had no place to keep the animal at school, and feeding it would just be an added expense in his frugal budget. Leo knew that he could not afford the luxury of owning a horse. One night, about a month before Leo was to depart for Dibrell College, he said to Smith,

"You know, I don't need my horse. I think I'll give it to Laura."

Smith answered him, "Leo, you have a good horse. If you don't want him, I'll buy him from you. How much do you want for him? I know that you can use the money."

Leo spoke, "No, Smith, I don't need the horse, but he is not for sale. I'm going to give it to Laura. It's not right for the girls not to be given a horse too."

Laura accepted the horse. Soon she got married, whereby she also earned the milk cow that came to her under the custom of the Cumberlands.

Chapter VIII

A PEDAGOGUE'S PROGRESS

The past two years had been the hardest of Leo Boles' life. He had done such a vast amount of manual labor that he had little time for anything else. He would come in from the fields dead tired at sundown, eat supper, and fall into bed. Then before sunup the next morning he would eat his breakfast, and be back in the field by daylight. This procedure is not conducive to the improvement of one's intellect.

Leo had tasted the sweet water of wisdom at Center College. He had taught as an assistant to the scholarly Professor Potter in the Bildad public school. He had brushed lightly against the great flowering plant of knowledge, and some of its pollen had fallen on his sleeve as he had passed, and the fragrance of its flower was destined to haunt him the remainder of his days. In the solitude at Bear Branch Leo Boles had determined to drink as deeply as possible of the perennial spring of wisdom.

One of the best of the "colleges" of the Cumberlands lay almost upon his doorstep. Dibrell College, located in Warren County, was only about seven miles from Jeff Boles' place on Sink Creek. It is a fine commentary on the roads in the rural regions of this era, that although most of the students who attended this school lived within a radius of fifteen miles. The students were compelled to reside in the college dormitories, or board with some family who lived in the immediate neighborhood of the school. Today, with hard surface roads, it is possible to drive from the Sink Creek community to Dibrell in perhaps ten minutes, but in 1896, it was more profitable for Leo to live in the dormitory, rather than attempt the task of staying at Jeff's and attending the school as a "day student."

Leo had saved enough money from teaching at Bildad and farming his rented acres to see him through his first term at Dibrell. After that, something would have to be worked out before he could again attend the Dibrell school.

Shortly before Leo entered Dibrell, he went to see his old teacher and friend at Bildad, F. J. Potter, whom he respected very much. He told Professor Potter about his ambition to get an education, and humbly asked him for any assistance that his former teacher could give him.

As the two talked, a plan was worked out whereby Leo Boles could eventually emerge with a college education, *if* he had the tenacity and determination to see it through. It would take between five and six years to accomplish, and in the interim Leo would not have a nickle to waste, or spend foolishly. Leo would have to use everything that he could scrape together during these years to pursue his education. It was a matter of having the "guts" to live in poverty all the time until he finished his education.

The plan that Professor Potter helped his student work out was extremely simple. Leo had saved enough money to pay for the ensuing winter term at Dibrell (1896.) After Dibrell College closed in the spring, Leo would again become Professor Potter's assistant teacher at Bildad. With the money *earned* and *saved*, Leo would pay his expenses through his second semester at Dibrell during the winter term of 1897. The summer and winter of 1897 would be spent teaching, during which Leo would save the money for his winter term at Dibrell in 1898. The routine of teaching school, saving his money thus earned, and applying this money in further study at college would be repeated until, at last, the goal had been attained.

It must be noted here that Leo Boles was no longer considered exactly a young man. He had been married and was a widower with an infant son. Very probably throughout Leo's college career he would be the oldest member of his class. Professor Potter had pointed out to Leo he would be perhaps twenty-six years old before he got through going to school, and that he was open for nicknames such as "Pop" and "Grandpa." However, no classmate of H. Leo Boles ever cast aspersions at the ambition or determination that this brilliant fellow student possessed.

The plan that must be followed entailed a great amount

of personal dignity on the part of the budding pedagogue. After careful consideration, it was decided that the name "H. Leo Boles" would be more suitable and dignified than either "Leo Boles" or even "Henry Leo Boles." People who knew him well enough to simply address him as "Leo" would continue to do so, while the rank and file of his school constituents would be more impressed by the introductory phrase, "Our new Professor will be H. Leo Boles, who has been attending Dibrell College, etc."

The most important extracurricular activity, in not only Dibrell, but also other schools of the day, were the "literary societies." Professor J. B. Clark, the president of Dibrell College, was a strong believer in the work done by the literary societies. He considered the opportunities presented in these meetings most valuable in the development of leadership among his students. Professor Clark was convinced that his students would go forth from Dibrell College to take their place in their respective communities quite proficient in the art of reasoning. It was also important that they be able to express their thoughts concisely in public speech. Professor Clark furthermore believed that engaging in formal debates was the best method by which an individual might develop orderly thinking. Accordingly every Friday night was set aside for the meeting of the school's Literary Society.

The programs of the Literary Society were not confined merely to debates. Devotional exercises, group singing, vocal and instrumental numbers, as well as orations, declamations and readings were also included on the Friday night programs. It was the idea of the college authorities to have *as many* students participate in the activities as time would allow. The boys and girls were allowed to sit together during the meeting and they would dress up and make dates for the occasion. The Literary Society meetings were always well attended as the public was invited. The Friday night meetings were not only for educational purposes, they were also social gatherings.

As soon as H. Leo Boles had enrolled in Dibrell College he lost little time in establishing himself as a leader in the school's activities. Officers in the Literary Society were elected monthly. The rise of H. Leo Boles in the club had been so meteoric that the election of officers for May (1896) found this first year man in the chair of the Dibrell Literary Society as its president.

Dibrell College furnished H. Leo Boles with better educational advantages than he had even dreamed existed. For the first time in his life he had access to an excellent library. Here he formed a love and respect for good books that were never to leave him. In the Dibrell library, H. Leo Boles formed the reading habits and fashioned the research patterns that enabled him to develop later into a great independent scholar.

H. Leo Boles never forgot for a moment why he was at Dibrell, and he was loath to squander even a moment of his time. He consequently developed an ability to concentrate upon his subjects that few of his contemporaries were able to accomplish. The skill of bringing all of one's mental powers to focus on a certain topic is most difficult to achieve, but once attained the solution of many problems is facilitated. The corrolary of concentration upon one's studies is excellent grades in all subjects. According to G. W. Hinkley, long time Dibrell resident and principal of the Dibrell High School for thirty-two years, H. Leo Boles made the highest grades in the history of Dibrell College!

Part of the Commencement Exercises of Dibrell College was the traditional annual political debate. The subject of these debates was always a current political problem that had nationwide implications. The four best debaters in school were selected by the faculty for these discussions. This debate always attracted a large crowd. It was designed as a public service in which the citizens were offered an opportunity to become better acquainted with existing national politics. However, it was also regarded as an occasion in which the institution definitely wished to "put its best foot forward." It was a signal honor that H. Leo Boles was chosen each of his three years to participate in this debate. It also casts a light upon the respect and esteem in which he was held by his college faculty.

It was at Dibrell College that H. Leo Boles made

many friends and acquaintances. There he met S. H. Hall, and they remained on most intimate terms throughout a lifelong friendship. Davis Chaffin, who enlisted as a private but rose through the ranks to become a General of the Army, was another close friend. Dr. John Mitchell, one time President of the University of Oklahoma was another of his classmates at Dibrell.

S. H. Hall relates this incident of his first engagement in argument with H. Leo Boles:

> I entered the school at Dibrell, Tennessee, in the fall of 1897. H. Leo Boles had been there the year before, but did not attend the fall semester. When he came into the school in January 1898, I was warned that he would "take over" the Literary Society. A young man by the name of Womack and I decided that we would try to head him off.
>
> Boles did not disappoint us. He was by far the strongest man in school. Since the students knew that I had done some preaching, and was fairly well known as a public speaker, a drive was made to get me lined up with the group designed to stop Boles.
>
> Boles and I opposed each other on every issue and we soon had the literary society divided into the Boles party and the Hall party.
>
> The real head-on collision with Boles came when I was president of the society. One of the girls, a sweetheart of mine, violated the rules of the society by failing to come up with her assignment. I imposed a fine of $5.00 on her. Boles, as soon as he heard of it went to the girl and offered his services as her lawyer to defend her in court. Believing that I was the only one in school as hardheaded as Boles, I resigned the presidency and played the role of the attorney for the society. Professor Tom Turner was appointed as judge. We liked to have scared the life out of the judge as we had at each other. If there is a word in our vocabulary that could be used in villifying another, it must have been used. . . . But I lost the trial.

During his last year at Dibrell College, there happened to enroll a rather tall, trim, auburn-haired girl of eighteen. This brown-eyed lass was vivacious, cheerful and mischievous. Her name was Ida Mae Meiser.

It so happened that H. Leo Boles and Ida had a class together in American History under Professor Clark. One day, he asked the question, "Who invented the steamboat?"

H. Leo Boles immediately answered, "Robert Fulton in 1807."

Ida interrupted, "Oh no, it was John Fitch in 1785."

At once an argument ensued. Some of the girls in the class took Ida's side of the dispute, among them being Jackie Potter, a distant relation of Professor Potter of Bildad. Bob Mullican, who really didn't know about the steamboat, but who did know about the scholarship of H. Leo Boles, argued vehemously that nobody but Fulton could have invented the steamboat. Finally, Professor Clark intervened.

"This seems to be a good subject for a debate. Suppose Ida, you and Jackie debate this subject at the Literary Society next Friday night. H. Leo, you and Bob take the other side."

As soon as school was out that afternoon, Ida and Jackie made a bee line for the library. But they were too late. The boys had been there ahead of them. H. Leo and Bob had checked out all the American History books that they were allowed, then they had some of their friends check out *all* the rest of the books that had any reference to steamboats.

The girls went over to Professor Clark's house. They told him of the trick that had been played on them. He laughed a little and told them that they could use his personal library if they wished. After perusing the histories in Professor Clark's home, they could find *nothing* that would help them on their side of the argument.

The picture was this: Here were two Freshman girls, inexperienced in the wiles of debate, being pitted against the most formidable opposition in the college. Both Boles and Mullican were Seniors, and they were crafty, skillful and experienced. The girls were really up against the "first team." Capping it all off, the girls were completely without supporting material from any reference books! What were they to do? They certainly did not feel like conceding the debate after the boys had treated them the way that they had.

The story now becomes a little obscure. Whether it was Professor Clark's idea, or whether it occurred to the girls first is not clear. However, Professor Clark had one real old American History book that was out of print, and he was sure that the library did not have a copy of this old relic. This the girls borrowed and doctored up considerably. Within the covers of this venerable copy, they proceeded to simply *write their own history*. Cleverly concealed within their one reference book was the fictitious "history" that they had just written.

The night of the debate, Ida got up and made her speech. She proceeded to read "quotations" from the obscure volume. When it was Jackie's time to speak, she based her emphatic arguments on the same book. It was their only argument, but it was good enough to win a split decision from the judges. H. Leo Boles in his rebuttal "smelled a mouse" and demanded to see the book that was being quoted so liberally by the girls; but they demurred, and his time was up without his getting a look at the questionable text. Just as soon as the meeting was over, H. Leo ran across the stage and grabbed the book. As he did so, all the fake history notes fell out upon the floor! It was the only debate that Boles and Mullican lost all year. They had been swindled, and by a couple of Freshman girls at that! That night the Hall party held a parade around the dormitories.

When Leo rode up to Professor Potter's house on a weekend in February in 1897 to talk about being the assistant teacher again that summer, the Professor said, "Leo, you have become well established here. The school people in the county seat have heard good reports concerning you. Why don't you apply for a school of your own this year?"

Leo Boles answered him, "Do you think that I can handle a school by myself?"

Professor Potter replied quickly, "Of course you can! Now is the chance for you to more than double your salary."

65

H. Leo Boles became very serious at the mention of earning more money. After a little silence, Leo said, "All right, if it pleases you to write me a recommendation, I'll ride over to Smithville next Saturday and apply for a school."

Here is what Professor Potter wrote, under the date of February 7, 1897:

> The bearer, Mr. Leo Boles, has been a pupil and an assistant in my school at New Bildad, and as a pupil he has been studious, polite, and logical; and as an assistant he has proved himself possessed of tact, learning, enthusiasm, and a high degree of patience. I cheerfully recommend him to a position as teacher in our public schools.
>
> Very respectfully, F. J. Potter.

Professor Potter was well established as an educator. He was known to be most conservative in his recommendations of his pupils. Therefore, the letter when presented to the DeKalb County school board was not taken lightly. H. Leo Boles was duly appointed the principal (it was only a one-teacher school) of the Mountain Ridge School for the following term at a salary of $40.00 per month.

As he and Smith had done at Center College, H. Leo Boles did his own cooking and housekeeping in the Dibrell dormitory. About every third or fourth week-end H. Leo would go home to Sink Creek and bring back his food supplies. Laura, or one of his sisters, would do his laundry for him on these visits home.

One Sunday afternoon, his brother Smith was to drive Leo back to Dibrell. H. Leo put his freshly laundered clothes, including every shirt that he owned, except the one that he was wearing, in the back of the buggy. All went well until they came to Mountain Creek, then a near tragedy occurred. A cloudburst in the middle of the day had caused a considerable rise in the creek. As Smith was attempting to ford the creek, all of Leo's laundry got wet, and most of it floated off down the creek, never to be retrieved.

After teaching the term at Mountain Ridge, H. Leo Boles attended Dibrell his final semester in the winter-spring of 1898. He was never again to teach in his home county of DeKalb. After his graduation as an honor student, with the prestige of Dibrell College behind him, he was appointed principal of a two-teacher school at Green's Cross Roads, Warren County. This was a richer county and H. Leo Boles now drew a salary of $50.00 per month.

While teaching at Green's Cross Roads, Professor Boles made his home at Ike Grizzle's house. Ike was a prosperous farmer whose home was located adjacent to the school. During the two years that H. Leo taught at Green's Cross Roads, he and Ike became fast friends. There were three things that Ike Grizzle loved above everything else: fine livestock, doing a friend a favor, and a good practical joke.

One day when the Professor was busy teaching school, Cain Golden, Adina's brother and consequently H. Leo Boles' step uncle, brought his threshing machine and crew of six men to harvest and thresh Ike Grizzle's wheat. During the morning, one of the men working on the thresher had lost his hat as it had blown off and had been mangled in the machinery. It was too hot a day to work in the fields bare-headed. When the hands came in to eat their noonday meal at the Grizzle's, the man who had lost his hat went into the school teacher's room and helped himself to a hat. He found Professor Boles' "hard hat" and promptly stole it. In those days, what people called a "hard hat" was a derby. Many years later, Cain Golden still got a hearty laugh when he recalled how silly that man looked running his thresher and wearing H. Leo Boles' brown derby hat.

After H. Leo Boles had received his second pay check for teaching the Green's Cross Roads School in the fall of 1898, he borrowed one of Ike Grizzle's fine saddle horses and rode up to the Sink Creek farm for the week-end. His son Cleo was now three years old. Cleo was a frail and quiet child, but he seemed to be growing as rapidly as a weed. There were other children in the family about his age with whom he happily played. Leo offered to pay his father for Cleo's keep, but Jeff would have none of that. Leo then left $20.00 with Adina to spend on Cleo's clothes, medicines, or in any way that she thought necessary.

67

That Saturday night, Leo rode on up to Bildad to counsel once more with his old friend and teacher, Professor F. J. Potter. Professor Potter was most happy to see him. They looked each other over carefully. Professor Potter had many grey hairs and was beginning to be stooped a little; Professor Boles was young, vigorous, eager, well-dressed, with money in his pocket and riding one of the best horses in Warren County. The old professor let Leo enjoy his moment of triumph, then suddenly and with crushing effect, he asked Leo, "Now that you are *through going to school,* what do you plan to do?"

The question stung his former pupil like a yellowjacket. Leo falteringly answered, "Professor Potter, you know that we both planned for me to graduate from college with a bachelor's degree."

Professor Potter stung him again, but this time he used a more kindly voice like he was explaining the "Q.E.D." of a geometry problem to a class of near-morons, "All right you are going to graduate from College. What are you going to use for money if you squander it on clothes and high living? On your salary, you ought to be riding one of your father's mules instead of that fine animal out there."

Feeling the rebuke acutely, H. Leo Boles, was quick to change the subject, "That's what I came over here to see you about, Professor Potter. Now that I have graduated from Dibrell, what college do you think that I should attend?"

Professor Potter was now convinced that he had put his former pupil back in line, so he allowed the new trend in the conversation to develop further, "Leo, are you convinced that the college I attended did a good job on me?"

Professor Boles was far too tactful not to rise to the occasion. "Oh, yes Sir!" Leo replied, "But you were a very exceptional student. I feel sure you would have probably been a very well read man, if you had never attended any college at all."

Professor Potter smiled at the artful answer his erstwhile pupil had given him, then seriously he said, "Leo you have come again to my door for advice. The best advice that I can give you now is the same advice that I gave you three years ago. Why not paraphrase John Bunyan's great epic and call your life, "A Pedagogue's Progress"?

Professor Potter continued, "You have followed the routine of teaching in the summer and fall so that you could earn the money to attend college in the winter and spring. Dibrell College has given you all that she has to offer. I feel sure that my old friend, W. N. Billingsley, who has just been elected president of Burritt College will allow you two full years of college credit if you want to finish your schooling at Burritt." Then he added in a voice full of pride, "If you graduate from Burritt College, you will have graduated from the best college in the Cumberland Mountains."

H. Leo Boles left Professor Potter's house that night determined that he would seek an interview with President Billingsley just as soon as the Warren County schools let out that Christmas. More than once the renown of Burritt College had reached his ears. Besides that, Professor Potter had said that Burritt College was the "best" college in the Cumberlands. That alone made Burritt most desirable to Leo.

One thing in particular that H. Leo Boles had learned in Dibrell College was that he was a very ignorant person. The more he learned, the more ignorant he realized that he was. As hitherto unknown doors were opened to him, the longer the corridors of his incomprehension became. He realized exactly what Sir Isaac Newton meant when in the twilight of his scintillating career, the great scientist stated that he had merely strolled along the beach of the sea of truth and here and there he had picked up a few shiny pebbles that had seemed most obvious.

When Leo had left Dibrell for the last time, he determined that he was not finishing his schooling, he was merely passing another milestone in the everlasting lane of learning. The desire to acquire more education became an obsession with him. Shakespeare once said, "The sea hath bounds, but deep desire hath none." It was inevitable that as soon as his pocketbook would allow it, H. Leo Boles would enroll in Burritt College.

Chapter IX

THE FOUNTAIN ON THE MOUNTAIN

President W. N. Billingsley of Burritt College had received a letter of application for admission from H. Leo Boles early in the fall of 1898. President Billingsley had written H. Leo, then the principal of the Green's Cross Roads School, that Burritt College could accept two years of academic credits from a graduate of Dibrell College, consequently, H. Leo Boles would be admitted to the Junior Class at Burritt, subject to making up certain work that the Burritt College faculty required for graduation.

H. Leo Boles had then written a second letter in which he had inquired about the chances of doing some work by which he could partially defray his expenses for board and tuition. President Billingsley had answered this question with a short letter in which he replied that a few jobs were open for deserving students, but that the students who received this help were picked by him pending an interview. President Billingsley advised H. Leo to come to Spencer for a personal interview if he was further interested.

As the result of the correspondence, on New Year's day 1899, H. Leo Boles stood before President Billingsley's office door awaiting his interview. Several young men were there ahead of him. While waiting, H. Leo fell in conversation with the nattily dressed man just ahead of him in the line. This young man was very impatient at the delay and kept muttering about being thusly held up. Finally H. Leo's time came to see Mr. Billingsley. A deep bass voice within the office said, "Next, please!"

H. Leo went in, "President Billingsley, I'm H. Leo Boles. We have had some correspondence, Sir."

President Billingsley turned steel grey eyes upon H. Leo Boles. He seemed to see completely through the applicant standing before him. So much depended upon this interview that Leo's knees were shaking. Presently President Billingsley spoke again and the room rumbled, "Why do you want to try to work your way through Burritt College? It will be much better if you do not have to spend time away from your studies working at a job. You may not make it here scholastically anyway. Many boys do not have what it takes here."

H. Leo Boles was no longer frightened. "President Billingsley," he said slowly but firmly, "I will make it scholastically. Never fear about that part of it. As for why I need to work my way through Burritt College, I have to because I am a very poor man. May I take some of your time to tell you how I made it through Dibrell?"

President Billingsley looked the applicant over again. His eyes locked with the light blue eyes of H. Leo Boles that steadily looked into his own. "Please be seated, Mr. Boles. Now tell me how you made it through Dibrell."

Briefly, but with the logical simplicity as if he were explaining a mathematics problem, H. Leo Boles outlined the financial structure of what Professor Potter had called "A Pedagogue's Progress." H. Leo finished with this statement, "If it were practical to get supplies here from my father's farm, I could do my own housekeeping like I did at Center and Dibrell, I would not need to work. I, too, am very desirous of spending all my time on my studies here."

President Billingsley then said, "The boy who was here ahead of you applied for the job of building fires in my office. What kind of a job do you want?"

Again the steel-grey eyes locked with the light-blue. There was no give, either way. H. Leo Boles answered, "President Billingsley, I desire an education, and I am willing to do anything to get it. If you have *any* kind of work that I can do—I don't care what it is—I will do it to help pay my expenses."

President Billingsley then exhibited the sound judgment that marks all able school administrators. He was quick to recognize a worthy young man. The office this time did not rumble, it thundered, "Mr. Boles, you may build the fires in my office."

H. Leo Boles walked the Burritt College campus his first week there as if it were hallowed ground. He listened with pride as the traditions of Burritt were explained in the school chapel. Burritt College had an illustrious past. It was founded in 1841. It was the first co-educational college in the South in that young women as well as young men were taught in the same classes. Under the leadership of men like William Davis Carnes and R. L. Gillentine, Burritt had risen to the academic heights. Now under the direction of the gifted Billingsley, Burritt was entering into its golden era of scholastic achievement. He was surrounded by a faculty of excellent academic men standing who like the brilliant Gillentine would have been an asset to any school.

Located on the very top of Spencer Mountain, in Van Buren County, in the town of Spencer, Tennessee Burritt College had been erected. Spencer was a unique place to build an educational institution. It was a small isolated community in the heart of primitive Tennessee. This state today follows the system of assigning automobile license tags in the order of the gallons of gasoline sold in each of the ninty-five counties that compose Tennessee. The Van Buren County tags today begin with the prefix number, "95-".

In 1899, Spencer was almost entirely cut off from the outside world. Communication was by horseback, the mail being delivered three times a week. The students were carried up the mountain by special stagecoach. A student running away from Burritt College without the knowledge of the college authorities was not only improbable, it was next to impossible! But Burritt College was no jail or reform school where a parent could put a spoiled or pampered adolescent. Students were present at Burritt by permission of the faculty only. Anyone who squandered either his own or the college's time was promptly expelled by President Billingsley.

The reason that Burritt College was built in such a secluded place was that its founders were determined that *nothing* should interfere with the college work. President Billingsley believed that the remoteness of Spencer Mountain was a great boon to education at Burritt. He considered that boys in other colleges, located in cities such as

72

Nashville or Knoxville, who were turned loose from three o'clock in the afternoon until the school hours of eight or nine o'clock the following morning would certainly "bankrupt their morals and lead only to ruin."

Looking down the steep sides of the mountain, one could not fail to be impressed with the scenic beauty of the virgin timberland, waterfalls cascading over pallisade bluffs and the untold wonders of the valleys that lay below. As the students ascended the mountain, an interesting botanical laboratory was paraded before them. In the lowlands, oak, elm, maple and beech trees abounded; while in the highlands and atop the mountain, chestnut, ash, pine and mountain laurel thrived. It was truly a wonderful setting for an institution designed to improve the mind, body and soul of its students.

The buildings on the campus of Burritt College were made of red brick. Rather than accomplish the most tedious task of hauling the brick up the precipitous mountain, the founders of the college had erected brick kilns on the school grounds. There the brick had been burned in the old-fashioned way, making use of local clay.

Professor W. N. Billingsley served Burritt as its President from 1899 to 1911. President Billingsley was one of Tennessee's most distinguished educators. He held many honors which were conferred upon him by grateful contemporaries. He was President of the State Association of Public School Officers (1888-1899). Governor Benton McMillin appointed him as a member of the State Textbook Commission (1899-1904). His friends were very proud of his fine work on the textbook commission. Governor McMillin chose Professor Billingsley to represent the State of Tennessee at the Paris Exposition in 1900. Billingsley traveled extensively in Europe and England, studying the school systems in many countries on this trip. Among other duties, he served as President of the Tennessee Teachers Association and was, for many years, a member of the State Board of Education. President Billingsley was a conscientious educator. During his regime, Burritt College reached the zenith of its famous history.

H. Leo Boles, in describing the work of W. N. Billingsley wrote, "He gave his life to the people of the mountains and he served them faithfully to the end. Professor Billingsley's contribution to education and his service for the betterment of teaching service was the greatest blessing the people of the Cumberland Mountains had ever received."

H. Leo Boles was overjoyed at the rich blessing that he felt was his as he attended to his daily duties. He was far happier than he had been since before he had lost Cynthia. The privilege of drinking at the fountain of learning in his present surroundings atop the mountain was both exhilarating and exalting. He drank deeply at the fount that freely flowed, and the more he drank, the more liberally the fountain seemed to flow. H. Leo was reminded of the line of J. G. Saxe, that he once memorized:

At Learning's fountain it is sweet to drink.

As he continued to drink of the waters of knowledge, the name of H. Leo Boles began to appear more frequently at the head of the weekly scholarship rankings that each teacher was required to file in President Billingsley's office. The deep bass voice chuckled as he remembered the soft-spoken words of the slight built, blue-eyed man who had stood before him on New Year's day and said, "I will make it scholastically. Never fear about that part of it."

A perusal of the Burritt College catalog of 1899 (Gospel Advocate Publishing Company) reveals that the 3 R's were taught in the primary and secondary departments, but one infers that these were only a means to the end of studying Greek, Latin and the early sciences. If anyone is skeptical regarding the caliber of academic achievement that the students attained in this curriculum with that pare the Burritt College curriculum with that offered by some of the more modern colleges of today. An examination of the 1899 catalog shows that young Boles would complete the following courses that were required for his graduation:

Mathematics

1st Year   Robinson's Higher Arithmetic and Algebra
2nd Year   Robinson's Plane Geometry and Trigonometry

3rd Year	Robinson's Surveying and Robinson's Analytic Geometry
4th Year	Norton's Natural Philosophy and Robinson's Astronomy

Latin

1st Year	Sallust's Catiline and Cicero's Orations
2nd Year	Virgil, Six Books of Aeneid, Livy, Horace, Select Odes
3rd Year	Horace, Epistles, Satires, Art of Poetry
4th Year	Cicero's Treatises on Friendship and Old Age

Greek

1st Year	Bullion's Grammar, Reader to Fables and and Dialogues
2nd Year	Grammar, Reader (complete), Xenophon, Anabasis, Cyropaedaea
3rd Year	Extracts from Isocrates, Demosthenes, Plato and Longinus
4th Year	Homer's Odyssey and Sophocles Oedipus

English

1st Year	Hart's Rhetoric, with Exercises in Composition
2nd Year	Kames' Elements of Criticism, Sir William Hamilton's Lectures on Logic
3rd Year	Cleveland's English Literature, American Literature, and Readings in the English Classics
4th Year	Metaphysics, Hamilton's Lectures, Moral Philosophy, Alexander's Lectures

Natural Science

3rd Year	Anatomy, Physiology and Hygiene, Chemistry
4th Year	Geology, Zoology, Botany

In 1899 the year that H. Leo Boles entered, there were 231 students enrolled in the college. The degrees conferred by Burritt College, under its charter rights granted by the Tennessee Legislature, were Bachelor of Arts and Bachelor of Science; Mistress of Arts and Mistress of Science.

75

Here is the schedule that H. Leo Boles followed at Burritt College in 1899 and 1900.

4:30 Arising Bell—30 minutes to dress and prepare room
5:00 Study for one hour in classrooms
6:00 Breakfast
6:30 Gymnastic Society (physical exercise)
8:00 Chapel
9:00 Group Singing
9:30 Regular Classes
10:00 Morning Recess—20 minutes
10:20 Regular Classes resumed
12:00 Dinner
1:00 Regular Classes
3:00 Afternoon Recess—20 minutes
3:20 Regular Classes
5:00 Afternoon Vesper
5:30 Prepare for Supper—15 minutes
5:45 Supper
7:00 Boys in Dormitory, Girls in respective homes for study
8:40 Warning Bell—20 minutes to prepare for bed
9:00 Retiring Bell—all lights out

The catalog of Burritt plainly said, "No young man is permitted to leave the college premises, day or night, unless it is known where he is going and what he is expecting to do."

Students who "slipped out" and went to town after the retiring bell rang were almost invariably discovered and disgracefully denounced from the chapel pulpit the next morning.

The student body was unified by the ringing of a huge cast iron bell that was mounted in a tower on the campus. All school activities were signalled to begin and end by the ringing of this bell. In the still, cool quiet of the mountain air, when the atmospheric condition were right; the tolling of the Burritt bell could be heard throughout the valleys below for a distance of perhaps thirty miles.

On Saturday morning the Literary Societies would meet. The attendance at these meetings was excellent, inasmuch as membership in one of the societies was compulsory. Saturday afternoon, the boys were encouraged to engage in games, or some other "innocent amusement."

H. Leo Boles had joined the Calliopean Literary Society and, as might be expected, he soon began taking an active part in the work of this group, especially the debates. He became a leader on the campus, and he was selected by the Calliopeans to represent their society in the Commencement Exercises of 1899 by delivering an oration. It was a definite honor that he should have been chosen to give that speech because at the time he had been at Burritt for only a few months.

During the summer-fall of 1899, H. Leo again accepted the principalship of the Green's Cross-Road School in Warren County. In January, 1900, he again entered Burritt College. He was very desirous of having the full year at Burritt, but his financial condition was such that he had to earn the money so that he could graduate.

President Billingsley, and other members of the faculty had made H. Leo the proposition that if he would study his textbooks and could learn enough in absentee during the summer, and while teaching school in the fall to pass the first semester examinations, they would allow him full credit for the courses. They did not think that he could do it! However, they had not reckoned with the tremendous thirst for knowledge that H. Leo Boles possessed. Neither had the Burritt College faculty, at this time, a true insight into the dogged determination, the driving courage and the brilliant intellect of their student. It was, therefore, a surprised group of professors who graded H. Leo Boles' examination papers in early January of 1900! It was decided by unanimous vote of the Burritt College faculty to allow him to enter the Senior Class, now in its last semester.

It was the custom and tradition at Burritt College that each member of the Senior Class should prepare and deliver before the faculty and student body, four orations or essays during the last semester of the year. The subjects of H. Leo Boles' orations were: "The Achievements of Youth," "Napoleon, the Conqueror," "Progressive Development" and "An Ideal Character." It was also customary for each member of the Senior Class to deliver an oration on Commencement Day as a part of the graduating exercises. His subject for Commencement Day was, "The Decline of Myths and the Rise of Science."

President Billingsley, on behalf of the Trustees and Faculty of Burritt College, and the power vested in him by the Legislature of Tennessee, conferred degrees on five young men and three young ladies. Billingsley then hurried home to finish packing his clothes into his trunk. Early the next morning he was off on the first leg of his journey to France to attend the Paris Exposition.

Thus, it occurred that on June 3, 1900, a dream came true for Henry Leo Boles. Through work, sweat and stubborn tenacity of purpose, a goal had been reached, and sweet victory was at last won. H. Leo Boles had graduated from college without one red penny being given him by anyone. He had literally "worked his way" through school. He had financed his way through college by backbreaking work on the farm, and by difficult teaching during the fall in the public schools. He had "lifted himself by pulling up on his own bootstraps." And now, he had a title that he could truly and proudly write after his name; he had justly earned the appellation, "Henry Leo Boles, Bachelor of Arts."

Chapter X
DECISION IN TEXAS

An honor graduate of Burritt College in 1900 who desired to teach school experienced little difficulty in finding employment. Armed with a letter of recommendation from President Billingsley, written the week before graduation, H. Leo Boles went forth from Spencer Mountain in search of a better teaching position than he thus far had been able to procure.

Professor Boles' early teaching experiences had met the approval of both the pupils and patrons in the communities where he had worked. An old adage says, "Nothing succeeds like success." A cardinal principle of psychology states that one tends to enjoy and repeat an act that has been successful. Consequently, it was only natural that H. Leo Boles should continue his teaching career after he received his degree from Burritt College.

H. Leo Boles seems to have been a "natural" teacher. Most certainly, he was one of the best classroom instructors that Tennessee has produced. It is realized that the foregoing statement is most complimentary, because the Volunteer State is renowned with the names of excellent teachers. However, there are hundreds of men and women today that will testify that Brother Boles was by far the most able instructor that they ever had. He had a way of presenting a lesson, especially in the Old and New Testament classes that he later taught, in which the point that he was making was almost inescapable for the student to see and understand.

Professor Potter, as early as 1897, seems to have summed up the teaching qualifications of Professor Boles, after he had taught only three terms, far better than any later day author when he described Leo Boles as possessing "tact, learning, enthusiasm, and a high degree of patience." One other attribute must be added; his ability to reason through complex problems step by step, until the answer appeared clear and simple in the minds of his students. S. P. Pittman, who was associated as a teacher with H. Leo Boles for 24 years puts it this way. "How often did we hear him say, pointing his index finger toward his listening audience, 'I do not know how to think otherwise than straight.'"

Above all other qualities as a teacher, however, towered Professor Boles' tremendous enthusiasm for the job that he was doing. He loved to teach. The sheer joy of watching a youthful face light up as his pupil began to "see through" a problem in mathematics, or the expression in the eyes of a student who was for the first time understanding the meaning of a beautiful poem, was the main reason that H. Leo Boles chose to follow a teaching career after his graduation from Burritt College.

While he was yet attending the Spencer school Leo had begun a correspondence with practically every county school superintendent in the Cumberlands. He was after the best paying position that he could get. At Burritt College, Leo had several classmates who were from Texas, and they had naturally told him about the public school system of that state. Not only did the Texas counties pay better teacher salaries, but many of them had school terms that ran for eight and even nine months of the year! This made the Texas schools pay double or triple the salary paid in the Cumberlands. Leo resolved that if he ever got a chance to teach in Texas, he would surely accept the invitation. However, his letters of application to the Texas school officials brought polite, but negative replies.

After much negotiation, Leo accepted the principalship of the school at Sykes, Tennessee. This was in Smith County, not far from the town of Carthage. There were two very good reasons that Leo finally decided on the Sykes school. Firstly, it paid more money than he was offered elsewhere; and secondly, his friend George F. Womack was teaching there.

Leo had formed a strong friendship with George Womack during the Dibrell days where they had been both classmates and roommates. It was well that the two young men were together in Smith County as Sykes was entirely too far away from their homes to visit during the week-end. This was the fartherest that either of them had been away from home, and both of them experienced a real case of "homesickness" before the school term was even a month old. However, the school work was heavy and the young pedagogues soon were so deeply engrossed in their teaching problems that they had little time in which they could long for home.

George Womack was possessed of a superior mind. Being associated together as they were, one acted as a tower of strength for the other. Each had confidence in the other, and in this neither was ever disappointed. They felt that together as a team that they could accomplish anything to which they set their hands. In this respect, these two young intellectuals, in the flower of manhood were very probably correct as neither of them ever failed to do anything that he had really determined to accomplish.

George Womack had a secret ambition to study law and become a successful attorney. The purpose became more deeply set as he watched H. Leo Boles concentrating on his books. George had not had the advantage of going to college further than the courses offered at Dibrell. As he watched Leo apply the study techniques that had been so successful in his attack on the Latin, Greek and Mathematics required at Burritt College, George Womack got a tremendous idea. He now had the answer to how he was going to accomplish his ambition to be a successful lawyer. All he had to do was to convince Leo that the two of them could study law together, and they could learn much about the profession by the inexpensive method of independent study and research. They could borrow, or maybe buy, a set of law books and using the study techniques that Leo had developed, they could go a long way toward teaching themselves the reading of law. This was the dream of George Womack. He would try to sell Leo the idea. Leo loved logic and public debating so well that the practice of law was a profession in which he could not fail to succeed. Yes, George thought, it should be comparatively easy to convince Leo that they should become lawyers.

Before George could really get started on his cam-

81

paign to convince Leo to study law, however, one of those unexpected events that mould and alter the course of people's lives occurred. It was now the last Monday in August, 1900. The school at Sykes was in its eighth week, and was running smoothly. Then the bombshell exploded! A letter from the school board at Moody, Texas, arrived at Sykes, addressed to Professor H. Leo Boles. The letter had been sent to the farm of H. J. Boles, in DeKalb County, and Jeff had immediately forwarded it to his son. Mails in that day were slow in the mountainous Cumberlands, and this letter was almost too late in its arrival. The letter stated that, while at the time of the former correspondence with Professor Boles there had existed no vacancy in the Moody schools, there had been an unexpected resignation of two of their teachers, and if Professor Boles was still interested in coming to Texas, would he please telegraph the Moody School Board immediately.

Leo and George held hushed discussions at frequent intervals in the corridor just outside their classrooms that afternoon. Finally, school was over for the day, and Leo and George went immediately home to where they were keeping "bachelor's quarters." There Leo related to George the benefit to be reaped by teaching in the Texas schools. It did not take long for them to arrive at a decision. Early that evening, Leo and George borrowed a horse and buggy, drove into Carthage, and sent the Moody School Board their answer. The wire stated briefly that H. Leo Boles was available for the position, and that he would accept the proposition provided his associate teacher, George F. Womack, for whom he personally vouched, was appointed to the other vacancy. They requested the Texas school board to answer immediately.

The next day Leo and George were nervous and fidgety, but they said nothing to anyone there at Sykes about what they hoped was developing. That evening, they again borrowed the rig and rode into Carthage for their answer. The telegrapher had the message. The Moody superintendent had duly appointed H. Leo Boles to be the principal and Womack the associate teacher. Their salaries were to be $100 and $75.00 per month for an eight month term. The telegram stressed the fact that schools in Texas opened the first Monday in September, and asked the direct question, "Could you be here on time?" Now that posed a good problem. It was then Tuesday night, and they were due in Moody by the following Monday. That gave only five days to make a clean break in Smith County and get to Texas. Fortunately, Moody is located in the eastern part of the state and there was a through train from Nashville to New Orleans. From New Orleans to Dallas was another day by train. Leo and George calculated that they could make Moody by Monday *if* they cleared out of Carthage (Smith County) by Wednesday night. Consequently, Leo and George jubilantly wired back that they accepted the positions and that they would be there in time for school opening on Monday!

That night the young men almost completed their packing before they retired at about two o'clock. They were up early the next morning, and before school began they offered their written resignations to the local trustees at Sykes. An awkward situation arose immediately when the trustees refused to accept their resignations. Then H. Leo Boles and George Womack got angry and asked just how they (the trustees) proposed to hold them at Sykes. The Trustees went into session. Presently a two-horse wagon was hitched up and all three trustees drove into Carthage to consult with the County Superintendent. About noon the trustees were back in Sykes with the superintendent in town. The superintendent then proceeded to show the qualifications of a good politician. He was shocked and dismayed that two such fine Christian young men with such promising teaching careers ahead of them should even consider doing such a thing as running out and leaving all the children without teachers. The superintendent was sure that the boys had just been carried away for the moment without considering the seriousness of the situation. He asked Leo and George to reconsider, and not throw away their teaching future. If they did this dastardly thing they could expect never to be hired again to teach in Tennessee!

The boys went into a huddle. Neither had been particularly impressed by the threats of the superintendent. They had signed no contracts. They decided to stand pat on their decision as the distant green pastures of Texas still beckoned. However, Leo and George realized that they were in a serious predicament. Granted they had moral obligations in Smith County, but by the same token they had committed themselves to the Moody School Board. They realized that they had acted too hastily in accepting the Texas appointment before they had been released from their present position. But now that they were in the middle of a mess, somebody was going to be disappointed. It would probably be called "rationalization" today, but Leo reasoned that since he had applied for the Moody school previous to his application for the Sykes school, and even though it had been a mistake on his part, he *had* given his word in the telegram, and since his and George's blunder was going to discommode either the school authorities in Texas or in Tennessee, he and George had the moral right to pick the place that would best suit their own personal interests. Consequently, the two teachers, who had just become most unpopular in the Sykes community, left Smith County behind by boarding the evening stagecoach bound for Nashville, from which they traveled by rail before taking the stage again, to their destination. They made it to Moody about midnight Sunday.

The boys had made their decision so suddenly that there had been no time for a final visit to their homes in the Cumberlands. Everyone around Sink Creek knew that H. Leo Boles was a right stubborn young man once he "set" his head on something, so when word finally seeped through the community that Leo was principal of a school in Texas and had taken George Womack with him, no one seemed particularly surprised. The three who were not in the least surprised were his brother Smith who was shortly to depart for Arkansas, his father Jeff, and the venerable Professor Potter of Bildad.

Professors Boles and Womack were not neophytes in organizing a school. They were right personable young men. They were hard workers. The native state from which they had come had furnished many of the early settlers of Texas, and the memory of the Tennesseans, Crockett, Bowie and Travis, among others, were enshrined in

84

the Alamo. The author of Texas independence, Sam Houston was twice elected Governor of the Volunteer State. The young teachers were welcomed to the Lone Star State by the natives. They were accepted as Texans in Moody. No greater compliment could be paid them as they threw themselves into their adopted community's activities.

In Dibrell, H. Leo Boles had joined the fraternal orders of the Masonic Lodge, and the Odd Fellows. He transferred his membership in these to the Moody chapters. He rose in Masonic work until he took the order's thirty-third degree. George Womack was also a member of these lodges.

As Leo and George proceeded to build themselves into their school community their popularity increased. They soon had their school running "as smoothly as a top." They liked the Texas town and their neighbors "took a liking" to the "right smart" young professors who worked with them so enthusiastically. The patrons of their school were not long in realizing that they had acquired two capable young schoolmen from Tennessee.

After Leo and George had found a house in which to dwell, and had become comfortably established in their home, George began in earnest to unfold his plan of operation for making his life-long ambition become a reality. He persuaded his friend Leo to share his intentions of becoming a lawyer. He and Leo bought a set of second-hand law books, and began reading law while they were teaching school. The long winter nights were spent together in studying the statutes. They made plans to save their money until they had enough to attend the Law School at the University of Texas, in Austin. Their plans were well made and were sound in every respect. Lawyers they were going to be!

When school was out about the first week in May, 1901, George returned to Tennessee for the summer. He had left in such a hurry that he had some personal affairs that needed his attention. Leo remained in Texas to try his hand in selling books in a house to house canvassing campaign. Leo had only mediocre success in this venture. True, he made enough money so that he did not have to dip into his savings in order to defray his summer living expenses, as he had done each summer heretofore, but he soon saw that salesmanship was not one of his better accomplishments. With only three weeks of his summer vacation left, H. Leo had saved from his summer work, just about enough to pay for a roundtrip train ticket to McMinnville, Tennessee; this being the closest railroad station to the Sink Creek farm.

Leo had only about ten days at home. All seemed well. Cleo was frail but apparently healthy. Jeff cut short a protracted meeting in order to see his eldest son. In spite of his apparent aloofness, the "old man" was quite clannish in his behavior, especially toward those who bore the name of "Boles."

Leo and George returned to their same job, and soon the school year of 1901-1902 was well under way. The year was marked by intensive study of the law books by the two teachers, and a formation of a debating society in Moody.

During the spring of 1902, Leo asked the school board for a raise in pay. He was told that they would all like to see him and George get a raise but there was no money to do so. Accordingly, Leo and George started a correspondence with the school superintendents of other Texas counties. One of the school trustees was the Moody postmaster. When he saw how much mail the boys were getting from school officials in other towns, he called the board together and told them that they were going to lose two of the best teachers Moody had ever had if they did not raise their pay. So it came to pass that during the school year, 1902-1903, Leo received $125 and George was upped to $100 per month.

It turned out that the spring of 1903 was the pivot point in the life of H. Leo Boles. During the second semester, Leo received word of the death of his younger brother, Roscoe. This news greatly affected him and caused him to think more profoundly about the spiritual side of life.

With the news of Roscoe's death, Leo began to consider religion a very serious matter. He remembered the

H. LEO BOLES, 1905

pious environment in which he was reared. He recalled the spiritual discussions and the talk about the contemporary problems of the church that he had heard as a boy when itinerate preachers had stayed overnight with Jeff Boles. He recollected the several years of his boyhood when he was kept out of the fields in order to read the Bible for six hours a day to his father, when Jeff's eyesight was failing. He thought about the sacrifices and hardships that Jeff was enduring while he was furthering the word of God among the poor people of the Cumberlands. Finally, he considered the day when he and his wife, Cynthia Cantrell Boles, had gone forward to accept the teaching of Christ during the annual "protracted meeting" held at the Olive Church of Christ in DeKalb County. He reflected upon his confession that Jesus Christ was the Son of God, and his baptism into his name.

Atheistic doctrine was as far removed from the innate emotions of H. Leo Boles as the poles of the earth are from the equator. The minor prophet, Joel, calling upon the children of Judah to repent, uttered these words:

. . . the day of Jehovah is near
in the valley of decision. (Joel 3:14)

Two incidents occurred during this time when Leo was struggling to find his way in Jehovah's valley of decision. These events helped to crystallize his thinking concerning things spiritual, and greatly facilitated his decision to become a preacher.

In the late winter, George Womack was seized with a bad cold and subsequently developed pneumonia. It was "touch and go" for a few days. The Grim Reaper was standing ready to claim the body of George Womack. During this time, Leo stood watch over George, and prayed for his recovery almost constantly.

George awoke from his fitful, feverish sleep while Leo was uttering a prayer. Said George, through parched lips, "Leo, read to me please." Leo gently asked, "What shall I read, George?"

George then replied by quoting the eloquent Ingersoll's deathbed confession, "There is but one book . . . Read me your Bible."

The second event that helped Leo reach his decision to renounce the practice of law and become a minister happened shortly after George recovered from his sickness. It was customary for the good people of Moody to hold a "union prayer meeting" on the Sunday evenings when there were no preaching services. This group was called "union" because it was composed of people from the several church denominations represented in the community.

On this particular evening, a steward of the Methodist Church made a talk in which he expressed his thanks to God that people from all denominations could assemble and worship together as "they were all bound for the same place anyway—heaven." After finishing his talk, he called on Professor Boles to conclude the meeting. This Leo did in no uncertain way. He arose and in a few sentences condemned denominationalism, and declared it to be "a curse on the community." Leo finished his talk by giving a few choice quotations on the unity of God's people.

After Leo had closed his remarks, the Methodist steward arose and attempted to defend his position. He ended his rebuttal by challenging Professor Boles for a debate on the subject of denominationalism.

Now challenging H. Leo Boles for a public debate was almost like inviting a fish to a swimming contest. Of course the challenge was accepted. The fame of the earstwhile debating champion of both Dibrell and Burritt colleges was far-flung among the Cumberlands. But this was Texas, far removed from the Tennessee hills and hollows, and H. Leo Boles was just another school teacher invading the domain of religion, as far as the church people of Moody were concerned. The debate was set for two weeks from that Sunday night.

When the regular Methodist preacher returned the next day, his steward related the matter to him and asked the minister if he would take his place in the debate. The preacher replied, "I will be glad to meet the Professor on that question."

When some of Leo's friends heard about the switch in debater they urged Leo to back out of the discussion on the excuse that he had been challenged by an amateur, like himself on a religious question. Now that a professional preacher had been substituted, Leo could rightfully and honorably quit the field by refusing to go on with the discussion. This suggestion was, of course, scoffed at by both Leo and George. H. Leo Boles even in those days, was a master logician. He was tough competition in a debate when he did not have the Truth on his side of the argument. Here, however, Leo was on the *right* side of the question from the start. He wouldn't even have to depend upon twisting and confusing the arguments of his opponent to win because he had Bible teaching that he could quote. Furthermore, H. Leo Boles had heard Jeff quote the scriptures that old "Raccoon" John Smith, Alexander Campbell and David Lipscomb had used in discussions with denominalists. Leo knew most of the passages of scripture that he would use by memory, it remained only for him and George to find them in the Bible so that he could read them directly from the New Testament.

Professor Boles as the challenged had the privilege of stating the question. He accordingly submitted the proposition, "Resolved that Denominationalism is Contrary to Christianity," and chose the affirmative. Leo was skillful enough to know that he wanted the first speech so he could rock sectarianism back on its heels from the very beginning. In his speech he pointed out that the bloody religious wars of Europe were fought by monarchs attempting to force their particular secular beliefs upon their subjects. He dwelt briefly upon the evils of the Spanish Inquisition. Leo brought out the fact that the Man of Galilee was a Man of Peace. Then Leo brought forth his imposing array of scriptures for Christian Unity, and gave book, chapter, and verse for each quotation. Finally, he closed his argument in a most dramatic fashion by declaring that Jesus only established one church. His voice reached a thundering crescendo, then his tone began to soften until at last his voice was barely audible as he reached his climax. Then in well-controlled tones, Leo closed his discourse with the "One God, One Christ, One Church" argument; only the church as set up on the Day of Pentecost was ordained by the Trinity, and all denominationalism must be considered not only unscriptural, but a downright curse upon the community of Moody.

Leo had delivered the best oration of his life. It was such a masterpiece of speaking that anything the Methodist preacher could say would fall flat on the audience's ears. Everyone in the house was impressed. However, Professor Boles lost the decision of the judges.

It seems worth relating here how it came about that after such a speech Leo could lose. The answer was in the simple mechanics of how the judges had been selected. It had been agreed upon that each disputant would make thirty minute speeches, and they would each have a ten minute rebuttal. The Methodist preacher insisted upon having judges instead of moderators; these judges were to render a decision as to whether Professor Boles had proved his proposition. The Methodist was to select one judge, the Professor another, and these two judges were to select the third judge. The preacher selected the steward who had started the debate as his judge. Since there was not another member of the church of Christ in the community, Professor Boles chose a man who was not a member of any denomination as his judge. These two judges selected a man who belonged to the Baptist Church to be the third judge. As was to be expected, the two judges who were members of denominations voted against Professor Boles, while his judge loyally voted for him. Never again was H. Leo Boles to debate a religious question without moderators instead of judges presiding.

One of America's foremost educators and philosophers of the twentieth century, John Dewey, once said, "Man thinks only when he comes to a fork in the road. Only when a person must make a choice does he really think." The incidents related in the foregoing pages did much to cause H. Leo Boles to decide which fork of the road he would follow. He re-evaluated his choice to study law, and he arrived at the decision to devote all his life to preaching the gospel.

90

Shakespeare, in the play *Julius Caesar*, said:

There is a tide in the affairs of men,
Which taken at its flood leads on to fortune;
Omitted, all the voyages of their lives
is bound in shallows and in miseries.
On such a sea we are now afloat,
And we must take the current when it serves,
Or lose our ventures.

H. Leo Boles' DECISION IN TEXAS was the turning point of his life. The tide of his life was taken at its flood, and henceforth all the future voyages of his life followed the course that he believed a Christian should take.

Once Boles had made his irrevocable decision to become a preacher he realized that he had wanted to preach since his early childhood. He could see that he was already leaning toward the work of the Lord before George Womack had persuaded him to study law. All at once, Leo saw that he, like his father before him, had merely been sidetracked from preaching for a while by curcumstances.

George Womack carried out his plan to study law. He steadfastly followed the course that he had charted for himself. He saved his money from teaching school, attended the Law School of the University of Texas, graduated with honors and made an eminently successful attorney. George rose in his profession until he served for many years on the Supreme Court bench of the State of Oklahoma. Whenever, Tennessee friends looked up Judge Womack, George never failed to inquire about the welfare of his old friend, H. Leo Boles. Then George had a habit of looking over the heads of the people with whom he was conversing, and murmur with a distant tone in his voice, "The man who would have made the most brilliant attorney in the country turned out to be a preacher."

When the school closed in May, 1903, Professor Boles resigned his position in the Texas school and returned to the home on Sink Creek. He told his father that he had fully made up his mind to consecrate his life to the preaching of the gospel, and doing what good he could in the world. Jeff again did not act surprised, but he was definitely delighted that his son should make the choice to preach.

91

Jeff Boles had an appointment to preach at Sunny Point, Tennessee, on June 7, 1903. Jeff asked Leo to accompany him to Sunny Point and to preach that day in his place. Leo prepared his sermon on "The Human Side of Salvation." In an article written for the *Goepel Advocate*, June 6, 1943, entitled, "Forty Years as a Gospel Preacher," H. Leo Boles describes his first sermon thusly:

After he (H. J. Boles) had read a portion of Deut. 28 and commented on it, he led the people in prayer. Praying for "the speaker that he might speak so as to please God," my father then announced; "My son, H. Leo Boles, who has just returned from Texas, where he has been engaged in teaching will now preach for us." I had prepared to speak on "The Human Side of Salvation." I spoke forty minutes, I was not frightened, but spoke rapidly. I knew what I was going to say, and I said it.

On June 21, 1903, H. Leo Boles preached his second sermon at the Olive Church of Christ, where he had been baptized. His subject was "Whatsoever a Man Soweth that Shall He Also Reap."

H. J. Boles had arranged to evangelize during the months of July, August and September of that year. It fitted in very nicely for Jeff to take his son, Leo with him on this mission. In this way, Jeff could help Leo in his study of the Bible.

The development of H. Leo Boles as a gospel preacher was rapid. Leo was already well recognized as an excellent public speaker, but he realized that his knowledge and understanding of the Bible were entirely inadequate. It was therefore a great blessing that the young preacher could be associated with his father at this time. Jeff Boles was a splendid Bible scholar and he was a successful gospel preacher. The experience of the father was a benediction to his son. Jeff's piety, prayerfulness and loyalty to God were examples that blessed his son far above the ordinary benefits of life.

The companionship of Jeff Boles and H. Leo Boles during the summer of 1903 was similar to that of Paul and Timothy. There were age and youth in league with each other; age instructing youth and youth revering age. It was a union of autumn with its fruit ripe with experience, and the springtime of youth with its hopes and ambitions. There were enthusiasm and experience yoked together in a holy cause, and there was tender expectancy and rich assurance combined in the affection of a father and son. Very few young preachers have experienced such advantages as to be associated in the proclamation of the truth in such close relationship as existed in this combination. The result of their labors in the vineyard of the Lord that summer was the baptism of over a hundred repentant sinners.

Chapter XI
ZION IN NASHVILLE

H. Leo Boles, now aged twenty-nine, had made his decision between becoming a lawyer and a preacher of the gospel. His choice made on the plains of Texas in the spring of 1903 was unalterable. His decision was final, the Rubicon was crossed, and the "point of no return" had been passed. Henceforth, the life of H. Leo Boles was to be dedicated to the service of the Lord.

Upon the return to his native Cumberlands, late in May of the "year of decision," H. Leo Boles lost little time in launching his preaching career. He had experienced a full summer of pioneer evangelism when he accompanied his father, H. J. Boles; and together they preached to the people who lived in the more isolated parts of Cannon, Putnam, Fentress, and Overton counties of Tennessee.

The young preacher was willing and eager to do the service of the Savior, but after a season of preaching, he could see very clearly that he was woefully unprepared to preach to others until he, himself, learned much more about the Scriptures. He was well aware of Apostle Paul's simple statement to the church of Corinth, "Woe is me if I preach not the gospel"; but he was equally familiar with the punishment that was promised those who preached false doctrines. H. Leo Boles also knew the result that occurred when the "blind led the blind." He fully realized the significance of the words of God, spoken through the prophet Hosea, when he said,

> "My people are destroyed for lack of knowledge; because thou hast rejected knowledge, I will also reject thee. . . ."

H. Leo Boles was an educated man in 1903. He was, in fact, rapidly developing into a classical scholar. Following the study habits developed at Burritt College, he had read voluminously and almost ceaselessly throughout his teaching career. Being an individual who was already well read and who had an insatiable curiosity to learn, the more keenly he felt his deficiency in knowing and understanding the written Word of God. To paraphrase an old adage concerning education, one might say,

Knowledge of the Bible without preaching is futile;
Preaching without knowledge of the Bible is fatal.

In order to gain an understanding that is essential for the correct interpretation of the Bible, so that the true meaning of the Scriptures might be revealed unto him, the logical mind of H. Leo Boles could accept only one answer: *"I must go to a Bible school."* He knew that schools existed where the Bible was taught as the center of the curriculum where all the other subjects were grouped around the One Great Book. Such an institution H. Leo Boles determined to attend.

The history of education is replete with examples of schools that were organized and existed for the sole purpose of furnishing a Christian education for the youth of the land. After the founding fathers of this country had established themselves in their Colonial homes, they almost immediately began to plan for the education of their children. Since religion was a major motive for the colonization of America by the English, it was only natural that provision for the indoctrination of the spiritual beliefs of the founders should be inculcated in the curricula of the early schools and colleges.

The first immigrants to this country brought with them their preachers, ministers, and priests, as well as laymen who were strongly saturated with the doctrines of their sect. As the older people began to die out, it was necessary to train young leaders to perpetuate the tenets of their particular secular order. Some of the prospective young ministers were sent back to England to be educated there; but as time went by a vast majority of the religious leaders were trained on the American side of the Atlantic in schools set up especially for this purpose.

In order to educate young Puritan preachers, Harvard College, just outside of Boston, was founded in 1636, just sixteen years after the Pilgrims landed at Plymouth Rock. Yale, Princeton, Kings (Columbia), Brown and other universities were founded by ecclesiastical bodies seeking to perpetuate certain theological beliefs. In fact, all of the nine colleges that existed in the thirteen English colonies were established for specific religious purposes.

It was natural on the American frontier, that the free people who read their Bibles and studied the Word of God for themselves would have their own interpretations of the Scriptures. It was also to be expected that when the preaching of the backwoods ministers did not conform to the teachings of the Bible, certain devout individuals would "have their say" about what their Bible taught them concerning the subject. When sectarian ignorance and prejudice, bigotry and dogmatism reached its height, the providence of God overruled the bitter theological wranglings, and there arose simultaneously, in widely separated sections of the country, small groups who threw off the yoke of denominational bondage and began to follow the New Testament teachings in all particulars. This was the beginning of the "Restoration Movement."

Soon after the Movement began, religious groups organized themselves into churches according to the pattern described by the Apostle Paul in the New Testament. It was inevitable that soon schools and colleges would be established whose curricula would stress teaching the Bible in all its wonderful simplicity and truth.

Alexander Campbell was by far the most scholarly and the most distinguished leader of the independent groups who initiated the "Restoration Movement." He had received a splendid education in the University at Glasgow, Scotland; and he thoroughly understood the invaluable assistance that a church school could give the Movement.

It was common in the early days for preachers to begin small schools in their own homes. Some of these schools eventually grew into independent colleges and universities. As Mr. Campbell was a teacher, as well as a preacher, he established a school in his home, in 1818, at Bethany, in what is now West Virginia. He named his school Buffalo Seminary. The school grew and in 1840 it became known as Bethany College.

Alexander Campbell's motto was "Let there be light."

He emphasized the importance of educating young men who would be able to teach the Bible, and he offered educational advantages to the youth who were preparing to preach the gospel.

The educators in the church have been most potent factors, as they have trained young men who have become leaders and defenders of the truth. Without these leaders, the church could not have made the progress that it now enjoys; for *without trained leaders, no cause can make much progress*. This truism holds for all political, sociological and religious movements. No cause among civilized and cultured people can thrive on ignorance and superstition; its progress demands efficient and educated leadership. The cause of Christ is no exception to this rule!

Many young men who had enthusiastically and zealously accepted the gospel, and who had a burning desire to tell "the old, old story" came to Bethany to sit at the feet of Alexander Campbell. Among these was Tolbert Fanning, a native of middle Tennessee, and a man of strong intellectual powers. Mr. Fanning was equipped with a university training, and he had traveled through parts of Ohio, New York, Canada, and the New England states during the spring and summers of 1836 with Alexander Campbell. They had discussed fully and frequently the advantages of a Christian education. Mr. Campbell encouraged Tolbert Fanning to go back into Tennessee and open a school that would fulfill this purpose.

In 1837, Tolbert Fanning opened the Franklin Female Seminary, in Franklin, Tennessee. After two years in Franklin, Mr. Fanning moved his school to a location on the Couchville Pike, five miles southeast of Nashville. There he began building Franklin College, which was completed in 1844. Tolbert Fanning was its first president. Tolbert Fanning proved to have a clearer vision of Christian education than did Alexander Campbell, which eventually found the greatest practical embodiment in the vision of David Lipscomb and J. A. Harding in establishing the Nashville Bible School.

Many men who distinguished themselves as leaders in different professions of life received their education in

Franklin College. Among the graduates of this institution were: David Lipscomb (1849), James E. Scobey (1855), E. G. Sewell (1859), T. B. Larimore (1867), and E. A. Elam (1874). H. Leo Boles once stated, "If Franklin College had done no more than to give to the world these five men, the money expended in this institution must be reckoned the greatest investment for the cause of Christ that has ever been made!" But it did much more than this. Hundreds of faithful men and women trained by Tolbert Fanning became active workers in the church, while working at other occupations to make their living.

As early as 1869 David Lipscomb began to emphasize Christian education in the religious weekly publication *Gospel Advocate*, that had been co-founded in 1855 by his brother, William Lipscomb and Tolbert Fanning. David Lipscomb had caught the unique vision of a complete Christian education in that he believed that Christians should educate their own children. It was important that those who wanted an education should receive their academic work in a school where the Bible was honored and respected as the word of God and where each teacher was a dedicated Christian.

The long cherished dream of David Lipscomb to have a school where all the various subjects of education would be offered and the Bible taught daily to every Christian, male and female, saint and sinner, was fulfilled in the autumn of 1891. David Lipscomb and J. A. Harding had not planned to establish a school especially to train preachers, but to train young people for life who would be wiser, happier, and more useful in their society as Christians.

In J. A. Harding, David Lipscomb found a staunch ally who was completely convinced that the children of the church should not be subjected to religious influences contrary to the teachings of the Bible, but that they should be provided with an opportunity to acquire an education in a school where their faith would not be weakened, but made strong by the constant teachings of Christianity. The first announcement of such a school appeared in the *Gospel Advocate* in the spring of 1891.

On October 5, 1891, David Lipscomb and J. A. Harding opened the Nashville Bible School at 105 Fillmore Street. David Lipscomb had rented a large comfortable old brick mansion and he financed the school himself, paying the rent out of his own pocket.

The aim of the Nashville Bible School was to teach the Bible as the word of God to every student, every day. Academic subjects were required as in any other school, but the Bible was exalted above every other textbook. The other courses were related and correlated to the Bible, as the Bible became the hub around which all the academic subjects revolved.

Only a handful of Christians worshipped in Nashville at this time. The congregations established then were known as the College Street Church, Foster Street (now Grace Avenue), Woodland Street, Line Street (now Johnson Street), and North Spruce Street (now Eighth Avenue). None of these churches showed any interest in building a Bible School. As a matter of fact, no announcements regarding the school were made from their pulpits. This did not alarm either Lipscomb or Harding; neither was of the opinion that churches should operate schools.

Only nine young men showed up the day school opened; however, the number increased to thirty-two during the session. David Lipscomb and J. A. Harding were the instructors in the Bible; languages, literature, and the arts were taught by William Lipscomb and J. A. Harding. The founders were greatly encouraged; men of little faith would have had small cause to be. Though the opening was little larger than a cloud "the size of a man's hand," the spiritual drought in the land would be quenched by an ever growing flood of preachers pouring from the halls of the Nashville Bible School.

A few days after the school opened the founders were encouraged to report in the *Gospel Advocate* that the "Bible School opened on Monday of last week with very encouraging prospects. The opening was good and there is no reason why the brotherhood should not build up here a very thorough and flourishing school." The naming of the school was an afterthought. Lipscomb and Harding simply purposed to begin a school where the Bible as the principal text would be daily taught. Since the institution's location was Nashville, it only seemed natural to give it the name of the Nashville Bible School.

David Lipscomb had no confidence in the theological school whose sole purpose was to educate preachers. With the closing of the first school, twenty of the thirty-two who enrolled in the course of the year planned to preach. Counting all students who attended that year—regular and irregular—the number came to fifty-three. Only two or three young ladies were enrolled as regular students.

The first school year passed with little fanfare. There were no programs, holidays, or banquets. Student discipline presented no problems and the regulations were few indeed. No financial help came from the outside nor was any solicited. The trial run of the new school was entirely supported by the students and teachers.

The second session opened on October 4, 1892, on South Cherry Street (now Fourth Avenue). The total enrollment came to forty-two. Because so many of the students came as aspiring preachers to study the Bible and get an education, the critics of the Nashville Bible School labelled it a "preacher factory." What may have been the intentions of the founders regarding a school to train preachers, the attendance gradually increased and most of the students who came intended to preach.

For the first time the students in the Nashville Bible School who enrolled October 2, 1894, were furnished with a school catalog. The catalog had this to say about degrees: "We confer no degrees. It is vain to use empty titles; and the degrees, D.D., A.M., B.S., Ph.D., in this country are just that, they are so common and so easily obtained." This was stated notwithstanding the fact all the teachers held degrees. In lieu of degrees the students were presented with diplomas containing the periods and fields of study covered.

The school continued for the first decade with no matters of great event. The students were privileged to hear from time to time such preachers as M. C. Kurfees and Dr. T. W. Brents. Meanwhile the faculty changed, and when the school entered the tenth year, nine men and two ladies made up the faculty roster.

Other than the faculty and the handful of young men and woman who came for instruction, no one seemed especially interested in the new institution. No opposition came from the general public because the school attracted no attention on the outside. There were no other rival schools of its kind in Nashville, or the world, for that matter. If educators in Nashville schools were aware of its existence, they took no notice of it.

Indeed, criticisms were voiced; and strangely enough, they originated among members of the church. They either did not understand the ideals and purposes of the founders, or they lacked their courage and conviction. Their objections are easily guessed—that the school would rob the church of its mission and glory. Loyal churches were yet in the powerful wake of the residing struggle over the missionary society that had split and splintered the church. Both Lipscomb and Harding were aware of the difference between a school whose sole purpose was to educate young people and the society whose asserted purpose was to supplant the church and its mission. David Lipscomb had combed every inch of society controversy for a quarter of a century.

To alleviate the fears of such brethren, David Lipscomb wrote in the *Gospel Advocate* soon after the school's opening: "We never saw the day we did not believe every church ought to have a good Bible school in which the Bible would be taught to all who would receive the instruction. As to what we teach, the name expresses it. We teach the Bible the only and sure guide to religion."

H. Leo Boles commented in later years: "These brethren knew what they were doing when they began this work. David Lipscomb had for a number of years encouraged Christian people to give their children the advantages of a Christian education. These brethren knew that the school was not an institution like the Missionary Society. It was intended to aid Christian fathers and mothers in educating their children."

The critics of the school served a good purpose. Had not they voiced their objections, Lipscomb and Harding

101

would not have had such favorable opportunities to inform publicly the purpose and work of the new school. And it was their stout defense of the school that insured its stability. It was against this background that H. Leo Boles first became a student and later its greatest leader to win a complete victory for the ideals of David Lipscomb.

While J. A. Harding remained with the school, he managed its academic affairs, and David Lipscomb ran the business side. In time a decision was made to incorporate the school. J. A. Harding did not like the idea and David Lipscomb was not very enthusiastic about it. But Lipscomb was willing to do so to further the cause of Christian education. So on February 2, 1901, the institution received its corporate name, the *Nashville Bible School*.

Harding had already announced his intention to leave the Nashville Bible School. By 1901, J. A. Harding, cofounder of the Nashville Bible School, had rounded out an even decade as the president of this institution. Some brethren at Bowling Green, Kentucky, noting the good work that was being done in Nashville determined to emulate the example set in Nashville by founding a Bible school of their own. They raised the funds and bought a large farmhouse on several hundred acres of rich farming land. Here they established the Bowling Green Bible School. They invited Harding to become president of the Kentucky school.

Since the Nashville Bible School was well established by this time, Harding felt that he could accomplish more good by moving to the new school. The experience he had gained in the Nashville school would help breathe life into the venture at Bowling Green. Consequently, Harding resigned from the school in Nashville and took up the work of administrating Christian education in the Bible School at Bowling Green in June 1901.

David Lipscomb served on the Board of Directors and served as president until his death. H. Leo Boles said in the history of the school there were those who said David Lipscomb was the "Board." The school's charter granted the privilege to confer the B.A., B.L., B.S., and the M.A. degrees. The first year of the chartered Nashville Bible

School was generally regarded a successful one under the tutelage of William Anderson, the successor of J. A. Harding.

A dour prediction that the school would experience a decline in enrollment when Harding went to Bowling Green never materialized. The yearly growth of the Bible School exceeded the most hopeful expectations of David Lipscomb. As a matter of fact, he did not care to see the institution grow so rapidly as he said: "We have had no desire for a very large school. We had rather see a dozen moderate-sized schools distributed through the country."

H. Leo Boles had determined to attend either the Bible school at Nashville or at Bowling Green, but he had not yet decided which it would be. Since J. A. Harding had delivered an outstanding class address at Burritt College the year H. Leo had graduated, he preferred to go to the school headed by a man already proven excellent. He talked the matter over with his father, but Jeff offered very little help saying, "Both are Bible schools and if you study hard, either should teach you the Scriptures."

H. Leo Boles packed his two suitcases, September 22, 1903, and Jeff hitched the horse to the buggy that had taken them through the highways and byways of the Upper Cumberlands while they were doing their evangelistic work. Together they drove to the depot at McMinnville. Leo had about decided to attend the Bowling Green school; but when he went to buy his train ticket, he found that the fare to Bowling Green was almost twice as much as that to Nashville. H. Leo Boles decided to save the additional train fare and enter the Nashville Bible School.

How small the incident that sometimes determines the life of a man! Except for the $2.73 difference, H. Leo Boles would have passed on through Nashville, and never have studied the Bible under David Lipscomb.

It is interesting to speculate what would have happened if H. Leo Boles had gone on to the Bible school in Bowling Green. Would the great educational institution that today honors the memory of David Lipscomb exist? Would an equally strong college under another name with all its towering influence be flourishing in the Blue Grass of Kentucky? But for the hand of the Lord stopping H. Leo Boles in Nashville on that last day of summer, probably he would have never even attended the Nashville Bible School, and who knows whether or not David Lipscomb College would have become one of the great bulwarks of Christian education that it is today.

H. Leo Boles had saved enough money to pay his expenses for one year, and he had definitely decided to remain that long in the Bible school, but as the plan of his life unfolded, he was destined to stay at the Nashville institution for more than thirty years. Henceforth, the biographical sketch of H. Leo Boles is closely interwoven with the history of the Nashville Bible School and subsequently, David Lipscomb College.

At the time H. Leo Boles appeared on the campus, the character of the young school was crystallizing. The catalog for the school year, 1900-1901, carried the statement:

> Nine years ago we started here in Nashville with 6 students, and already the influence of our work has reached to the ends of the earth. Thousands of people have been led to Christ by our students, and dozens of churches have been planted by them. . . . If the school were to perish today and every cent invested in it be lost, it would, nevertheless, have been a grand investment.

By 1895 young men from the college had baptized over 1400 people and established ten or more churches. Although the school had never intended to be a "preacher factory," the training of preachers always has been a major preoccupation of the school's officials. Indeed, H. Leo Boles never made a wiser decision when he stopped short of Bowling Green, Kentucky.

Chapter XII
AT THE FEET OF THE PATRIARCH

William Anderson, of Maury County, Tennessee, was selected to succeed J. A. Harding as the head of the Nashville Bible School. The minutes of the board meeting of July 2, 1901, show that David Lipscomb, as Chairman of the Board was authorized to "employ Professor William Anderson as the principal of the Nashville Bible School for the ensuing year." It was thought that the school was too small for its head to be designated by the term "President." However, the catalog of the school that year lists William Anderson as its "Superintendent."

Mr. Anderson had made such a success as a teacher and was such an outstanding educator in his county that David Lipscomb thought that he would make a success with the Nashville Bible School. He had been co-principal with T. E. Allen of the Hillsboro High School in Williamson County, Tennessee, for several years. From its advertisement in the *Gospel Advocate* in 1901, the Hillsboro school was "A good school for both sexes, in a good neighborhood, free from the temptations to vice and extravagance which abound in towns and cities . . . cheap board and first class advantages. No saloon or gambling houses. Eight miles from Franklin, Tennessee."

Prior to teaching in Hillsboro, William Anderson had been superintendent of the Carter's Creek Academy, in Maury County. Many students were educated there under Mr. Anderson who turned out to be leading citizens of various Maury County communities.

The Nashville Bible School had moved from its original place to a location on Spruce Street. The property there consisted of about two acres of land on which there were four rather large buildings. This location was inadequate for the growing needs of the school. Anderson proved to be a good administrator and it was apparent that the school must have more space and larger buildings.

Now that David Lipscomb saw that the Nashville Bible School was growing out of its swaddling clothes, and seemed to be firmly established as an educational factor, he determined to see the school established in its permanent home. The property on Spruce Street was estimated to be worth about $20,000. This sum was augmented by the addition of some $12,000, a gift by the will of Mrs. Fanny Pond, of Nashville. David Lipscomb's farm consisted of about seventy-five acres. He proposed to give sixty-five acres of his land to the school provided that the other members of the Board of Directors would agree to see the property on Spruce Street and erect buildings on the farm. This was quickly agreed upon and planning for buildings was begun.

In the summer months of 1903 the school was moved from South Spruce Street to David Lipscomb's farm—a beautiful acreage lying south of the city limits. In deeding his farm to the school, David Lipscomb stipulated the conditions that the property shall:

be used for maintaining a school in which, in addition to other branches of learning, the Bible as the recorded will of God and the only standard of faith and practice in religion . . . shall be taught as a regular daily study to all who attend said school, and for no other purpose inconsistent with this subject.

The Nashville Bible School had pursued its course almost unnoticed by the public until its removal to the new location. Then the daily press of Nashville, August 24, 1903, announced the location of the new school with the date for the opening of the thirteenth year: "Nashville now boosts another educational institution, which, outgrowing its swaddling clothes, promises to take high rank among the institutions of its class."

It was planned at first to erect three buildings; a Boys' Dormitory; Girls' Dormitory and Recitation Hall. However, it turned out, only enough money was available for the Boys' Dormitory and a Recitation Hall that contained the Chapel and eight classrooms. This emergency was met by David Lipscomb giving his own home, a large two-story frame building, which was enlarged to serve as the Girls' Dormitory. He built a small two-story brick building for himself.

106

The new buildings were constructed of substantial red brick with absolutely no effort being made for ornamentation. The ideas of David Lipscomb prevailed, and he wished the buildings to be as simple and commodious as possible for the amount of money that was invested in them. The structures were not modern; they were not even as convenient as might be expected. David Lipscomb had just one idea in the construction of the buildings; that was to provide rooms for the young people who attended the Bible school. The rooms were well lighted and suitably furnished, but nothing else could be said for them.

The chapel itself was interesting in that it was on the second floor of the Recitation Hall building. It was reached by three separate entrances and stairways; there was a stairway for the young ladies, the young gentlemen and the general public.

The Nashville Bible School opened school in its new location on the Lipscomb farm in the fall of 1903. When H. Leo Boles arrived the buildings were far from finished. The Boys' Dormitory was incomplete and carpenters continued to work throughout the winter. Recitations were held in classrooms improvised in the vacant rooms of the Boys' Dormitory. Since the Chapel Hall was not finished, the daily chapel exercises were held in the Boys' Dormitory dining hall. The window sashes and glass panes were put in after school opened. No satisfactory arrangement was made during the winter for heating the buildings. Large stoves were put in the dining room and halls on the first floor; these were supposed to heat the rooms on the second and third stories! However, as H. Leo Boles remembered it years later, "There was very little grumbling on the part of the boys who occupied these rooms as they were in school there for the same reason that I was: to study the Bible." On particularly cold mornings, the hardships endured by the Apostle Paul and the early Christians seemed to have a special emphasis for the boys living in the dormitory of the Nashville Bible School.

Superintendent William Anderson was now in the third year of his administration. David Lipscomb commented thusly upon the success that he had with the Bible school, "Brother Anderson is one of the best managers of boys and girls that I ever knew; he gains their confidence and becomes an intimate associate with them without forfeiting their respect."

When the thirteenth year of the Nashville Bible School opened on September 23, 1903, there was a total enrollment of one hundred sixty-four. This showed about a twenty-five per cent increase over the previous year.

The faculty that the Superintendent had assembled for the 1903-04 school year was listed in the catalog as follows:

David Lipscomb, Bible
William Anderson, Bible and English
J. S. Ward, Natural and Physical Sciences
John T. Glenn, Latin, French, and German
E. E. Sewell, Greek
O. W. Gardner, Mathematics and Astronomy
J. Paul Slayden, the Bible and Philosophy
S. P. Pittman, Elocution and Sight Singing
Miss Ora Anderson, Instrumental Music
Miss Effie Anderson, Academic Department
Mrs. Ida Noble, Art
John T. Haines, Vocal Music
M. C. Kurfees and E. A. Elam, Lectures on the Bible
George A. Klingman

The total expenses for the year for a young man was $110.00 and $128.00 for a young lady. The difference in cost was due to the "uniform" that the girls were required to wear in all public appearance. The catalog declared:

It is the fixed purpose of the management of the school to avoid all extravagance in dress. As a matter of economy and to banish from the school all distinction, save that of merit, our young lady boarders are requested on public occasions to conform to a neat, plain uniform dress. The fall and winter uniform will be selected after the school opens. This will be a black or blue material, plainly made without fancy trimmings. The total cost of the uniform, including hat, will be about fifteen dollars. No uniform is required for daily wear.

H. Leo Boles, as has been said, had received an excellent education at Burritt College, and he was present at the Bible school for the purpose of studying the Bible. But this did not deter him from trying to get as much out of his other classes as possible. His innate thirst for learning was never satisfied, and he continued to learn even while repeating subjects that he had taken previously at Dibrell or Burritt. S. P. Pittman, who was on the campus as a teacher when H. Leo Boles arrived characterizes him, "Among the pupils that registered and suffered the inconveniences of a cold, unfinished dormitory was a modest young man with some teaching experience. No one who met him at that time would have surmised that this stranger, who made no claims to superiority, would gradually push through the motley crowd to become a leader of men in the fields of education and religion." And Pittman added in later years that H. Leo Boles came closer to epitomizing the ideals of David Lipscomb than any person connected with David Lipscomb College.

When H. Leo Boles arrived on the campus, no one knew that he was a descendant of the doughty "Raccoon" John Smith. He wore common but good clothes. At that time he had not preached long enough to have a reputation. There was nothing either for or against him by way of criticism other than he was high tempered. He was a conscientious man. Few have ever surpassed him in determination. Boles was not the sort to tell people he meant to make something of himself. What some mistook for rudeness was simply his manner of abruptness in dealing with people. As long as he lived he would be somewhat of an enigma even to those who knew him best.

G. C. Brewer, a classmate of H. Leo Boles in the old Nashville Bible School has this to say:

When I first knew Brother Boles, he had a very humble appearance and seemed to be sad over his experiences in life, but he was a very positive and emphatic man in his statements and would stand firm for what he believed to be right. He, too, was struggling to gain more learning and polish than he had received in the early part of his education.

We had the habit of criticizing speakers on a certain morning set aside for this purpose. This consisted of a chapel exercise each week when the students would be called upon to report every mistake that they had heard public speakers make. It was conducted by Professor John T. Glenn. Criticism morning put a fright in the hearts of some who knew about it and they were careful about getting up before that school audience. They knew that if they made mistakes, these mistakes would be put on parade on the 'morning of criticisms.' Brother Boles himself was ever conscious of this critical attitude on the part of the students and teachers, and he, at times, showed some embarrassment in his public speeches.

H. Leo had learned how to do independent research. Since he was at the Bible school to learn the Bible, he devised his own plan of study. He read closely and prayerfully every word of the lesson assigned, then he read all of the commentaries that he could find on that subject. He had three classes daily in the Bible, and he also enrolled for Greek, English, and Elocution.

S. H. Hall had been assigned to room with H. Leo Boles during his first year at the Nashville school. They had been classmates and opponents at Dibrell College almost ten years before, but had lost touch with each other during the time intervening. The friendship between George Womack and Leo Boles was well known in the Cumberlands. It was also widespread that George Womack professed to be an atheist. Again, H. Leo Boles had just returned from Texas and but recently had made his decision to preach the gospel instead of becoming a lawyer as George was doing. Putting these facts together, some friends of Sam Hall, who had been preaching for some time in Warren County, asked Sam to look out for Leo while in Nashville, and they requested Sam to do all that he could to strengthen the faith of his classmate.

Sam Hall, accordingly, secretly maneuvered with Superintendent Anderson for the two of them to room together. S. H. Hall reports the outcome of the plan in these words:

Just before leaving McMinnville for the Nashville Bible School, I met W. G. Cummings, one of the elders of the church there. He stopped me for a short talk about Brother Boles. Brother Boles' father was one of the most loved and faithful preachers that we had in those parts, and we were all interested in his son. He informed me that Brother Leo had just left for Nashville to enter the Nashville Bible School, and knowing that I would soon be there, suggested that I take a wholehearted interest in him. Brother Boles was an independent thinker, he had read Tom Paine and some other infidel literature. He had at times said things that indicated that he had been influenced by it.

Soon after we began to room together, all my fears soon disappeared. . . . When I discovered Brother Boles' prayer habits, all fears that he would drift from God left me. His prayers at night before retiring dispelled all my doubts about him.

Being a member of the Bible class that David Lipscomb taught, was perhaps the greatest blessing that could come to a young preacher. David Lipscomb was best known to the public as a preacher and editor of the *Gospel Advocate,* but he was best known to his students as a peerless instructor of the Bible. For almost a quarter of a century he taught the Bible daily in the Nashville Bible School. It was his arrangement to teach two classes each day in the Bible; one in the Old Testament and one in the New. In his Old Testament class, he would begin with Genesis and then follow the books in order throughout the school year. In his New Testament class he would begin with Matthew, then study John. The other books of the New Testament followed in their order. He would have his Old Testament class recite first and then the next hour he would teach his New Testament class.

As a teacher of God's truth, Lipscomb very probably had no superior. In his class work he had his own way of getting his students to study. No one was able to exactly analyze the methods that he used so successfully to get the students to prepare the lessons that he assigned. Perhaps it is best to say that he *inspired* them to study God's Word. Students who slighted their lessons, ever other Bible classes, seldom came to Brother Lipscomb's class unprepared. The earnest, kind look that he gave a student who missed a question was sufficient to bring self-condemnation to the student, and when the class was over, the student usually left the room with a strong determination to be better prepared next time. David Lipscomb seldom, if ever, gave a sharp rebuke in words to one of his students for not being prepared to recite; his kind sympathetic look was enough.

The conduct of students in his classes was always the

111

best. Much of the good behavior was due to the respect that the students had for him. He was gentle and courteous to boys and girls and this won for him their love and esteem.

David Lipscomb did not require his pupils to do very much memory work. Occasionally, he would have them memorize a few verses, but whole chapters were not required to be memorized as was the method of some other Bible teachers in the school. Brother Lipscomb desired, most of all, to get the truths of the Bible clearly and firmly fixed in the hearts of his students that they might bear fruit in their lives. He was more interested in getting the gospel into the *hearts* of his boys and girls than he was to keep the language fixed in their *memory*.

David Lipscomb was very careful not to teach any theory *about* the Bible, but he was exceedingly anxious to teach *the Bible*. He studiously avoided expressing his own opinion, even when he was asked to do so. He would bluntly say, "'I am not teaching my opinion, but I am trying to teach the word of God." He was little interested in the opinions of the commentators who wrote about the Bible. He refused to turn aside from the revealed truth of God to study the opinions, doctrines and commandments of men.

The method used by David Lipscomb to study a subject was to find and collate every scripture in the Bible on particular topics. He repeatedly told his classes, "We do not have enough on a question until we study *everything* that God has said on that subject." He impressed upon his students the great importance of not being satisfied with the investigation of any Bible subject until *every* related scripture had been examined.

Where the Bible was silent on a certain detail, David Lipscomb was careful to point out that God had not revealed himself on that point. As a teacher, he would sometimes ask such questions as; "Why did Nicodemus come to Jesus by night?", or "What was the thorn in the flesh that Paul received?" The students would usually give various answers, until Brother Lipscomb would say, "Well, I don't know; God has not spoken on that point; I was just wondering how you knew." Such a procedure would always impress the class that no one could believe or have faith on any point where God had not spoken.

Sitting at the feet of David Lipscomb two hours a day for seven years made a tremendous impression on the life and character of H. Leo Boles. From Brother Lipscomb's teachings Boles formed the habit of studying the Bible for several hours every day. Having studied the Bible H. Leo Boles, like his teacher, accepted and practiced it, irrespective of consequences. As was his instructor, Brother Boles was never on both sides of a question. He was not like the man up in Hickman County who made tracks on both sides of the creek when pressed to take a stand on one side of an issue. He was always in the open where he could be found on any Bible question. Like his illustrious teacher, H. Leo Boles was full of faith and knowledge of the word of the Lord—straight-forward, upright, and unswerving. He was determined to pursue the right course, and no matter what the cost he meant to bring men into submission to the gospel. Never did any material interest, or worldly gain, or fleshly comfort, or idle ease get between either David Lipscomb or H. Leo Boles, in the service of the Lord.

H. Leo Boles was a participant in Brother Lipscomb's Bible classes as long as he continued to teach. Even after, he had been made president of the Nashville Bible School, H. Leo Boles still sat at the feet of the patriarch until the grand old man's health finally gave way and he could teach no more. Then, H. Leo Boles in humility and meekness, took the Old Testament and New Testament classes of David Lipscomb, and continued to teach these as long as he remained with the college.

As long as David Lipscomb lived, his pupils sought his advice and guidance. The stamp of Brother Lipscomb was upon all those who had studied with him, but it seemed that H. Leo Boles had received a double portion of his spirit. The Christian love and fellowship that developed between teacher and pupil blossomed into a brotherhood like that which existed between the prophets Elijah and Elisha, and like the prophet of old, when God took David Lipscomb across the river Jordan, the mantle of the Lord's faithful servant fell full upon the shoulders of H. Leo Boles. These shoulders were made strong and sturdy as the hand of God braced them for the full defense of the gospel against which the gates of Hades shall never prevail.

Chapter XIII

FAVOR WITH GOD AND MAN

During the school year of '03-'04, David Lipscomb secured for H. Leo Boles appointments to preach almost every Sunday. It was customary in those days for the congregations in Middle Tennessee not to use the same preacher every Sunday. Numerous congregations were in the habit of having four different preachers speak to them on the first, second, third and fourth Sundays of the month respectively; a fifth minister might be called to preach when a month had five Sundays. Located preachers serving a church full-time were frowned upon because this had the "smack" of the professional pastor system. At the turn of the century, the "loyal churches" were against the missionary society, instrumental music and pie suppers. C. A, Moore did preach full time for the College Street Church of Christ where Lipscomb served as an elder. David Lipscomb was subject to a change of practice when he was convinced the Scriptures were not violated.

It is not the purpose here to discuss the merits or demerits of such a system. It is sufficient to say that this method offered many opportunities for the young preachers of the Bible school to gain the pulpit experience necessary for the development of a ministerial student.

Instead of having Saturdays free from classroom work as most schools do, the Nashville Bible School used a system that was far more advantageous to the teachers and young preachers who were in school. They held school on Saturday morning and Monday afternoon. There was no school on Saturday afternoon or on Monday mornings. In this way more time was allowed for the preachers to travel to and from their "appointments" and not miss their school work.

One of the places where H. Leo Boles preached monthly was the South College Street Church in Nashville. It was the custom of this church to send out young preachers during the summer to hold revivals in the more remote areas of Tennessee; "home missions" they called it.

After the Nashville Bible School had closed, May 26, 1904, H. Leo Boles took the canvas tent that belonged to the College Street Church and set out to hold seven meetings. He traveled alone and whenever he had to have aid in erecting or taking down the tent, he was dependent upon whatever help he could obtain.

It was a hot summer and hard work, but he baptized 153 souls into Christ, and established two new congregations. For his labors he received a total of $168.63.

H. Leo Boles had orderly habits. He seldom did things "on the spur of the moment." It is relatively easy for his biographers to trace the progress that he made in his evangelistic work because with his first "protracted meeting" he began keeping a ledger in which he wrote brief notes recording terse statements concerning his preaching accomplishments. The first meeting H. Leo Boles conducted in the early summer of 1904 was with the Scovell Street Church. As a matter of fact this was his first meeting though he had worked before in revivals with his father. This protracted meeting continued through four Sundays resulting in 17 baptisms and thirty dollars for his efforts. H. Leo Boles began a practice that summer according to B. C. Goospasture that would be true of him for the rest of his life. His meetings were booked as the invitations came—with large or small churches and little or no salary at all.

During the summer of '04, the tent of the Nashville church was pitched in what H. Leo Boles described as the "more destitute" places. The following extract from his ledger is typical of the kind of work that he did:

1904, Aug. 21, *Baxter, Tennessee*

I began a tent meeting at this place. Brother C. V. Cathey of Texas led the singing. No congregation here then. Meeting continued two weeks.

Results: *Preached* 30 discourses; *Baptized* 50 and 5 reclaimed—55 in all.

Organized a church—helped to appoint brethren Lewis Lee, Robert Gentry and Grundy Jackson as elders.—Arrangements made to build a house. Collected for preaching—$12.30. I agreed to preach once per month till the next meeting.

Other places in which H. Leo Boles evangelized that summer were: Cherry Hill and Cross Roads in DeKalb County, Patterson in Rutherford County, Cookeville in Putnam County and Antioch in Jackson County. If the young evangelist had any qualms about his qualifications to make a gospel preacher at the beginning of the summer, he would never have any again. H. Leo Boles all through life made his way by sacrificing time and energy. He learned how to prepare sermons in the early years and gradually acquired his matchless ability in their presentation.

When the fourteenth year of the Nashville Bible School opened on September 20, 1904, H. Leo Boles was present to continue his study of the Bible under David Lipscomb. Superintendent Anderson had appointed H. Leo Boles to the place of assistant teacher of mathematics. In return for teaching three classes, he received his room, board and tuition. The courses for which he was enrolled were two classes that Brother Lipscomb taught.

Other changes in the faculty that year were the addition of J. W. Shepherd, and Miss Emma L. Martin, who took charge of the Library and Primary Departments respectively. J. Paul Slayden was given a class to teach in the Bible. He was frequently a substitute in Superintendent Anderson's Bible class as the latter was not regular in his teaching due to poor health. S. P. Pittman remembers Slayden as a brilliant young man.

The school enrollment had increased so much that it became difficult to operate with only one literary society for the young men. With nearly one hundred male students enrolled in the Babylonian Literary Society, it was impossible for the society to function as it should. A young man simply did not get an opportunity to appear on the program often enough. Upon the request of a number of young men, the faculty decided to divide the Babylonian into two new literary societies.

Dr. J. S. Ward designated John T. Lewis and H. Leo Boles as the two young men who should "choose up sides" and organize the new societies. Accordingly, all the young men were called to assemble in the Chapel Hall on October 26. When they were seated, John T. Lewis took his place on one side of the auditorium and H. Leo Boles on the other side. Lewis had the first choice and he chose S. H. Hall. H. Leo Boles' first choice was J. E. Boyde of Oregon. An even division of the students was made. Lewis took his group into a recitation room and they were organized into the Caesarian Literary Society with John T. Lewis as its first president.

The Boles group retired to another room and organized into the Calliopean Literary Society. Boles was elected the first president of this group. These two literary societies became rivals in oratorical, declamatory, forensic, and athletic contests.

The next year the Caesarian Society changed its name to the Lipscomb Society. This "smart move" by the Caesarians created consternation in the ranks of the "Callios," but not for long. The name of Lipscomb was indeed potent, but the zeal of the "Callios" overcame the handicap.

The friendly rivalry that existed between the "Callios" and "Lipscombs," as the members of those societies were called, was something that kept the pot boiling in the student ranks of the old Nashville Bible School. H. Leo Boles and John T. Lewis, as leaders of the Callios and Lipscombs respectively, injected a keen competitive spirit almost every school activity.

G. C. Brewer, in an article written especially for this book, entitled, "Remembering," states:

Each of the literary societies was obligated to put on a public program once a month, and then on another Saturday night of the month, these two societies put on a joint program, which was a contest between the two groups. A Calliopean would give a declamation—a Lipscomb would give a declamation; then one from each society would read an essay, and then have an hour, or perhaps an hour and a half of entertainment.

Judges were appointed and the decision was given at the close of the program. Of course, each society was anxious to defeat the other in every point. Sometimes this was so. The decision was given to

H. LEO BOLES, IDA MAE MEISER BOLES, AND
LEO LIPSCOMB BOLES

every performer on one side or the other; at other times, the decision was divided, and a Calliopean would win the essay contest, for example, but the representative of the other society would win the oratorical contest, etc.

Always there was a debate, and usually this was the most sought after decision of the whole thing, because the debate appeared to be a greater test of skill on the part of the participants, whereas, the other might be decided upon the value or merit of the piece recited in the reading, declamation, etc.

The contest or joint programs described by Brother Brewer were arranged by a committee from each of the societies. John T. Lewis and H. Leo Boles, as the respective heads of their groups, along with several other members of each society formed the committee that selected the students who participated in the programs opposite to each other. This called for quite a bit of "horse-trading" as each side tried to put up somebody that the other society could not defeat. Brother Lewis has described the atmosphere of these committee meetings as follows:

> Boles and Lewis were competitors in the full meaning of those words. . . . Boles had an expression "A wheel within a wheel," and for three years he kept those wheels spinning, while I did everything I could to throw sprags in those wheels. The last year we were in school, Boles, Holland, Lewis and Brother Andy T. Ritchie constituted the committee to arrange the joint programs for the two societies. Sometimes when we met, the atmosphere in the room would get so hot that Brother Ritchie would say, "Now brethren, brethren," but Boles, Holland and Lewis seldom heard him, in those halcyon days of youth.

One incident, told by Brother Lewis seems worth relating here as it brings to light the antics displayed in the rivalry between the two societies. The third and last year that John T. Lewis and H. Leo Boles were students, the Lipscomb Society had Brother Lipscomb's picture hung in the hall of the chapel. The Calliopeans, in retaliation, got three sections of a small bookcase, put a few books in it, and set it across the hall in front of Brother Lipscomb's picture. The Callios then went about whispering that Brother Lipscomb could now look down upon a library.

The Lipscomb Society felt that something had to be done. John T. Lewis called his group together and raised quite a sum of money for those days. They planned to get a nice bookcase, go to Goodpasture's Book Store, (a relation of B. C. Goodpasture) and buy a nice lot of second-hand books. These were to be sent out the morning that school closed in the spring. It would then be too late for the Callios to do anything about it.

Two days before school was out, Lewis went to a Nashville furniture store to buy the bookcase. They had two beautiful cases, just alike, except that one was mahogany while the other had an oak finish. Lewis chose the mahogany bookcase, to be delivered early on the morrow. He then went to the book store and Mr. Goodpasture helped him select some appropriate books.

In the meanwhile, H. Leo sensed that something was going on, so while Lewis was in the bookstore, in walked Boles. Lewis wanting to act like nothing out of the ordinary was happening, waved his hand at the pile of books and asked, "Boles, what do you think of these books?" H. Leo thinking fast put the facts together and muttered that he guessed that they were all right. Then he went out of the bookstore and caught the first streetcar back to the school.

It was not too long before H. Leo was back in town. He bought the duplicate of Lewis' bookcase in the oak finish, and then at Goodpasture's store, he picked out enough books to fill the case. Boles ordered both the books and the bookcase delivered immediately. John T. Lewis' purchases arrived in the same delivery wagon as the Callios'.

Since Sam Hall was a member of the Lipscomb Society, chosen by Lewis, both Sam and Leo thought it better if they did not room together again. No rivalry or friction caused this decision; it was simply more harmonious for Leo to room with a fellow member of the Calliopean Society while he was engaging in "skulduggery" with the Lipscombs. Sam Hall and H. Leo Boles remained fast friends throughout life as they stood side by side in a powerful defense of the Faith.

A fellow Jackson Countian, T. C. Fox replaced Sam as Leo's roommate. This was fortunate as Leo and Tom had much in common. Boles and Fox made a good team. Tom was an excellent song leader, something that very definitely H. Leo Boles was not! Boles had many talents but singing was not his forte. Tom led singing in many meetings that Leo conducted.

Tom Fox was also a young preacher. Like his roommate, he had been sent out by an established church to do "home missionary" work during the previous summer. One night when Tom and Leo were studying their Bible lesson, Tom happened to notice the diagrams that Leo was making in his notebook. Tom remarked that preaching certain principles of the New Testament would be very much simplified if he had the advantage of diagrams large enough for the audience to see. That immediately started the fertile mind of Boles to work. He reflected upon Tom's remark for a few days, and it still sounded good. Leo next discussed the matter with Brother Lipscomb. After hearing his student advance the idea for a while, David Lipscomb slowly and cautiously said, "Brother Boles, a good chart, like a blackboard can be a help sometimes, but you must be very careful to show God's Word just as he has revealed it, not as *you* may interpret it."

While Leo was still thinking about using some charts in his preaching, Tom received a letter from the Murfreesboro Church in Rutherford County. The content of the letter was that the church wished Tom to take its tent and again evangelize in the rural areas of Middle Tennessee during the summer of 1905. Tom Fox wrote the Murfreesboro congregation that he would do so and that he would be accompanied by his roommate, H. Leo Boles. This commitment clinched the matter of constructing charts in Leo's mind. Accordingly, Leo and Tom made an agreement, Leo would get up the material for the charts and organize it, while Tom would do all of the art work and printing; the expense of the canvas and stencils would be met by each paying half. After many hours of back bending toil, Tom completed the thirty-five charts. These were used during the summer of 1905. Several years later when Leo and Tom finally went their respective ways, Leo

121

bought out Tom's share and continued to use the charts for many years.

School closed on May 26, as Leo completed his second year at the Bible school. The catalog shows that Miss Elizabeth Kittrell of Hampshire, Tennessee, was the only graduate in 1905. The program for the Commencement Exercise follows:

Opening Address.........William Anderson, Supt.
Oration—"The Value of Learning"....H. Leo Boles
Oration—"True Heroism".........John T. Lewis
Essay—"Influence of
   Literature".............Miss Elizabeth Kittrell
Presentation of Diploma...William Anderson, Supt.
Address—David Lipscomb, President of the Board

As soon as school was out, Leo and Tom began the first of the twelve protracted meetings that they held that summer. It was much easier for the two of them to travel and work together than it was for either of them to evangelize alone. Tom not only led the singing, and assisted in the preaching, but he and Leo frequently did the menial labor of circus roustabouts in that they frequently had to erect the tent on a new site on Saturday before they could begin the "tent meeting" on Sunday. After the meeting was ended, it was an all day's work to take the tent down, fold and pack it, so that it could be moved to the location of the next meeting place.

The following extract from the ledger of H. Leo Boles describes the work that he and Tom were doing. It also shows the results and compensation that they received:

1905—July 16—Lancaster, (Rutherford County) Tenn.

I began a tent meeting here continuing two weeks. Brother T. C. Fox leading the song service. The meeting resulted in 11 baptisms. Received $4.50—Brother Fox, the same.

One gets a clear idea of the good that was being accomplished by the following data taken from the ledger:

1905—Sept. 3,—Liberty, (Jackson County) Tenn.

Brother Fox began this meeting for me. I joined him on Monday and continued through two Sundays. This was a tent meeting and much interest was stimulated here.

Results: 21 Baptized and a committee for building a house was appointed and arrangements for the house completed.

Received $7.50—Brother Fox, the same.

It is astonishing that a pocket of infidels should be encountered in the heart of the Cumberland Mountains, yet the ledger contains the notation:

1905—July 30—Buffalo Valley, (DeKalb County) Tenn.

I began a tent meeting in this place. Brother T. C. Fox led the song service. Meeting closed Aug. 9. Came in contact with many infidels here.

4 baptized—Received $7.50—Fox the same.

Leo and Tom separated for two weeks during the middle of the summer. Each had made commitments to conduct a meeting close to their respective homes previous to accepting the Murfreesboro church's proposition. Consequently, Leo went to McMinnville, and Tom to Jackson County.

Sam Hall had extracted a promise from Leo to hold a tent meeting, near his mother's home in the Stiles Community, just outside of McMinnville. Sam was anxious for the McMinnville brethren who were dubious about the faith and consecration of H. Leo Boles to judge for themselves. The result of his meeting was the establishment of a congregation. The new church was named Mount Leo in honor of the young preacher who was dedicated to the Lord. Forever afterwards, the faith of H. Leo Boles was never doubted. Let Brother Hall tell the story of the meeting in his own words:

While my mind had been fully satisfied in the soundness of the preaching, and the faithfulness of his devotion to the cause of Christ, all possibility of doubt was dispelled during this meeting. While conducting this meeting, Brother Boles stayed at my mother's home. I noticed that he wanted to get away from everyone twice a day; once early in the morning and then again late in the afternoon, immediately before it was time to go to the meeting place. I wanted to know why, so I followed him one day as he walked up the road a bit then around a field into the woods in the back of our home. There I found him kneeling in prayer. After I saw this, I

123

told Brother Cummings about it. He loved Brother Boles, and I never saw a happier face than his when I told him of Brother Boles' prayer habit. People who do this do not get very far away from God.

The establishment of the Mount Leo congregation was modestly described in H. Leo Boles' ledger. If one did not know from other sources that the now flourishing church was named for H. Leo Boles, he would never surmise this fact from the terse description recorded in the ledger.

1905—June 25,—Stiles Community (McMinnville) Tennessee

I began a tent meeting across the river in the Stiles Community, continuing through three Sundays. The meeting resulted in 18 additions and a church organized and set in working order—Also arrangements to build a house were made. Received $14.25.

The large canvas tent seemed to be a special target for pranks. Ever so often, someone would cut the ropes which held the tent in an upright position. This would be taken in stride, as they would erect it again taking no notice of the happening; the trivias of life were of small moment to doughty H. Leo Boles. For example:

1905—Sept. 17—Double Springs, (Putman County) Tenn.

Brother T. C. Fox began this meeting for me. I joined him on Monday. This was an interesting meeting. Held under a tent. Continued through two Sundays. Some one cut the tent down here one night. I tied it up again early next morning before breakfast and continued on as if nothing had happened. Resulted in 13 baptisms. Brother J. P. Watson was present through this meeting. Received $14.40.—Fox the same.

The ledger shows that the summer of 1905 resulted in 170 additions to the church. For the thirteen meetings, H. Leo had received a total of $225.15 for his labors.

After concluding the Double Springs meeting, Leo visited the Sink Creek farm. He did not get to see Jeff as the latter was engaged in his final meeting of the season in White County.

Cleo was now ten years old. He had been well raised by Adina, as one of her own children, and she loved him dearly. However, H. Leo now had a place where he could keep Cleo with him. Arrangements had been made for Cleo to room with his father in the Boys' Dormitory. They would eat their meals in the Dining Hall, and Cleo would be enrolled in the primary department there at the Nashville Bible School. A heating system had been installed so the boy would not suffer from cold. H. Leo Boles had wanted his son with him the previous year, but he was afraid that the frigid dormitory would adversely affect the health of the spindly lad. But now that the rooms had been made more comfortable, H. Leo had made arrangements to teach an extra class to pay for Cleo's room and board. He again as an assistant teacher, received his own room and board as compenastion.

When the 1904-1905 school year of the Nashville Bible School had closed, the prospects were bright for another good term. William Anderson had not been in good health for some months. He left school after it closed and went to his country home near Columbia, Tennessee. The friends of the school were shocked to learn that on the morning of June 29, 1905, at eight o'clock, William Anderson had suddenly died from a heart attack while he and a friend were waiting for the arrival of the rural mail carrier. The Nashville Bible School had lost its beloved superintendent and Christian education a truly great leader.

When the Nashville Bible School opened its fifteenth year on September 19, 1905, the Board of Trustees had not made definite arrangements for a new superintendent to replace the lamented William Anderson. Dr. J. S. Ward, who had been associated with the school as a teacher since its third year was requested to act as superintendent until a suitable successor to William Anderson could be found.

The enrollment for the session was 181. H. Leo Boles and Cleo were among those present when school opened. He again registered for David Lipscomb's two classes in the Bible, and added a course in English. He also taught two classes in mathematics and one in history.

The school year passed quietly under the management of Dr. Ward, and the institution closed another successful year May 24, 1906. There had been only one graduate since J. A. Harding had left the school in 1901, but at the close of the fifteenth year, there were nine members of the graduating class. On Commencement Day each young man who was graduating gave an oration and each young lady read an essay. The program that day was as follows:

Ethel Blackman, B.L., Tennessee—"Essay, Self-Mastery"

H. Leo Boles, B.A., Tennessee—"Oration, Power of Influence"

Mary E. Bourne, B.L., Tennessee—"Essay, Each Moment a Golden Door Opens, then Shuts forevermore"

Lyde D. Bowers, B.L., Florida—"Essay, The Thoughts of Men are Widened with the Process of the Suns"

James E. Boyd, B.S., Oregon—"Oration, Uses of Adversity"

S. H. Hall, B.L., Tennessee—"Oration, The Tie that Binds"

John T. Lewis, B.L., Tennessee—"Oration, What Is your Life?"

David W. Shepherd, B.L., Tennessee—"Oration, Independence"

Jessie L. Wells, B.S., Tennessee—"Essay, Willst du Immer Weiter Schweifen?"

The diplomas were delivered to the class by Dr. J. S. Ward, the Acting Superintendent. Addresses were made by David Lipscomb and E. A. Elam. This was the largest class yet to graduate from the Nashville Bible School. The B.A. degree that H. Leo received was inferior to the degree bestowed upon him by Burritt College, in 1900. H. Leo Boles had remained in the Nashville Bible School for only one reason—to study the Bible under David Lipscomb!

At the close of the session a reunion of all former students was planned for May 23, 1906, and a large number attended. J. A. Harding and J. N. Armstrong were the guest speakers for the occasion. At this time E. A. Elam was officially elected to membership on the Board of Directors to make up the seventh member required in the by-laws of the Board; David Lipscomb made the recommendation, and as H. Leo Boles said when the will or wishes of

126

David Lipscomb pertaining to the school were made known, they were carried out without question. The decision to put E. A. Elam on the board of the Bible School would hold the greatest importance for young Boles in years to come.

Chapter XIV

THE ROCKY ROAD TO ROMANCE

The courtship of H. Leo Boles and Ida May Meiser was not without its trials. Leo had been a Senior at Dibrell College and Ida a Freshman when they first met in 1898. Their ages were twenty-four and nineteen respectively.

It so happened that Ida had her last period in the afternoon free from classes and with others she was put into a "study hall" in the back of the Dibrell College auditorium. Due to a shortage of space, the auditorium was also used as a classroom. It so happened that an advanced Latin class met in the front part of the auditorium during the sixth period. Early in the term Ida was struck by the fact that the best student in the class, by far, was a rather small boy with very blue eyes. The promptness of the boy's answers and his agile, brilliant mind made quite an impression on Ida. She spent much more time during that last period in watching Leo Boles recite Latin than she did in preparing her own lessons!

Ida Meiser had been influenced to attend Dibrell College by another of her former teachers, Miss Mary Lou Parker. Mary Lou had talked to Ida and her folks and she had promised that if they would allow Ida to attend Dibrell that the two of them would room together. One evening while they were at their studies, Ida asked her roommate, "Mary Lou, who is that rather small boy in the Latin class that is so smart?"

Mary Lou replied, "That must be Leo Boles. He's the best Latin student here."

Evidently Mary Lou then told Leo that Ida admired him, because it was not long after that when Leo asked Ida for a date.

Henry (Hank) Meiser, Ida's father, was a very sturdy and colorful personality. A famous wit once said, "The Lord makes each one of us different, and it is certainly good that he does." Hank, born 1839, on the Ohio frontier was a descendant of a distinct breed of pioneers whose raw courage and peculiar traits of character were required in order to wrest the west from the wilderness. His was the heritage of everwestward migrating emigrants from Holland. The Meiser family moved from Pennsylvania into eastern Ohio, thence onward into Iowa and Kansas. Not caring for the prairie country, Hank's father had then moved back to northern Ohio.

As with the Boles progenitors, there has been a Meiser in every war the United States has ever fought. Consequently, when President Lincoln issued his first call for 300,000 volunteers to repulse the Confederate attacks at Fort Sumpter and Bull Run, Hank rode into nearby Defiance, Ohio, and enlisted in the United States Army.

It is relatively easy to trace the activities of Hank's Company "F" of Ohio's 111th Infantry because of the excellent biography, MEMORIES OF THE WAR, written by its commanding officer, General Isaac R. Sherwood. The record gives a full account of the routes, campaigns and engagements of the 111th from 1862 until the war ended in 1865.

Hank's regiment was the General Burnsides' army in New Market, Kentucky, when it was ordered to attack the strong Confederate forces guarding Cumberland Gap. The only railroad directly connecting Richmond and Atlanta ran through this historic mountain pass, and its severance would tremendously cripple the Confederate lines of communication and transportation.

General Burnside was ordered to cross the mountains and attack Cumberland Gap from the rear thus outflanking the heavily entrenched Confederate force. Many students of war consider that in audacity and daring the scaling of the Cumberlands by an army with artillery was probably as difficult a task as the crossing of the Alps by Napoleon.

The rugged mountains and valleys of East Tennessee form a background of natural beauty that master painters of any age can at best only poorly copy. It is as if God himself is showing the Belascos and Urbans how puny are

129

their artificial efforts when Nature produces her own art.

The primal independence of the mountains, rising peak on peak, scraping the sky with rocky brow held a weird fascination for the men from the North. Etched against the backdrop of the variegated shades of green were the flame azalea, the purple rhododendron and the white blossoms of the mountain laurel. The virgin growth of giant hardwood trees watered by the overhanging, misty haze and the clear, quick streams impressed Henry Meiser tremendously. The sheer beauty of the Cumberlands so enthralled him that he vowed that if opportunity ever presented itself, he would here live out the remaining days of his life.

Henry Meiser returned to Northern Ohio after the war, married Rebecca Rex of solid Pennsylvania Dutch stock and settled down to a comfortable lumber and sawmill business in Defiance County; here seven of his eight children were born. Ida was the oldest; chronologically, there followed Elizabeth, John, George, Grover, Eva, Maude and Howard.

The wheels of Hank's destiny were again set spinning in 1890. The profitable mill and lumber yard of *"Meiser and Wonderly"* caught fire and burned to the ground leaving Henry Meiser and Henry Wonderly practically pennyless.

Hank remembered again the raw beauty of Nature's handiwork that was exhibited in the Tennessee Cumberlands, as he had fallen in love with their scenic beauty. He had repeatedly told his wife, "Becky, Tennessee is a healthy place to live." Consequently, Hank moved his family and belongings to Warren County, Tennessee where the Meiser family boarded with an old war "buddy", Jim Richardson, also of Company "F". After looking around for a while, Hank bought a farm near the Richardson's. Hank was soon to be joined by a third member of Company "F", Washington C. Ryan. "Wash", as he was known, was quite wealthy but he chose to live with the Meiser family until his death several years later.

Although the Meisers lived in the country it must not

be construed that they were not well informed people. They were well versed not only in the classics but also in current events. Hank subscribed to the mail editions of the *Cleveland Free Press* and the *Cincinnati Inquirer*. He was an active Democrat and he was well informed on local and national political issues.

It should be pointed out that Hank Meiser was a hunter par excellent, and wild game in the Cumberlands was abundant. Not only did he hunt as an amateur sportsman, but he also served as a professional guide to parties from the North who sought his services for two and three weeks' hunting trips into the more secluded parts of the Cumberlands. H. Leo Boles recounts, "Three meats were served at the first dinner I ate at the Meiser home; bear, venison and wild turkey."

Ida and Leo kept rather steady company throughout the remainder of the school year, and during the summer as well. Jeff Boles' farm was only about nine miles from the Meiser place and Leo visited Ida rather frequently during the summer.

That fall Leo, while teaching at Green's Cross Roads, managed to see Ida about once every two or three weeks. Leo was boarding at Ike Grizzell's place, and Ike was a prosperous farmer. Among other things, Ike owned about half a dozen good saddle horses. Leo had no difficulty borrowing a horse occasionally, and riding the fifteen miles to the Meiser home to see Ida.

One Sunday morning, Leo rode up to the Meiser farm to do a little "courting." After spending the day, he stayed on into the night for a while. Finally, about ten o'clock, he decided that it was time for him to be on his way. He went out to the barn and threw the saddle on the horse in the stall where he had left it that morning. He got about two miles down the road before he discovered that he was the victim of a practical joke played by John and George Meiser, Ida's younger brothers. The boys had switched horses in the stall while Leo and Ida were "sparking." Leo rode back to the Meiser place and called loudly for Ida, who fortunately had not yet retired. She lighted a lantern for him and he went out to the barn, and finally got started home on the right nag. Several years later, Bert Hinkley, who married Ida's sister, Libbie Meiser, agreed with Leo that the Meiser home was a very tough place to go courting.

Ida and Leo had kept up with their letter writing. They wrote and received about two letters per week for several years. The only interruption that occurred was when Leo had hurriedly rushed off to Texas. There was a year during that time when there was no correspondence between the two whatsoever.

During the Christmas of 1905 Ida and Leo had become engaged to be married. The wedding was to be the following September, after Leo had graduated from the Nashville Bible School. While evangelistic work in Rutherford County during the early summer of 1906 was progressing, the tempo of correspondence with Ida had increased. Finally, the marriage date of September 23 was set.

The elders of some of the churches of Christ in Rutherford County were highly pleased with the success of the evangelistic programs that they had supported during the last two summers. They felt that it was their duty to continue to provide laborers to till the fields nearest home. Consequently, H. Leo Boles was sent again into the rural areas of Rutherford County with a tent and a song leader assistant. This time David R. Nickell of Wenatchee, Washington, went with him.

On June 3, 1906, they began a meeting at Milton which lasted three weeks. They set their tent in Lascassas (June 24) and Sharpeville (July 8) with only moderate success. However, when one casts his bread upon the water, he knows not what will become of it. For example, one would not guess that a thriving congregation would be established from the following entry in H. Leo Boles' log:

1906—July 22—Jefferson, (Rutherford County) Tennessee

I began this tent meeting under very unfavorable conditions.—Raining first Sunday. Brother Nickell led song service.—Continued meeting through two Sundays.—Baptized six—Put a little band of brethren and sisters to keeping house for the Lord.

During the meeting I preached to *three women* at their home and baptized *two of them.*

Received nothing—Brother Nickell the same.

On August 5, 1906, at Sulphur Springs, Rutherford County, H. Leo Boles began what was to be his last meeting of the summer, and it came within a hair's breadth of being the last of his life. He became stricken with typhoid fever, and he lay in a most critical condition for over a month. Traveling around the rural areas as he did; eating and drinking different things in many homes is, at best, very hard on an evangelist. Although he survived, H. Leo Boles carried to his death the effects of the typhoid disease suffered that summer. During the late summer, Boles lay at death's door. The typhus infection kept Leo's fever so high that he remained either unconscious or delirious for over a month. Slowly Leo, with the help of God, regained his health.

D. R. Nickell described Leo's sickness as follows:

During our first summer together, Brother Boles was stricken with typhoid fever, and for five weeks lingered on the brink of the river that separates time from eternity. I am glad that I had a small part in assisting him to remain on time's side. I shall always remember very kindly and affectionately the fine Christian home of Brother and Sister Charles N. Haynes near Murfreesboro, Tennessee, where we were so very hospitably kept during those strenuous five weeks, and the visits of other good brethren during that time.

Being close-mouthed seemed to be an inherent trait in most mountain people. In this respect, H. Leo Boles was no exception. In matters pertaining to his personal affairs he was positively secretive. He had told only his father, Jeff, and David Lipscomb about his engagement and marriage plans.

Leo's illness, of course, stopped his correspondence with Ida. She did not have an inkling of an idea that Leo was sick as neither Jeff Boles nor David Lipscomb had themselves been notified that H. Leo Boles was ill in the rural areas of Rutherford County.

This firsthand account is taken from H. Leo Boles' personal ledger. He belatedly logged this:

1906—August 5—Sulpher Springs, (Rutherford County) Tennessee

I began this tent meeting sick. Continued it two days. Brother Nickell led song service. Brother Nickell, W. L. Logan, and Brother Allen continued the meeting and closed on the 2nd Sunday night of the meeting.

Five were baptized.

And still later this:

I had typhoid fever and did not preach any more till 2nd Lords day in Oct.

While sick I was kept at the home of Brother C. N. Haynes. They were as kind and good to me as they could be.

Before I fully recovered I went home, Dibrell, Tenn., and was married to Miss Ida Meiser, and then went to the Nashville Bible School where we were both selected as teachers. I was married Sept. 23, 1906.

Ida did not hear from Leo from August 4 until September 20. She continued her preparation for the wedding, nevertheless. When she finally received a letter from Leo on September 20 written with a rather feeble hand, she was all ready for the ceremony on the twenty-third.

Elder Perry G. Potter, of Dibrell married them and they set out for Nashville immediately as school there had already started.

Leo, after graduation from the Bible School, accepted David Lipscomb's invitation to become a full-time teacher. As Ida was an accomplished elementary teacher, having taught seven years in the schools of Warren County, Leo experienced no difficulty in arranging with Lipscomb for Ida to teach the primary department of the school. Leo and Ida taught together as members of the faculty of the Nashville Bible School during the school year 1906-07.

On May 23, 1906, the Board of Trustees had met at David Lipscomb's home and discussed the vacancy left by the untimely death of Superintendent William Anderson. After much discussion, E. A. Elam, a member of the

Board, was elected to the position of Superintendent of the Nashville Bible School. Elam accepted the responsibility, but insisted that he could not reside on the school ground until the school term of 1907-08. It was agreed that Dr. J. S. Ward should continue as the Acting Superintendent until E. A. Elam could move to Nashville from Lebanon.

The faculty for the sixteenth year (1906-07) was listed as follows:

E. A. Elam.......................Superintendent
J. S. Ward........Acting Superintendent, Science
John T. Glenn............Latin, French, German
E. E. Sewell.......... Greek, English, Philosophy
O. W. Gardner.....History, Mathematics, Pedagog
S. P. Pittman.......Bible, Elocution, Vocal Music
H. Leo Boles..Academic Department, Mathematics
Miss Effie Anderson......Music and Voice Culture
Mrs. Ida Noble............................Art
Mrs. Ida Meiser Boles.......Primary Department
Miss Lucy Dodd....................Expression
J. W. Shepherd......................Librarian

The enrollment for the sixteeth year of the school reached 192. This was the largest enrollment yet. The total expenses for a young man had risen to $137.00 and for a young lady $146.00.

E. A. Elam was a graduate of Franklin College, class of '72. He had graduated from Burritt College in 1879. Elam had taught several years before he had started preaching. He was a Bible scholar and an eloquent preacher. He wrote the Sunday School literature on the Uniform Lessons for nearly thirty years. During the vacation of 1907, E. A. Elam moved his family to live on the campus of the Nashville Bible School, and he took full charge of the school upon his arrival in Nashville.

During the Christmas holidays of 1906, instead of resting or taking it easy, H. Leo Boles was to be found in a religious debate at Hickory Grove, Warren County, Tennessee. His opponent was a Seventh Day Adventist by the name of O. W. Burnell. Two propositions were discussed on December 26-29. Following is an extract from the Boles' ledger:

First Proposition: The Scriptures teach that God has ordained and sanctified Saturday, or the Seventh Day of the week as a special day for worship for Christians under the Christian Dispensation.

> O. W. Burnell, Affirmative
> H. Leo Boles, Negative

Second Proposition: The Scriptures teach that God has ordained and sanctified the First Day of the week as a special day of worship for Christians under the Christian Dispensation.

> H. Leo Boles, Affirmative
> O. W. Burnell, Negative

This was strictly a one-sided contest as the Boles technique and skill of debate, armed with irrefutable Biblical evidence, was entirely too much for Mr. Burnett to combat. Again, this debate was held on Boles' "home grounds" as Ida had been a most popular school "marm" at Hickory Grove for the four years just prior to her wedding. Burnett was no match for the educated professor.

When school closed May 23, 1907, H. Leo Boles and D. R. Nickell were again sent to evangelize in Rutherford County. On June 2, they began by erecting their tent in Christiana. This was followed by meetings in the communities of Barefield and Blackman.

They took up where they had been forced to quit the summer before by the untimely illness of H. Leo Boles. Boles and Nickell simply considered the work temporarily interrupted by an unavoidable circumstance and started out with renewed vigor.

The entry of H. Leo Boles into his ledger of the Blackman meeting is interesting because it tersely chronicles the birth of his second son:

> 1907—June 30, Blackman, (Rutherford County) Tennessee
> My father with Brother Nickell began this tent meeting. Baby "Leo Lipscomb" was born June 29, so I did not begin this meeting. Continued two weeks. Had five additions.

Success does not always crown the efforts of the gospel preacher no matter how hard he may try. Paul and Barnabas were unsuccessful in many places because the people did not believe, but this was not the fault of the apostles; it was the same gospel that Paul preached in Philippi and Corinth as he preached in Antioch of Pisidia and Iconium. H. Leo Boles tried two years with practically no success at Milton. One does not make a hit every time he goes to bat, even when he has the truth on his side. Following is another quote from the ledger:

1907—June 3—Milton, (Rutherford County) Tennessee

I began a tent meeting at this place and preached day and night for three weeks. No additions.

Brother D. F. Nickell was with me and led the song service. Much prejudice here against the truth as I presented it.—Received nothing.

1907—July 14—Milton, (Rutherford County) Tennessee

I began my second tent meeting at this place, continuing two weeks—preached day and night. Brother Nickell with me again and led song service.

Baptized one during this meeting who had been a member of the Methodist Church.

—Received nothing.

In contrast with the Milton efforts, in his next meeting, H. Leo Boles went back to Sharpeville where he had baptized only four in 1906. The entry reads:

1907—July 28—Sharpeville, (Rutherford County) Tennessee

I began my second tent meeting at this place and continued through two Lord's days. Brother Nickell led the song service.

It rained the first week, but crowds were very large.

Had thirty-one additions.

Many years later, D. H. Nickell has this to say regarding his association with H. Leo Boles in working the rural portions of Rutherford County:

Two very profitable and enjoyable summers in meetings were spent with Brother H. Leo Boles in Rutherford County, Tennessee. He did the preaching and I led the song services. I heard as much gospel in those two summers preached by Brother Boles as most people are privileged to hear in a life time. I also saw how a well-informed man is enabled to meet error and opposition to the truth.

When the 1907-08 school year began, H. Leo Boles,

137

teacher, doing full time work, teaching philosophy and mathematics, yet again he sat at the feet of David Lipscomb for two classes a day, one in the Old Testament and one in the New Testament. He continued to do this for seven years in succession. Practically the same courses in the Bible were covered each year, but he considered that it was time well spent to repeat these Bible courses. The "old, old story of Jesus and his love" was truly old, yet ever fresh to H. Leo Boles.

H. Leo Boles was one of the principals in yet another debate during the summer of 1908. At Walter Hill in Rutherford County a Baptist preacher named W. J. Watson, was holding a meeting simultaneous with the tent revival that Boles and Nickell were conducting during the summer of 1907. It was decided that W. J. Watson and H. Leo Boles would be invited back the next summer to debate some of the essential points of doctrine where these two differed. Watson agreed to debate Boles at Walter Hill on May 26-28, 1908. Of course, H. Leo Boles consented. There were four propositions to be argued. These were:

First Proposition: The kingdom, or church of God, to which H. Leo Boles belongs, was set up on the first Pentecost after the resurrection of Christ.

H. Leo Boles, Affirms
W. J. Watson, Denies

Second Proposition: The church of Christ with which I, W. J. Watson am identified, was set up during the personal ministry of Christ on earth.

W. J. Watson, Affirms
H. Leo Boles, Denies

Third Proposition: The Scriptures teach that a sinner may pray for pardon of his sins and may expect the answer to his prayer after he has repented of his sins and believed on Christ before his baptism.

W. J. Watson, Affirms
H. Leo Boles, Denies

Fourth Proposition: The Scriptures teach that baptism to a penitent believer, out of Christ, is unto the remission of sins.

H. Leo Boles, Affirms
W. J. Watson, Denies

J. W. Shepherd acted as moderator for H. Leo Boles and A. Malone was the moderator for W. J. Watson. The Walter Hill Baptist Church, where the debate was held, was crowded for every meeting. After the debate closed, F. B. Srygley read aloud a petition from the Lascassas community requesting the debate to be repeated over at their place. Boles immediately accepted but Watson declared that it was not feasible for him to waste further time in such prattle!

The summer months of 1908 and 1909 offered little that was new by way of experience. On February 22, 1909, Boles had turned thirty-five. He was no longer a young man and he barely would have qualified for that description at the time of his arrival on the Bible School campus. His last meeting for the summer of 1909 was with the Arlington church in Warren County. A Methodist revival had been in progress a week when Boles began, September 12. Back in those days evangelists such as Boles were pretty generally known as "Campbellite preachers." The denominations never welcomed their presence in a community because too often they lost their best members to the "Campbellites." The preacher promised to return for another meeting, and he did eleven years later. Boles wrote in his journal—"My father and step-mother attended nearly all the time which was a source of great joy to me."

H. Leo Boles continued to develop his talents as a gospel preacher in the summers of 1910 and 1911, and preaching monthly while school was in session. As the next school year neared the June closing in 1911, Boles was readying for a full summer of evangelism as he had done in each of the preceding summers. Nothing of marked importance happened that summer. H. Leo Boles was about as human as most people and reacted in about the same fashion. He knew country people and their ways; they always take 'coon hunting and politics seriously. In a meeting at Oak Grove in Wilson County, Tennessee, his meeting was spoiled because nearly all the church members "talked politics day and night." "Well, they made," as Boles put it, "strong solicitations to a third meeting for them next year." He responded—"No definite promises."

The summer of 1912 found H. Leo Boles closer to a day about which he could have had no inkling—the presidency of the Nashville Bible School. He was now standing on the threshold of a life of unprecedented service to the school and church.

Of the nine meetings H. Leo Boles conducted in the summer of 1912, two are deserving of attention. The evangelist should be remembered for a mission meeting he conducted in Mayfield, Kentucky, beginning June 16, 1912, which continued over three Sundays. No loyal group of the members of the church of Christ was meeting in Mayfield at that time. According to J. C. "Cliff" Emerson, a life-long resident of Graves County, Kentucky, the first congregation of disciples was organized into a church, June 18, 1853, at Spring Creek in Graves County; a store at that place is now called Dogwood. As the years passed some of the members moved to the county seat. In 1868 the Christians built their first meetinghouse at the cost of $8,000.

Along toward the close of the century, the more progressive young members of the congregation wanted instrumental music in their worship. The elders contended the practice was unscriptural and refused on those grounds. But the young people would not let up in their demands. Finally the elders agreed for an organ to be used in the Sunday School, but demanded that a cover be placed over it during the worship hour. Later the organ was brought into the worship; and at the close of the century only the "Digressives" had a church in Mayfield.

The meeting Boles conducted was at the "cock crowing" of a new dawn for the church of Christ in that city. The Christian Church had little or no success in the outlying rural areas of Graves County. From Memphis, through Jackson, and into Paducah, the Illinois Central Railroad split the country. Preachers from Freed-Hardeman College evangelized the whole region. But a little-known preacher from Nashville won the day for the cause of Christ in one of the best known cities in Western Kentucky. Boles baptized eighteen people, receiving $80.00 for his efforts, and set in order a congregation of thirty-two who signed the following statement drawn up by Boles:

140

CHURCH OF CHRIST, MAYFIELD, KENTUCKY
ENROLLMENT OF MEMBERS

We, the undersigned members of former congregations, not finding a church in Mayfield, Kentucky, worshipping and serving God as it is written in the New Testament, do agree to meet together for work and worship as God, our Father, has ordained in the New Testament. We express our determination to take the Word of God, without any addition, subtraction, or modification whatever, as our guide in all work and worship and pray God's blessing upon us in doing his will, we understand that we must leave off all instruments of music in the worship and all human organizations for church work, such as Missionary Societies, Christian Endeavour Societies, Ladies' Aid Societies, etc. The church, without any of these societies, is God's ordained institution for preaching the gospel and doing good unto men.

The original copy of the agreement has long since been lost and there is no record of those who signed the agreement.

In late July of this summer, the evangelist conducted another meeting at Walter Hill in Rutherford County, Tennessee. As is the general rule, little attention is paid to a revival in an urban area. But this was not the case two generations ago when activities were limited in the rural sections and such as there were proved to be of interest to most everyone—particularly in matters of religion. When Boles came into a community the folks flocked to hear him.

The Methodists heard of Boles' coming and planned a meeting to run concurrently. No reason was given by the Methodists, but H. Leo Boles thought he knew. He proposed to the Methodist preacher that they conduct a union meeting together. It came of no surprise to Boles when the Methodist preacher declined; and it was probably a fortunate decision for the Methodists.

H. Leo Boles closed his journal at the end of the summer of 1912; and this is no mystery since newly appointed as President of the Bible School, he would devote his weekdays to the school and preach Sundays.

141

Chapter XV

THE MANTLE OF DAVID LIPSCOMB

The Elam administration spanned the years from 1906 through 1913. The Nashville Bible School differed little from that of other years outside of President Elam's never ending efforts to raise money to operate the school. He urged Christians in the *Gospel Advocate* to contribute toward the improvements continually being made on the campus. David Lipscomb and his associates had no idea of running the school for profit. David Lipscomb gave the better part of his energy to the *Gospel Advocate*, and the savings of his lifetime to the Nashville Bible School.

About this time a criticism was directed against the school because the word "Bible" appeared in the title of the institution. Though David Lipscomb was growing feebler he was still busy and interested in the school. He replied to the criticism simply saying—"All that is meant by the expression, 'Bible School' is that God's Book is taught here more universally than any other. A school that does not do this ought not to call itself a 'Bible School.' " Students were no exception and some of them looked on the institution as a training ground for preachers.

The administration of E. A. Elam was not especially marked; the school catalog listed Elam as "President" for the eighteenth session and all subsequent heads of the institution have worn the title. Some weeks before the closing session of the school in the spring of 1913, E. A. Elam tendered his formal resignation to the Board of Directors. His devotion to the Bible School had not been questioned, and his loyalty to Christian education was deep and sincere. Until the day of his death his interest never wavered in promoting and sustaining the Nashville Bible School.

Some strong feelings on the part of students and faculty attended the resignation of E. A. Elam as school head because of differences with some students the previous school year. H. Leo Boles refused to take sides in the petty complaints directed against President Elam. Though

142

young Boles was not particularly close to the older men at the time, E. A. Elam became Boles' great friend and staunch defender as long as Elam lived. While H. Leo Boles took his stand on the side of Christian charity in this instance, it was never Boles' nature to be controlled by his emotions. E. A. Elam never thought of himself as a school man and was relieved to be freed of the school's responsibilities so he could devote more of his time to preaching and writing.

After President Elam offered his resignation, the Board of Directors promptly met urging him to reconsider his intention to resign. His wishes were that his resignation be accepted. He suggested that the school needed a man who would devote full time to the position remaining on the campus to direct the affairs of the school. At this same meeting David Lipscomb nominated H. Leo Boles to succeed E. A. Elam at the close of the current session; the motion was seconded by the retiring president. J. C. Mc-Quiddy, another of Lipscomb's "favorite children," a member of the board, recommended that the Boles election be unanimous. The Board of Directors so acted and H. Leo Boles moved into the main stream of Restoration history.

When H. Leo Boles became president of the Nashville Bible School in the spring of 1913, the institution needed capable hands to guide it. By now David Lipscomb was an old man of eighty-two and failing rapidly. No one was more surprised at the growth of the school than Lipscomb, and he was, no doubt, reluctant to let his ideas of yesterday which guided the school go by the board. What the school needed was a president who would open the doors of progress, and at the same time, retain the confidence of David Lipscomb. H. Leo Boles filled that bill and David Lipscomb never made a wiser decision. David Lipscomb could have no higher confidence in a man than to place his mantle upon him as the president of the Nashville Bible School. No other position was held more sacred by him— not even the editorship of the *Gospel Advocate*.

When the school opened on September 9, 1913, David Lipscomb began teaching his classes in the usual manner.

143

But his health soon became such that he could not continue, and Boles assumed the responsibility to teach his Bible classes. David Lipscomb frequently attended classes that year and commended Boles as being an excellent Bible teacher. Lipscomb had taught his Bible classes sitting in a large cane-bottomed chair with arms. The chair was placed on a platform so that he might better observe his students. After he gave up his classes, the chair was kept reserved for him. He was always punctual when he came and the students could hear the sound of his shuffling feet along the hall way. As he entered with his broad-brimmed black hat and walking cane clutched in his hand, Boles would say, "Come in Brother Lipscomb." Brother Lipscomb would hang his hat on the hook, take hold of the chair post and step carefully onto the platform, take his seat, and slowly lay his walking cane on the floor. Then he would adjust the Bible on his knees to enjoy the hour. Seldom did Boles ever question the old gentleman about the Bible lesson under discussion.

Whatever reservation some of Boles' associates may have had about the qualifications of the new president were soon dispelled. Over the span of a lifetime H. Leo Boles cultivated the mental habit of carefully planning each step with the most exacting care. An apt description of the stout-hearted Boles in those days was that "he doeth all things well. . . ." There had been harder days in his life than these. The stubborn rock-studded soil of DeKalb County had yielded to his plow. Here he had lost the tender wife of his youth dying in the birth of his first born child. He had saved his son, always frail, for a brief, but useful life. Some powerful intangible force stirs deeply the hearts of such men who face suffering and the paradoxical problems thrust upon them by an inscrutable fate. If Henry Leo Boles ever sought the easy life, he never found it. And there is no evidence that he did. That he sought the high and hard road of usefulness to God and man is patent to all who knew him.

An often repeated cliche that hindsight is better than foresight had little application in the life of the "last of the pioneer preachers." Even in his youth he had resolved that he would give purpose and meaning to his life. The image of this "granite man" is becoming more sharply focused with the passing of the years. His incalculable service to the church and school he loved is only now being fully evaluated.

When Boles became president he expected that all he did would pass under critical eyes both to praise and find fault, but he proved himself equal to his responsibilities and accepted without stumbling every challenge. As long as H. Leo Boles served the school, he gave the lion's share of his time to it. This does not mean that he slighted either his preaching or writing. He was an extremely gifted person and nothing he ever did in one thing went begging in another. The control of the Bible School passed into Boles' hands in the early summer of 1913. During those summer months he travelled extensively soliciting both students and funds and he continued to use his summers in this manner as long as he served the school.

All who knew David Lipscomb found him to be sparing with words and never given to superlatives when praising a deserving person. He wrote in the *Advocate:* "We do not doubt that the care and energy of Brother Boles as President of the School will promote its success at several points. Brother Boles knows how to give close and needed attention to business to succeed with it." The practical aspects of the everyday affairs never escaped David Lipscomb's attention; he was himself a good business man, and could recognize the same qualities in another person.

H. Leo Boles differed from E. A. Elam in several respects. The latter had little patience with the tedious and endless details of school administration since he was first a preacher, and next a writer. These activities took up most of his time. While serving as president of the school, E. A. Elam never maintained a public office—a bedroom in the boy's dormitory served that purpose. Whatever problems faced him as a school president stemmed out of the fact that he was not a trained educator and had never planned to be!

Soon after becoming president, Boles equipped an office always open to the students, faculty, patrons, and the public. With the same enthusiasm and energy that marked him in everything else he did, President Boles began to give his new office the best he had. Boles assumed that a college's business is education. He assembled a good faculty to help him, and he strove for a better teaching staff as long as he served the college.

H. Leo Boles promptly demonstrated his ability to operate the school which celebrated its twenty-third opening in the fall of 1913. By Christmas the school had enrolled one hundred and forty students; five young men and an equal number of young ladies made up the senior class. H. Leo Boles is remembered in those very first years as a man with a sharp tongue, and there were occasions when he was less than gentle. Some students did not like him at first acquaintance. They had to learn to appreciate him. He was always neatly dressed with his "high collar" and shoes shining to a high gloss. Students say his eyes were as blue as the heaven above and could bore a hole right through you.

Back in those days, and the rest of his life for that matter, he wanted things done right and right then. As Annie Porter Delk Kennedy remembered him—he was "all fire and tow." His temper sometimes got the upper hand but Boles was never ruffled even when he displayed his high displeasure. He stood up to teach a class and it was an ill-advised student who came unprepared for the recitation. He would snap his finger at a student, "You were absent last class meeting"; and he generally knew why. A student could expect a scolding for being tardy; and if he were kept over time in another class no sympathy was extended. President Boles was severe in his attitude toward "horse-play" in his classroom; outside of class he had a keen sense of humour. Even in class he enjoyed a humourous episode that arose out of a class situation.

President Boles began his second year with high hopes, and it proved to be a banner year. At the end of the last session more than two hundred students had enrolled. Where he had gone in "out of the way places" to hold meetings, he was now going to solicit students and support for the school. The Board of Directors approved the plan for the college quartet to accompany the president on those tours. During the summer months of 1916, the president and the quartet were engaged almost every night at some church building.

It was becoming crystal clear that H. Leo Boles as an administrator was both an authoritarian and disciplinarian in dealing with faculty and students. The image of the head schoolmaster in American education until well into the twentieth century was that of a patriarch whose position was respected and his words never questioned. H. Leo Boles was such a schoolmaster—always stern and sometimes plain stubborn. He required faithful and exacting work from his teachers and that they should require quality work from their students. He had one problem he never solved and that was to enroll paying students. It seemed that everybody wanted to work his way through school.

H. Leo Boles was a highly intelligent man who developed the highest appreciations for the finer graces of life. Such qualities come easily for men who belong to that breed of natural aristocracy that history is so generous to recognize. This was the period when Lyceum and Chatauqua artists appeared on stages in the hinterlands all across the country. When world famous artists and celebrated preachers came to Nashville, President Boles saw to it that his students were afforded the privilege to see and hear them.

Each school year was marked by advancement and change. The teaching of the Bible remained paramount and the classics and fine arts were taught, but the useful arts such as home economics were finding their way into the curriculum. President Boles began to promote the fact that the college was a co-educational institution where young people were taught their true mission in life.

When H. Leo Boles took office, the school was poorly equipped. From the beginning the school had been operated in a somewhat loose fashion. The president meant to change this and began to re-organize the school along the lines of good business procedure. Some of the teachers were paid a salary while others were paid at the end of the year after all operating expenses. What was left of

147

the receipts went into a common fund that was divided among the teachers. This was called taking "potluck"; all shared equally in little or nothing. When Boles came to the faculty, he paid four hundred and fifty dollars in cash so as to share equally with the others. President Boles changed the policy and a new member was not required to pay anything into the common fund. All shared equally with the president and the faculty at the end of the school year.

President Boles changed still another custom that had been a practice in the old Franklin College. The faculty claimed an interest in the furnishings and school equipment. The campus and buildings were under the control of the Board of Directors who assumed responsibility for their upkeep and this included new constructions and capital improvements. When E. A. Elam left the school he gave all of his interest in the furnishings to the faculty. To prevent the disposal of the equipment and to insure its care, the president brought up the interests of the faculty and then prevailed upon the Board of Directors to purchase the fixtures. A resolution was passed by the Board of Directors, May 19, 1915, to purchase all of the school's furnishings. For the first time in the school's history plans were laid for the faculty to receive fixed salaries.

Other poor business practices were corrected. Even the utility man purchased whatever he thought was necessary for operating the plant. That practice was ended with a new procedure to centralize all school purchases. The school's services were expanded and its usefulness was implemented by an ever expanding offering of subjects. All of this was reflected in the catalog for the school year (1915-1916); student expenses were listed at two hundred dollars and students were advised there would be extra charges for art, music, voice, and the domestic arts of cooking and sewing.

For many years a farming operation was carried on the farm and continued toward the close of Boles' second administration. Boles was general farm manager in addition to his other duties. A letter to the Board of Directors dated May 17, 1919, reflects some of his numerous problems:

148

I have been at the expense of operating the farm, having three hired hands all summer and boarded two of them. I have canned several hundred cans of tomatoes and beans to be used for the school; have housed several tons of hay and will harvest about 75 barrels of corn. I will furnish the exact invoice of this and should have pay for all of these.

Working students assisted on the farm doing general work. Like the students, mules came and went. Two were called "Nig" and "Walt"; but their names never meant a great deal to the students. The laziest mule was always called "Callio" by the Lipscomb boys, and the Callios dubbed the same mule "Lips" well out of earshot of Brother Boles. One of the early memories was of the farm wagon clattering down the cobblestone streets of Nashville to the Union Station to pick up the luggage of incoming students.

About this time the boy's dormitory was re-named Lindsay Hall in honor of a Texan who had given a substantial sum toward the erection of the building. The girl's dormitory was named Avalon Home, and the Chapel Building was called Harding Hall in memory of James A. Harding. Another footnote is added to the history of the Boles' family with the Bible School with the graduation of the president's eldest son, Cleo, who finished with the B.S. degree in a class of twelve in the spring of 1917.

When the school opened the following September, World War I, mounting in savage fury was soon to reach its bitter climax. In spite of the national crisis and the preoccupation of everyone with the world's shame, President Boles continued to set up new milestones for the school. He made arrangements with Vanderbilt University, George Peabody College, State Normals, and other colleges in the South to accept credits from the Nashville Bible School without entrance examinations. Boles was employing so many part-time teachers being trained by Vanderbilt and Peabody that for those institutions to refuse to accept the Lipscomb students being taught by their teachers would have, in effect, reflected on the institutions' graduate schools. The Nashville Bible School demanded that its students give a good account of themselves elsewhere in seeking advanced education in other colleges. The academic respectability of first the Nashville Bible School and consequently David Lipscomb College has seldom been questioned.

Many of the boys and girls worked their way through the Bible School on a "self-help" basis. After two years of such hard work to gain an education, few of them were willing to squander their time somewhere else. Every student who was willing to work with a need born out of necessity was given that opportunity. These students, for the most part, placed a high value on academic knowledge.

The school year (1917-1918) would be a memorable one; David Lipscomb died November 11, 1917, at the age of 86. His death deeply moved the student body. Whatever the Nashville Bible School had given to enrich the lives of the hundreds of young people who passed through her halls, David Lipscomb had not only given all his earthly possessions but now his life. He never drew a cent from the school and frequently had been known to pay a teacher's salary from his own pocket.

President Boles was paid a signal honor by his faculty soon after the death of David Lipscomb. The faculty presented the Board of Directors with a resolution requesting that H. Leo Boles be elected a member of the Board of Directors. Mrs. David Lipscomb gave her approval to the resolution with a brief note: "If this meets with the approval of the Board of Directors, it will be agreeable with me." It was not deemed advisable by the Board at the time to add the president to the Board of Directors. The minutes of the meeting show that "it is the wish of the Board that Brother Boles, President of the school, be invited to any and all of the meetings of the Board, and that he confer freely with the members."

Following the passing of Lipscomb, the faculty in a regular session petitioned the school directors to change the name of the school to David Lipscomb College. The president presented the resolution to the Board at a meeting in the *Gospel Advocate* office, May 4, 1918. On this occasion President Boles pointed out that the institution had so grown that "school" was no longer an adequate description; that in view of the work being done, "college"

150

OFFICE OF H. LEO BOLES

would be more appropriate. O. P. Barry moved the name be changed from Nashville Bible School to David Lipscomb College and it was done. In his lifetime David Lipscomb would not allow the institution to wear his name.

At this same meeting, H. Leo Boles called the Board's attention to the need for a new girl's dormitory and other improvements. For the past three years more girls had applied than the school could admit. It was agreed to consider the matter and a committee was appointed to that end.

The last two years of Boles' first administration were marked as usual by progress. The Board had given the "go ahead" sign for the new dormitory. The *Gospel Advocate* joined in a vigorous campaign to call attention to the needs of the college for a new dormitory. A special meeting was held in the Ryman Auditorium, May 18, 1919, to interest the churches in Nashville in helping to raise funds for the new structure. E. A. Elam agreed to go into the field to raise the $50,000 needed for the building.

A reading of the Board minutes beginning in 1903 after the school was incorporated might leave the impression that its members mostly talked about financing the school which is largely true. C. A. Moore was serving as secretary of the Board in 1911 and the following statement was included in the minutes for January 24: "The treasurer then suggested the wisdom of having his books of the school audited as we have been careless in this matter since he had been keeping the books." The minutes disclose that there were periodical audits by the Board of Directors. The services of professional auditors were later used, and this became a standard practice in Boles' second administration. In the spring of 1919, all of the old accounts of the Nashville Bible School were cleared. The Board of Directors then assumed control of the school's furnishings and the buildings, and responsibility for new structures and other capital improvements. It was following these final transactions that all the members of the faculty began receiving a regular salary in September, 1919.

David Lipscomb College was now on the high road to greater service. H. Leo Boles had taken the school while it was still in its swaddling clothes and had given it academic stature and dignity. The difficult struggle to increase enrollment had been unrelenting. His "drumming" up students by going into the rural areas of Tennessee, Kentucky, Georgia, Alabama, and Mississippi was now bearing fruit. When Boles closed out school in the spring of 1920, the brand new girls' dormitory was about ready for occupancy. In short, the spade work had been done for David Lipscomb College to enter a grand new era of Christian education.

The year H. Leo Boles mounted to the presidency of the Nashville Bible School, there was little to suggest the institution was a college. Nashville then covered an area of some twenty square miles with about 100,000 inhabitants. The school was on a beautiful shady campus located on a farm of 160 acres. Most of the old farm is now one of the finest residential sections in Nashville.

The Board of Directors in 1913 included David Lipscomb, president of the Board of Directors, C. A. Moore, J. C. McQuiddy, E. A. Elam, and W. V. Davidson. The school was departmentalized after a fashion; but in comparison with the standardization required of present education it would be considered unorganized. Whoever hoped to enter the Collegiate Department according to the school catalog for the year (1896-1897) had to stand an examination in Reading, Writing, Common School Arithmetic, and other related studies. For those who were unable to pass the examinations, the Primary and Intermediate departments were set up, and the enrollments for those departments were always small. During Boles' first administration these were mostly attended by faculty children.

In the first years, the Collegiate Department offered Greek, Latin, English, Philosophy, Mathematics, and Modern Languages; such offerings were typical for the period. After the Bible School was moved to the farm, other changes came such as the awarding of degrees and a gradually changing curriculum to meet new educational demands. The college catalog pictures what the institution had grown to be at the time H. Leo Boles retired as president; the Primary Department included the first eight grades; the High School was made up with a four year program. The third and fourth years of the High School

152

were labelled "Freshman College"; and the fourth year was described as the "Sophomore College" year. The Collegiate Department added two additional years designated as "Junior and Senior" classes.

The relation to the organization of a standard junior college is too obvious for comment. One of the first steps made by A. B. Lipscomb, who succeeded Boles as president, was to do away with the program and establish a *bona fide* junior college with a supporting primary school and high school. As H. Leo Boles neared the close of this first tenure, he was attending Vanderbilt University working toward his M.A. degree in Philosophy, Psychology, and Sociology. When Boles returned to the college in 1923 as president, he came back a university graduate with the added prestige that goes along with such.

The Nashville Bible School began on an experimental basis. The history of Christian colleges established in the first scant years of the Restoration Movement promised little to the future of other such institutions. The classic models were Bethany College, an instrument of the Christian Church; and the College of the Bible, which opened in Lexington, Kentucky, October 2, 1865. These proved to be sad disappointments. Franklin College had long since closed its doors.

David Lipscomb devoted some thirty years to thinking about a Christian school before he and James A. Harding took action. There is little cause to wonder at the wisdom of David Lipscomb when he started a school of his own. He had all the facts of Franklin College, Bethany College, and the College of the Bible in mind. He had good reason to distrust an entrenched clergy and the religious seminaries that trained them. David Lipscomb never intended to establish a "preacher factory" and he would not let his brethren forget that fact as long as he lived.

When David Lipscomb deeded his farm to the Nashville Bible School, he stated in a few words in this brief document what has since become the classic *magna charta* of Christian education: that the property shall "be used for maintaining a school in which, in addition to other branches of learning, the Bible as the recorded will of God

153

. . . shall be taught as a regular daily study to all who shall attend such school . . . ."

At the time H. Leo Boles was appointed by the Board of Directors to direct the Nashville Bible School, David Lipscomb was rapidly failing in health as he had suffered a stroke in 1909. The fact is known that Lipscomb personally selected young Boles to succeed E. A. Elam, and some felt that the decision at the best was an unwise one. The minutes of the Board meeting fail to record that H. Leo Boles was elected to the presidency of the Bible School. Some may have thought that Boles was a "stop gap" president, but as long as David Lipscomb lived no one ever said anything about it. H. Leo Boles had to prove himself to a good schoolman and he went about that task as he did everything that occupied his interest. His contemporaries looked upon the "mountain man" from the Cumberlands as somewhat of a rural provincial. Even those who both thought and said so were hardly sophisticates and would have added little grace to the ivied halls of Harvard. Nashville in the early part of the twentieth century was described as a "big country town." So H. Leo Boles without any popular support went his way slowly and deliberately building David Lipscomb College better than he knew in his lifetime.

Following the death of David Lipscomb several moves were made to replace him as president of the Bible school. As a matter of fact, H. Leo Boles never felt any security with the school even while David Lipscomb was living. In 1915 David Lipscomb was growing feebler by the day. To express his concern, Boles wrote a letter dated May 19, 1915:

> I would like to have some understanding in regard to the length of time I am to stay with the school. The nature of the work and the welfare of the school require that I plan and arrange a year or two ahead to make the school successful. I suggest that the term of five years be fixed or agreed on.

The statement was added that should either the Board or Boles be dissatisfied with the arrangement to give a twelve month prior notice.

On February 11, 1918, A. B. Lipscomb presented to

154

the Board of Directors a suggestion from Jesse P. Sewell, President of Abilene Christian College, that the Nashville Bible School standardize its academic offerings so that degrees from the institution might be recognized by other institutions. Sewell also suggested in his letter that the Nashville Bible School add a graduate department and that the graduates from the western colleges would be pleased to finish their education in Nashville. The Board of Directors invited Sewell to come to Nashville and outline his plan at a board meeting.

At a called board meeting for February 25, 1918, Jesse P. Sewell, a graduate of the Nashville Bible School, explained the need for a standardized four year college in Nashville, Tennessee. Sewell stated what has long since been recognized—that Nashville was the logical place for such a school. J. R. Aust, at that meeting, moved that the Board of Directors take such steps as would be necessary for the creation of a standard four year college. At a later Board meeting, March 4, 1918, A. B. Lipscomb, president of the Board, presented to the Board of Directors a copy of a proposition from Jesse P. Sewell to take over the management of the Nashville Bible School provided certain conditions were met. The Board declined the offer and wrote Sewell they thought it best not to make a change in the administration at that time.

During this same meeting O. P. Barry moved that a committee of three be appointed to study the matter of putting the school on a better financial footing. A. B. Lipscomb appointed O. P. Barry, W. V. Davidson, and C. A. Moore to make up the committee. Later the Board of Directors met in A. B. Lipscomb's *Gospel Advocate* office, April 6, 1918. At the meeting Lipscomb said that O. P. Barry was willing to take over the management of the school and be responsible for its operation and to accept as his pay whatever was left over at the end of the year after operating expenses were paid. H. Leo Boles did not favor the plan to share with O. P. Barry the joint operation of the college. When the Board requested Boles to submit his plan, he said that he had none of his own to offer but would cheerfully consider any plan the Board would suggest.

155

The matter of a change in the presidency hung fire until the Board meeting on January 12, 1919. E. A. Elam reported that he had found in a conference with the faculty a willingness on their part to continue with Boles as school head, and he was appointed to serve the ensuing year. Following the death of David Lipscomb, the Board minutes disclosed that the tenure of Boles was never secure, but he was never in the dark about the matter. H. Leo Boles was always philosophical about such matters. His turns in life never amounted to reverses but to new directions!

When the Board of Directors met a year later, January 6, 1920, O. P. Barry moved that A. B. Lipscomb be elected president of the college and for H. S. Lipscomb to serve as dean. The change was planned to take place at the end of that school session. The Board minutes of that meeting show that "Brother Elam gave a frank expression of his views concerning the proposed change. He did not consider it to be for the best interest of the school but was ready to yield to the judgment of the other members of the Board." Whatever the feelings H. Leo Boles may have had about the change, no one ever knew and this included the members of his own family.

These were the growing years of the college and most everyone on the Board and faculty felt he knew best how the college should be managed. None were trained school men and this was the classic experiment in Christian education with no precedents and traditions to serve as guide lines. It is now clearly recognized that the Nashville Bible School (later David Lipscomb College) is the mother institution of all such schools, and from her they still draw their inspiration. If David Lipscomb was first in the Nashville Bible School, and he was, then there can be no question that H. Leo Boles was first in David Lipscomb College. There has not been a period since that the memories of both men have not been honored, and what they thought and said is still regarded.

Chapter XVI
SWORD OF THE SPIRIT

No member of the church of Christ so powerfully wielded the "sword of the Spirit" in this century as did H. Leo Boles. No other person so stoutly championed the cause of apostolic Christianity and so profoundly shaped the image of the New Testament church as David Lipscomb at the turn of the century, but he had a worthy successor in H. Leo Boles. All who were acquainted with H. Leo Boles knew him in one or more of his varied roles. There are those who say that he was a better preacher than a writer while some hold the opposite view. What is more nearly the truth, Boles was incomparable in the multiple roles of evangelist, scholar, writer, and educator.

Thousands of church members who never knew Boles personally or heard him preach learned about him through the *Gospel Advocate*. And the story of the life and times of H. Leo Boles in the last forty years of his life may best be told on the pages of the *Advocate*. Here the rich and colorful strands of his life merge to form a complex figure in the tapestry of the later days of the Restoration.

The *Gospel Advocate* is the oldest religious journal among the members of the church, dating from its origin and the number of years of its publication. The first issue of the *Gospel Advocate* was published in July, 1855, by Tolbert Fanning and William Lipscomb. The paper was published monthly until the Civil War closed it down in 1861. It resumed publication in 1866. David Lipscomb soon became the sole owner and publisher of the *Advocate*. The Lipscomb family came from pioneer stock and have distinguished themselves among Tennessee's finest citizens. No one could have guessed in 1867 that David Lipscomb was destined to become the family's most famous son.

Whatever direction the Restoration Movement may have taken in the South, had it not been for David Lipscomb its course could not have been the same. The direction it did take resulted largely from the efforts of Tolbert Fanning and David Lipscomb through the *Gospel Advocate*. E. G. Sewell became co-editor with David Lipscomb and the two men worked side by side for fifty years. Later they were joined by F. D. Srygley and J. C. McQuiddy. After these stout champions had grown old, they were referred to as the "Old Guard." As these brethren passed away one by one, their deaths were especially noted in the *Advocate*. The cause of the ideals of New Testament Christianity never owed so much to so few in the course of the Restoration Movement in the last half of the nineteenth century.

From the very beginning Tolbert Fanning meant for the *Gospel Advocate* to investigate honestly and candidly the scriptural integrity of every religious issue facing the church. That practice was continued by David Lipscomb until he become too feeble to be a shaper of Advocate policy. David Lipscomb not only addressed himself to those outside the church but to its members as well. One particular adversary whom Lipscomb addressed was Daniel Sommer who led the anti-Christian college movement among the churches. Sommer is still regarded as the "grandaddy" of the "antis" who trouble the church now in much the same fashion as their predecessor did in that early period. When Lipscomb became convinced that Sommer had only one side to argue, he never again troubled himself to answer the Indiana preacher. But Lipscomb could learn from anyone, and he thought that Sommer's proposal to exclude the use of instrumental music in Christian worship in deeding church property was a sound proposal.

It never occurred to either Fanning or Lipscomb that religious controversy was somehow bad; the two men had something to believe and defend if necessary. The pages of the *Gospel Advocate* were freely opened for an opposing point of view provided that the point of view and its advocate were honest. David Lipscomb never allower the paper to be used to express one side of a question or to become the sounding board or propaganda medium for the "ax grinders."

David Lipscomb perhaps did not know how successfully he had stemmed the tide of "digression" in Middle Tennessee. One fact surely stands out; the victories won by the "Old Guard" through the pages of the *Advocate* were led by Lipscomb. Their success was finally sealed by the establishment of the Nashville Bible School.

In just eight years after Boles came to the Bible School, David Lipscomb wrote in the *Advocate:* "Brethren Boles and Glenn have studied the Bible closely while in school. I have heard their lessons as they recited them in class and as they heard these classes. I know no better teachers of the Bible." Occasionally the name of Boles would be mentioned in connection with a preaching appointment or a revival and the school after becoming its president.

Although H. Leo Boles wrote but a little for the *Gospel Advocate* after immediately coming to the Nashville Bible School in 1903, here and there tucked away in the pages of the *Advocate* are scattered articles written by the young man through 1915. He was already a good writer when he was first trying his editorial legs. In the issue of the *Gospel Advocate* dated March 2, 1916. H. Leo Boles wrote the lead article in a special issue under the general heading "Faith and Works." His article was titled "What Is Faith?" Clearly discernible at this early date is the touch of the master's hand. From his first day in Nashville it was apparent that Boles was no journeyman apprentice in command of the English language. It would be impossible to measure the magnitude of the life and efforts of Boles if the pages of the *Gospel Advocate* were not reviewed to this end.

Just as the nomadic wanderings of the Biblical patriarchs could be traced by the fires rising from their sacrificial altars, the passage of Boles down the years of his life may in no other place be so clearly followed as on the *Advocate* pages. At the very beginning of his career as a religious journalist and pamphleteer, two salient facts emerge: the English sentences of Boles at the very outset were marked by a classic beauty unmarred by a flowery or stilted rhetoric; and of even greater importance was his certain and exact knowledge of the Bible evidenced in his writings. Boles was a more eloquent writer than speaker.

This is not meant to imply that he lacked in either gift. Sitting at the feet of Lipscomb had taught Boles to talk and write in plain, simple language. He very seldom used a three syllable word if a one syllable word would suffice.

H. Leo Boles reached another journalistic milestone in 1918. For the first time he moved massively into the field of religious journalism. No less than fifteen signed articles issued from his pen in the *Gospel Advocate*. Among other subjects he was writing on Old Testament characters. His students in the Nashville school, and those who heard him during the Freed-Hardeman lectures on the same theme, carry an indelible memory of this great teacher.

One of the early articles was titled: "Cain, An Enemy of God"; the typical Boles prose is clearly discernible at this time in the following lines:
of God"; the typical Boles prose is clearly discernible at

> Satan has stood by every altar erected to Jehovah and tried to pollute it; he has had his representatives in every assembly of the saints and in some way or another has tried to defeat the will of God. He has mingled his voice with the music and praise of Jehovah; he has invented instruments to imitate and vitiate the harmony of the praise of Jehovah. . . .

Whatever he meant to say, the reader was not in doubt and never read very far to learn what was on the writer's mind.

H. Leo Boles gave a repeat performance in 1919 with another fifteen articles appearing in the *Gospel Advocate*. But an even greater honor came to him the following year. The publishers of the *Advocate* announced that Boles would be added to the staff of writers with a description of his unfailing energy to do several jobs well and with dispatch:

> This does not mean that he will cease to devote his energies to the development and improvement of David Lipscomb College. This he regards as his duty, and he has proved his faith by his works. He is a man who does things and appreciates the responsibilities that rest with him. Busy men do things. He does not neglect his work for other things, no matter how important they appear.

A promise was made along with the statement that the *Gospel Advocate* would continue to support all such schools as David Lipscomb College.

At first Boles mostly wrote about Bible personalities, but other articles now followed playing over a wide sweep of Bible subjects. His writings ranged from "Deism" to "modesty" in Christian apparel. The *Advocate* pages reveal numerous fascinating facets about this remarkable man. Some of Boles' brethren called him one of the finest scholars in the brotherhood while others ranked him in first place. He was a knowledgeable man, and the search to explain this fact does not lead far. He not only knew about books and great scholars, he read their works and understood them. While preparing a series of articles on the divinity of Christ, he cited eleven eminent authorities. Although an avid reader of religious works, the range of his intellectual interests were those of any well educated man of his day.

Boles quoted Disraeli who said, "A book may be as great a thing as a battle"; and Boles added, "but sometimes a book is a battle—a conflict between two giant intellects, or a combat between two great lines of thought, or the expression of a contest between truth and error." B. C. Goodpasture told how H. Leo Boles read a book—"He never laid a book down once he had begun to read it even though the book was proving to be of little or no value." What he thought was never guessed because at the conclusion of the book, he would scribble such statements: "a good book," or a "poor book," or "a worthless waste of time." He was fond of repeating that "A good book is a good friend; and if it is a good book, it is a great friend." He encouraged Christians to build a good home library with a generous number of good religious books.

After Boles left the school, he moved to a home he had bought on Cedar Lane located at the end of the Belmont streetcar line. The home was a large two story brick structure. Cleo and his wife, Lemma Perry Boles, lived in the upstairs of the home. The location of the home made it easy for H. Leo Boles to make his way to his *Advocate* office downtown and for Dr. Cleo Boles to go to his teaching duties in the Vanderbilt Dental School. Leo Lipscomb was attending Hume Fogg High School at the time.

While H. Leo Boles was away from the college he served as editor of the *Gospel Advocate*. He would give up that position when he returned to the college three years later. His temporary retirement from the college was rich and fertile as were all the years of his life. As a result, he entered into a policy making role of the *Advocate* by becoming not only its editor but also its part owner. Some twelve articles came from his pen in 1920. These were mostly a continuation of the study of the Old Testament characters. The following year passed in much the same fashion. Sixteen articles written by Boles were scattered through the *Advocate* in 1921. They concerned Bible personalities and other church subjects of general interest to his readers.

In the spring of 1922, his writings for the *Advocate* were like spring "bursting out all over." In addition to the normal range and number of his articles, H. Leo Boles wrote twenty-five editorials for the *Advocate*. G. C. Brewer complimented his friend: "Let me congratulate you on your management of the *Gospel Advocate*. You are giving us a good paper each week. I am glad that you are to have charge in the office. I believe that you are not only capable, but adapted to that sort of work." When his life is traced step by step, there is little cause to wonder that H. Leo Boles became spokesman for the brotherhood without portfolio.

If 1922 was a banner year for H. Leo Boles, so it was for the churches of Christ in Middle Tennessee and everywhere else. The church came to the general attention of Nashville as never before; a rising respect for the church began that year that has grown through the years. N. B. Hardeman and C. M. Pullias conducted the famed Tabernacle meetings in the Ryman Auditorium, which not only put the church on the map in Tennessee, but also gained recognition throughout the country. Two hundred people were baptized during the meeting.

A prophecy was made by F. W. Smith that "Harde-

162

man and Pullias will be sleeping with the fathers and perhaps their names forgotten before the influence of the meeting will be forgotten." During this meeting the incomparable N. B. Hardeman, master pulpiteer and Christian educator, took his place along side of David Lipscomb as one of the pillars of the church in this century. They would be joined in the scant years ahead by H. Leo Boles. Thousands heard Hardeman during the Tabernacle meetings, and tens of thousands read him in the daily press which carried his sermons verbatim. In deed the church was enjoying a new birth in the generous recognition and appreciation by the public.

This was also a year of sorrow for H. Leo Boles. His eldest son, Cleo, the son of Cynthia Boles, died of tuberculosis, May 22, 1922, at the age of twenty-eight. Cleo was a graduate of the Nashville Bible School and the Vanderbilt Dental College. He taught in the Vanderbilt College two years after his graduation, in addition to his professional duties as a dentist. He had just recently moved to Hohenwald, Tennessee, to practice dentistry when he died. H. Leo Boles was not the man to wear his grief openly, but he felt his sorrows more deeply than most knew, according to those in whom he confided.

Boles as editor was too busy to engage in speculative guessing about Bible teachings, with no time at all for "hobby riding." David Lipscomb's teaching had left its indelible imprint. However, at times he would get off on the lighter side and answer some query about something that would be of interest to the readers of the *Advocate*. He told in an article in early 1923 what happened to "copy" from the time it came to his hands as editor until it finally appeared in the *Advocate*. An editor must of necessity accept some copy and reject others from preachers who wanted to see their articles in print. This was the easiest way for a preacher to present his name before a large number of church members. In connection with this problem, and no doubt with a merry twinkle in his blue eyes, he wrote: "Some will send it (the article) with the comment, 'use it if you think best' or another with the bold threat and stern demand that 'if you don't publish this, I will stop the paper.' "

163

The paths of N. B. Hardeman and H. Leo Boles crossed often in the 1920's and 1930's in a period when each was the head of a sister institution and often rivals of each other. Boles was an admirer and staunch supporter of the Henderson schoolman. A second Tabernacle meeting was planned close after the first, and H. Leo Boles carried on a writing campaign in the *Gospel Advocate* to lay the groundwork for the meeting to be conducted by N. B. Hardeman and John T. Smith. The first Tabernacle meeting had not been sponsored by any particular congregation; Boles felt that a sponsoring church should be responsible for the undertaking with other sister congregations cooperating. The plan was adopted and Boles' favorite church at the time, Twelfth Avenue, assumed the responsibility.

H. Leo Boles returned to the college in the late spring of 1923 as its president. By now he was keeping the pages of the *Gospel Advocate* hot. A flood of articles poured from his pen in 1923, including nineteen editorials. The scope of his interests were ever widening; and he was writing on such subjects as evolution, war, and the English versions of the Bible. If he stood, as he did, on the threshold of even greater service to the college, this was likewise true of the splendid years of his service with the *Gospel Advocate* that continued to the time of his death.

Of all the famous names of the leaders of the Restoration movement connected with the *Advocate,* the name of McQuiddy has lasted longest. Neither the story of the *Gospel Advocate* nor that of H. Leo Boles can be told separate from that of J. C. McQuiddy. J. C. McQuiddy's long association with the *Gospel Advocate* ended with his death, August 3, 1924. A special memorial issue of the *Advocate* honored the life and works of this talented man. The younger generation is prone to forget their predecessors and benefactors. But J. C. McQuiddy, the younger associate of David Lipscomb, should not be forgotten. McQuiddy was not only a leading evangelist of his day, he was a staunch defender of the Christian faith as an editor, and a supporter of Christian colleges and orphan homes.

McQuiddy and Boles worked as yokefellows on the

164

Gospel Adovcate not only as writers but as co-owners. Mc-Quiddy showed his complete trust in Boles when the editorship of the paper was turned over to Boles' management. The two men had some characteristics in common. J. C. McQuiddy was misjudged on occasions and he was described as being a stubborn and an obstinate man, but so was Boles. As a matter of fact, those who knew McQuiddy realized that his firmness grew out of deep rooted convictions. No man could be more stubborn than McQuiddy or Boles when either was convinced of the rightness of his position. McQuiddy and Boles thought nothing of squaring off against one another over some vital issue when each had a differing point of view.

J. C. McQuiddy was born in Marshall County not far from Lewisburg, Tennessee. He was converted by the blind preacher, J. M. F. Smithson and baptized in Duck River at Leftwich Bridge. He began preaching when he was nineteen years. When he was invited to come to the *Gospel Advocate* in 1885 to become the office editor and business manager, he was preaching for the church in Columbia receiving $35.00 a month. Emma Unity Bell, McQuiddy's first wife, was born in Bedford County, Tennessee. She was the mother of nine children. David McQuiddy, Sr., her son, said, "Mother wrote the first copy of *Little Jewels* which is still being published by the *Gospel Advocate*." J. C. McQuiddy and his wife had been invited by David Lipscomb and E. G. Sewell to come to Nashville because the McQuiddys were selling so many subscriptions to the *Gospel Advocate*.

If no man contributed more to the *Gospel Advocate* than David Lipscomb, there is one respect in which J. C. McQuiddy contributed as much. McQuiddy was not only a great promoter of the *Gospel Advocate,* he was also an excellent business man. At one time David Lipscomb took the management of the *Advocate* out of his hands, but soon the paper was hopelessly in debt. Lipscomb called on the younger man to take over the paper, to run it, and get it out of debt. David Lipscomb had learned through experience that McQuiddy could get the job done.

In 1908 the McQuiddy Printing Company was established. The name was changed from the Gospel Advocate

Printing Company because the people in the courthouse and other places in downtown Nashville where McQuiddy went to solicit patronage found the name amusing. Leon McQuiddy, another son of J. C. McQuiddy, later suggested that the Gospel Advocate Company be set up so members of the churches of Christ could have their own publishing firm.

J. C. McQuiddy was a man with many splendid talents. He was among the leaders who established the Tennessee Orphan Home and served as chairman of the Board of Directors for several years. He was also interested in David Lipscomb College and served on the Board of Directors for a number of years. Unlike most preachers, but like David Lipscomb, McQuiddy had a business head. In Lipscomb's last years he had no interest in making money though he knew this was a part of life. J. C. McQuiddy was the man who sustained the *Gospel Advocate* and brought it safely through the breakers to shore. The McQuiddy Printing Company, one of the finest in the South, stands as a monument to the business acumen of J. C. McQuiddy. David Lipscomb, seldom ever delivering a eulogy, said of his associate: "He was the only man that had ever been able to run the *Gospel Advocate* without a financial loss." And H. Leo Boles recommended McQuiddy with these words: "J. C. McQuiddy was a business man; he was kind and considerate of those who worked for him."

In 1918 the *Gospel Advocate* contained a full thirty-two pages, and McQuiddy was able to do this without losing a single dime. J. C. McQuiddy shared the ownership of the *Gospel Advocate* with H. Leo Boles, A. B. Lipscomb, and S. F. Morrow. Each owned one fourth interest in the paper. They later sold their interest in the *Advocate* back to McQuiddy without losing a cent in the transaction.

Today the McQuiddy Printing Company handles the printing needs of the Gospel Advocate Company, which for a quarter of a century has been under the direction and editorship of B. C. Goodpasture, a good business man in his own rights. The McQuiddy Printing Company is managed by J. C. McQuiddy's grandson, David, Jr., who also serves as vice-president of the Gospel Advocate Company.

H. Leo Boles was not only a versatile traveller going down several roads at one time, but he also knew how to follow in the paths of great men. One reason for his success in life lay in his selection of the men whom he wished to emulate. After the death of David Lipscomb, E. A. Elam was always closest to Boles; and as Elam became older he, like Lipscomb, relied more and more on H. Leo Boles. The "Query Department" had long been a popular feature under Elam's care. So in 1925, he turned the task over to Boles with the comment: "We know of no one more competent in both heart and ability to do this work. He has no hobbies to ride or theories of his own to urge. He is a student of the Bible from beginning to end." Whatever role E. A. Elam filled in the church, *Advocate*, or school, H. Leo Boles followed closely in his wake.

The years, 1926 and 1927, were memorable ones for Boles in several respects. In the years since the death of David Lipscomb, his widow continued to live quietly in her home on the campus. Her interest in the school was as great as that of David Lipscomb. President Boles would often come by to question her about some of the views of her husband on the school or the church, or to pass the time of day with her. Boles wrote in the *Gospel Advocate* about the passing of Margaret Lipscomb, March 5, 1926; and in this connection Boles quoted a statement from David Lipscomb: "I am willing to repeat it as my last words to the world: I do not see how a parent can place a child where it will not be taught the Bible during its youthful and formative years."

H. Leo Boles did not write the usual large number of articles in the *Advocate* during 1927; and there were good reasons—he was carrying on a written discussion with R. H. Boll in the *Gospel Advocate*, conducting the "Query Department," managing David Lipscomb College, writing Sunday School literature, and preaching the gospel.

He engaged in a new writing venture the next year. A series of biographical sketches of pioneer preachers began to appear in the *Gospel Advocate*. It seems that Boles was a student of numerous and complex matters pertaining to the church and school. Boles, of course, included a biography of "Raccoon" John Smith with another story from the famous "Raccoon" repertory. John Smith had preached in Sparta, Tennessee, and a number of judges and lawyers were present in the audience. Afterwards he was asked if he were not embarrassed in the presence of so many learned gentlemen. He quickly retorted: "Not in the least, for I have learned that judges and lawyers, so far as the Bible is concerned, are the most ignorant class of people in the world, except Doctors of Divinity."

Like David Lipscomb, Boles kept his work with the paper and his management of the school separate, but he loved both and used each to implement the other. This same practice had been followed by Lipscomb. Large advertisements began to appear in the *Gospel Advocate* during 1928 saying that though David Lipscomb College is a liberal arts college, the Bible was still the hub of the curriculum as originally stated by the founders. It was during this year that E. A. Elam came to rely on Boles once more. Elam was an old man and his energy was flagging, but his spirit was burning as brightly as ever. It was announced that H. Leo Boles would become co-editor of the *Elam Notes* that had been for many years a popular feature of Sunday school literature published by the *Advocate*.

H. Leo Boles had traveled in the tributaries of Restoration history, but by 1929 he was moving into the mainstream. From this year until the day of his death a veritable deluge of articles poured from his pen. Most of them were printed in the *Gospel Advocate*. H. Leo Boles never wrote for publicity's sake. His writings show his vital concerns regarding the problems of the church, schools, and *Advocate*. He wrote on practically every subject of Biblical interest to his brethren, and they were interested in what he said.

This year ended in great sadness for H. Leo Boles. Grey ashes and misshapen hunks of blackened debris were the sad reminders of the two dormitories that had stood on the campus; the aftermath would become more grimly focused as the Depression Years set in. Such as had money in those days feared the next day a bank's closing would wipe out their life's earnings. The students of the college then, and those who worked with him on the *Gospel Advocate*, remember him as stolid and confident. H. Leo Boles was not the man to panic when the days grew long and the journey rougher.

H. Leo Boles had a way of pouring out his grief different from most people; he would work only the harder. In addition to a large number of articles in the *Advocate*, he wrote some thirty biographical sketches for the paper during 1930. The deep moving forces of the Depression were coming to the surface; the times were hard. The close associates of H. Leo Boles who studied him under great pressure said he seemed to do his best when the odds were the greatest. If he did not welcome those odds, he was never terrified by them.

H. Leo Boles began to feature his articles under such headings as "Fifty Years Ago and Now." About forty articles appeared under this title in 1931, and many of them were the biographical sketches. Another regular feature began to appear in the *Advocate* as Boles commenced writing comments on the International Sunday School lessons under the title, "Weekly Bible Lessons." He designed the lessons for elders, teachers, and the more advanced students of the Bible.

This year closed with the death of a great and humble saint of modern times, A. G. Freed, who died November 11, 1931. A. G. Freed was born August 3, 1868, in Indiana. He attended the public schools of Indiana; Freed entered Valparaiso University and graduated with distinction. He became a Christian early in life and soon began preaching the gopsel. His greatest contribution was establishing Freed-Hardeman College. As a result, he and N. B. Hardeman have taken their places in the hall of fame among the immortals of the Restoration Movement.

H. Leo Boles wrote that he had been blessed by the close association of three men—David Lipscomb, E. A. Elam, and A. G. Freed:

From David Lipscomb the writer learned the rugged truths of the Bible and received encouragement which strengthened his faith in the Word of God; through the association with E. A. Elam he learned to appreciate more the value of loyalty to the Word of God and service in the name of Christ; and through the association with Brother Freed he learned some of those finer graces of soul culture which adorn the Christian life.

H. Leo Boles signed his articles under another general heading in 1932—"Speaking as the Oracles of God." He was writing at great length on such subjects as church organization, the work of elders, deacons, and preachers. In addition to his work with the *Gospel Advocate* and preaching, he was in wide demand for college and church lectureship prgorams. The following year, he began to sign his articles under the general title, "Fundamental Facts," and continued the following year to write under the same heading.

H. Leo Boles marked up another busy year in 1934 unmarked by any spectacular accomplishments. Foy E. Wallace resigned from the *Gospel Advocate* and John T. Hinds replaced him as editor that year. Boles now had such titles as staff writer on the *Advocate,* editor of the *Gospel Advocate,* editor of the *Gospel Advocate Series of Sunday School Literature,* and a member of the *International Council of Religious Education.* His sundry religious articles were being signed under still another heading—"Bible Study Hour."

A different tone now began to characterize the pen of Boles; he is no longer the "fiery gladiator." Now he stands among his brethren as a solid champion. His counsel is being sought and his advice followed. No longer seeking personal honors, if indeed he ever sought them, they now came to him because he stood at the point of greatest honor—the desire to serve God and his fellowman.

When H. Leo Boles retired from the college, there were twelve years of his life remaining. Outside of the usual articles appearing in the *Gospel Advocate,* he wrote religious tracts and a series of articles on the history of the Nashville churches. He advised the churches and their

170

elders, and warned the Christian colleges and their leaders. In general Boles wrote whatever he felt moved to say about what the Bible taught on given subjects. Boles' writings between 1934 and 1939 still maintained his characteristic type of religious journalism.

One event in 1939 warrants special attention. Following the death of John T. Hinds the position for a new editor of the *Gospel Advocate* was open. Leo McQuiddy had not asked the advice of Boles in appointing John T. Hinds to edit the *Gospel Advocate* in 1934. Now it was different; the position of Boles with the *Advocate* was something like that of an elder statesman. Leon McQuiddy implicitly trusted the judgment of Boles regarding *Advocate* policy. Boles asked B. C. Goodpasture what he thought about taking over as editor of the *Gospel Advocate,* and persuaded him to accept McQuiddy's invitation. So in March, 1939, Boles proudly announced the new editor of the *Gospel Advocate* was to be B. C. Goodpasture. At this date Goodpasture is now rounding out his twenty-fifth year on the job. When H. Leo Boles spoke of "my boys" no one ever doubted that B. C. Goodpasture stood first in his admiration. Boles would tell on many occasions that Goodpasture had graduated from David Lipscomb with the highest honors of any student attending the college. Boles considered Goodpasture his most apt pupil.

In the introduction of the new editor, Boles said B. C. Goodpasture came from one of the finest pioneer tribes in Tennessee—the Goodpastures, a family that had produced some of Tennessee's finest leaders. Boles recalled that young Goodpasture had split rails, pulled fodder, and had done every other kind of farming in the best pioneer tradition.

The new editor never had a better friend or wiser counsellor than H. Leo Boles. Both had been reared among the high hills of the Cumberland Plateau and their families were friends. If one man can pass on the mantle of his greatness to another, again this was true in the relationship of Boles to Goodpasture. They were first brought together when Goodpasture came to the Nashville Bible

School campus in 1914. Their friendship began then and endured as long as H. Leo Boles lived; and the loyalty of the younger to the older man is undimmed with the passing of the years. H. Leo Boles singled out the three greatest personal friends of his life—David Lipscomb, E. A. Elam, and B. C. Goodpasture.

The last seven years of the life of Boles can be related from the pages of the *Gospel Advocate*. Had it not been for David Lipscomb and his writings in the *Gospel Advocate*, the present chapter of the Restoration Movement could be well summed up in the "modernism" of the liberal wing of the Disciples of Christ. In the late 1880's David Lipscomb was caricatured in the *Christian Standard* as an old woman futiley sweeping away at the oncoming tide of the sea. Lipscomb did not stand in the way of progress, but he did stem the tide of liberalism through the *Gospel Advocate* and the Nashville Bible School. His successor, H. Leo Boles, continued to wield the "sword of the Spirit" in the *Gospel Advocate*, and no one doubted that he had gained the day in the closing years of his life. H. Leo Boles was "strong in the Lord" because he had put on the "full Christian armor" at no small sacrifice.

Chapter XVII
RENDER TO GOD AND CAESAR

On one occasion Jesus countered his detractors by saying that whatever bore Caesar's stamp belonged to Caesar and whatever wore God's image must owe him first honors. H. Leo Boles had little interest in Caesar's possessions, but what belonged to God was of paramount importance. This is not meant to imply he took his citizenship lightly. He was fond of quoting the following lines:

I like to see a man proud of the place in which he lives. I like to see a man live so that his place will be proud of him.

What concerned men in the arena of politics was of passing interest to him, but whatever involved the church invariably drew him into the fray. "A carpenter is known by his chips." Likewise a man is known by what he will defend and controvert if he is called upon to do so. This chapter concerns the religious controversies of H. Leo Boles which began early and continued until the very end of his life.

This complex and "many splendored man" was blessed with superb talents. However, he may be remembered after his death, all who heard him were impressed with his clear and powerful logic in both the spoken and printed word. He was above all a master teacher, and his words are "echoes that roll from soul to soul, and go forever and forever." H. Leo Boles played multiple roles in the church spanning more than half a century; and as a result, he had clear insights into the intricate problems facing the church.

The life of H. Leo Boles was marked by a reverence for all things both of nature and the spirit. Church members found in him a faithful and sound teacher of the Bible. But this confidence was won at great cost. Down the passage of the years he was often weighed in the balance; seldom to his discredit and never to dishonor. Boles' brethren regarded him as the ablest religious debater in the brotherhood. Though religious debates have now passed

173

into something that resembles disrepute, the nineteenth century was the great age of the classic religious debates when men had something to believe and to defend. The history of religion, as well as profane history, is best told in the controversies that engage men of character and reputation.

It was not any one public debate that singled out H. Leo Boles, but a whole life devoted to driving home the truths of the Sacred Scriptures in the pulpit, on a lecture platform, or in a classroom. No man since Alexander Campbell was called upon with greater confidence by his brethren to tell what the Bible taught on a given subject; and Boles had something to say that was worthwhile.

Not everyone agreed with him on all he wrote and he was too magnanimous to expect them to do so. But he was generally on the right side of most questions if we may believe his brethren. The loyalty of H. Leo Boles to the Word of God, regardless of personal feelings involved, was never questioned. He had no use for debating purely for the sake of disputing: "When a great issue is at stake, then men of learning, spirituality, and forensic ability should champion the spirit of truth in the cause of righteousness."

Any person who ever heard Boles debate never doubted his determination to press the issue to some decision. His fellow students heard Boles in the mighty society debates when he was the undisputed champion of the Calliopeans. The story goes that once while he was debating on a team against two boys from Harding's school in Bowling Green, one of the Potter debaters used a chart to clinch his arguments. After demolishing his opponent's arguments in a fashion Boles thought was adequate, he pointed to the chart and said: "Now, take your rag down." He then pulled the chart down creating a somewhat tense and embarrassing situation for everyone. No doubt some of Boles' opponents thought he used his logic in a ruthless fashion. If this means that Boles approached his task without compromise, then it is true. It is also true that his dynamic personality was infused with sincerity, simplicity, and patience.

The younger Boles was dubbed a "red-faced" debater in those days because his face would be glowing as he drove "his nails." The story is told while Boles was in a religious debate not a long while after he came to the Nashville Bible School that his opponent repeatedly confessed his lack of knowledge about the Greek language. Boles was showing in his arguments the bearing that certain Greek words had on the disputed points. The preacher was a little on the ignorant side, and on several occasions he confessed his unfamiliarity with the Greek. Boles finally exploded with the remark: "Sir, I am not responsible for your ignorance."

This episode was not typical of H. Leo Boles in religious discussions. He never ridiculed his opponents nor sought public approval from his audience. Boles was a fair man in a controversy but a most determined one. I. C. Finley who served with Boles as one of the elders in the Reid Avenue church said that H. Leo Boles never expressed more self-confidence than when he spoke to a partisan audience especially when his supporters were in the minority. His stance was one of deliberate calmness and his spirit never suggested anger or conveyed either frustration or defeat. To overcome an opponent by force of logic was a cheap victory for this preacher.

H. Leo Boles followed certain ground rules in religious controversies. Such occasions he thought were not designed to provide public entertainment or publicity for the debater, and least of all to decide the issue. The primary purpose, however, should be to determine what the Bible taught on the subject and if at all possible to reach some common ground of agreement or position of unity. H. Leo Boles encountered the same objections that are always current—"We don't believe in debates"; or "We don't read our papers because there is so much discussion in them." When Lipscomb managed the *Gospel Advocate*, honest and candid investigations of Bible doctrine were carried on by high-minded, sincere men who had questions to ask and to answer when called upon. The nineteenth century was especially blessed with pioneer preachers with great forensic talent; and in many respects, H. Leo Boles was the last of that noble breed of men. Robert E. Lee has been de-

175

scribed as the last fine gentleman from the age of chivalry. H. Leo Boles may be aptly described as the last of the Christian gladiators.

The first classic religious discussion of Boles was precipitated by World War I when he declared that it was wrong for a Christian to take up arms against his fellow man or take his life and destroy property. Not since the Civil War had the church been troubled about Christians going to war. World War I was accompanied by a mass hysteria, and there were those who questioned Boles' loyalty to his country because of his position. Since the role that H. Leo Boles played in defense of the conscientious objector became one of the decisive factors that finally won official approval from Washington, it would be profitable to look at David Lipscomb on this count to see Boles better.

During the Civil War David Lipscomb stoutly championed the Christian liberty of church members who had convictions against going to war. Lipscomb experienced great personal grief over the Civil War believing such to be inimical to the highest spiritual and human values. He was convinced that war resulted in nothing but a malignant erosion of society in general. There are few now who would be inclined to dispute David Lipscomb.

Lipscomb preached with great boldness his convictions at a time when zeal was running high for the Confederacy, and much attention was directed to him. Some labeled him an enemy to the South, an abolitionist, or even a Yankee spy. When General Bedford Forrest occupied Columbia, Tennessee, the complaint was made to him that Lipscomb was an enemy of the South. General Forrest sent one of his staff officers to hear Lipscomb speak on the subject at one of his appointments. The officer sat directly in front of Lipscomb and gave close but respectful attention. The officer was moved to tears more than once and said after the services: "I have not yet reached a conclusion as to whether or not the doctrine of the sermon is loyal to the Southern Confederacy, but I am profoundly convinced that it is loyal to the Christian religion."

Much has been made by church historians on the effect

the Civil War had on churches both north and south. One fact is patent about David Lipscomb. He had no resentment for the North because of his sympathy for the war-desolated South. Lipscomb wrote after the Civil War: "Finally the years of sectional strife, war, bloodshed, destruction and desolation swept over the land, and the spectacle was presented of disciples of the Prince of Peace with murderous weapons seeking the lies of their fellow men." What Lipscomb best knew was that Christians who were rabid partisans on both sides lost face and influence; and in particular, the preachers who had taken a militant stand invoking the curse of God on their enemies.

David Lipscomb wrote his famous *Civil Government* to show that human societies organized under some form of civil government grew out of man's rebellion against God. Lipscomb believed that Christians were not under obligation to vote, sit on juries, and hold public positions created by the government. He thought that Christians should pay taxes, perform their duties laid upon them by the civil government that involved no violations of the laws of God. And he said: "A Christian can engage in active rebellion against no government . . . . Neither active support or participation, nor active opposition." Many think that David Lipscomb takes an extreme view, but such has been the convictions of a large number of Christians since Augustine's *City of God;* and both the apostles, Paul and Peter, admonished the Christians to be obedient and respectful to their rulers.

Just as David Lipscomb had personally argued his case before the military governor of Tennessee which was settled in his favor by Jefferson Davis, H. Leo Boles was a party to a similar move. J. W. Shepherd, J. N. Armstrong, and Dr. J. S. Ward were sent to the War Department in Washington, D. C. to interview General Crowder with some favorable results coming out of the matter.

H. Leo Boles never argued whether some wars were just and others unjust, or that some two hundred major wars fought by man were more or less just or unjust. His eye was single here. During the war the brethren were looking for leadership regarding the war participation question, and H. Leo Boles was able to satisfy most of them. The hour of truth came for Boles as it had for Lipscomb when he faced an officer of General Bedford Forrest. Christian participation was a burning issue in the spring of 1917 and preachers were warmly divided.

Finally Brother Haynes, one of the elders of the Murfreesboro church, set up a night for H. Leo Boles to state the Biblical position during the Murfreesboro meeting. It was the custom then for churches to hold "preacher meetings" for preachers and other interested brethren. The Murfreesboro meeting scheduled from April 29 to May 6, 1917, was such a meeting with some of the finest evangelists of the day on the program. The appointed night for Boles to speak came and feeling was running high. Long before the service began, standing room was no longer available and windows were opened by request for those standing on the outside.

The responses H. Leo Boles received were mixed; he got nasty letters and anonymous cards calling him a slacker. Others said he had not registered for the draft. H. Leo Boles weathered the storm, but he learned something from the experience; he found it wiser to discuss some matters before and after the storm. In the 1920's while the world was at peace, he published an extensive tract on the question. In the days just before World War II, H. Leo Boles was again heard. He said there must always be pacifists to insist upon moderation in human behavior. Some preachers took the position that Christians could bear arms, and Boles offered to meet the foremost preacher advocates of the time in a written or oral discussion, and each to the man declined. H. Leo Boles died in the year that peace and sanity were returning to the world. In the shadow of a fiery holocaust there is hardly a person alive today who would advocate war.

H. Leo Boles could well be called the "Great Controverter" because this was his major role in life. Other than the two public debates he conducted in the early years, he never had another similar experience. The *Gospel Advocate* was his "sounding board" and Boles was as devoted to the *Advocate* as he was to the college. He wrote that the *Gospel Advocate* "has been a synonym of loyalty to God's Word . . . and a humble defender of the simple order to New Testament Christianity." No one questioned that for twenty-five years he helped keep it so.

In 1878 David Lipscomb concluded that instrumental music in Christian worship was unsupported by the Scriptures. He never ceased to regard the practice as an unscriptural innovation. The question had been no larger than a "man's hand" after the Civil War, but time soon changed the picture.

How successfully David Lipscomb stemmed the Christian Church (Disciples of Christ) invasion into the South is too well known to need documentation. Whatever hopes the Christian Church leaders had were doomed by Lipscomb and laid to rest by N. B. Hardeman and H. Leo Boles. In the Ryman Auditorium N. B. Hardeman met Ira M. Boswell on the music question in 1923 from May 31 to June 5. This debate should have been the conclusion of the whole matter. Unfortunately for the Christian Church, it was not.

An agreement was arranged between H. Leo Boles to meet M. D. Clubb for a written debate on the music position to be carried on in the *Gospel Advocate*. Clubb was a Christian Church leader, editor of the *Tennessean Christian*, and Secretary of the Tennessee Missionary Society. The debate opened April 1, 1926 and closed with the issue the following July 1.

M. D. Clubb honored his opponent in writing: "H. Leo Boles is President of David Lipscomb College, Nashville, Tennessee, the leading college of the conservative brethren, and one of the editors of the *Gospel Advocate*. It will be seen from this that he is a man whom his brethren honor and in whom they have confidence."

The classic debate of Boles' colorful life came about in 1927 when he engaged his longtime friend, R. H. Boll, on the volatile "premillennial issue." H. Leo Boles suddenly found himself involved in a matter not of his own making. For some time there had been a question about what R. H. Boll taught on the subject of Old Testament prophecy. The

179

matter came to a climax in the middle of 1915 when R. H. Boll was dropped from the *Advocate* staff. J. C. Mc-Quiddy wrote a series of articles stating that the doctrines of pre-millennialism were especially troubling certain young preachers, and he singled out R. H. Boll as the promulgator of the teaching. In July, 1915, M. C. Kurfees charged in an editorial that R. H. Boll had been dropped from the staff because he taught, namely: (1) the kingdom of God has not yet been established and will not be established until Christ comes again; (2) Christ is going to come again in the very near future; (3) Christ will come in a body of flesh and bones without blood to sit on David's literal throne in a literal Jerusalem and rule with a rod of iron.

Another article appeared in the *Gospel Advocate*, February 24, 1916, containing letters from G. Dallas Smith, J. C. McQuiddy, and A. B. Lipscomb about an agreement they had with R. H. Boll in which he agreed to refrain from any teaching that might trouble the brethren. R. H. Boll had entered into such an agreement, but he thought he was being fenced in. When the articles came out in the *Advocate*, R. H. Boll reacted feeling that he had not been treated justly because he could not reply.

R. H. Boll wrote in the *Christian Leader* his thoughts about the matter:

> I think there should be a full, fair discussion of these doctrinal differences in the *Gospel Advocate*, in whose columns I faithfully labored for nigh seven years; and which paper in my judgment condemned me before its constituency and before the brotherhood in general without a fair hearing.

The issue continued to smolder and to flare up occasionally until the issue was discussed openly in the *Gospel Advocate*. S. H. Hall, who was a friend to both men made arrangements for the debate.

What the two men debated is one of the oldest stories in Christendom. In the early centuries of church history there was a notion that Christ would return to earth, set up his kingdom, and reign in Jerusalem for a thousand years. This expectation of the millennial reign of Christ was known as chiliasm. The doctrine was discounted by the Catholic church at a very early period, and from the fourth century ceased to be a living doctrine. However, chiliasm continues to crop up in one form or another. Alexander Campbell believed in a future millennial age when Satan would be defeated and the forces of evil would be destroyed.

The names of J. C. McQuiddy, G. Dallas Smith, and M. C. Kurfees appeared frequently in the running discussion with R. H. Boll who told in *Word and Work* his side of the question. F. B. Srygley finally brought the differences to the surface at a time when "premillennialism" had become a "fighting word." Anyhow this was the name given to those who believed that Christ would return to earth and reign a thousand years. After S. H. Hall initiated the proposal that R. H. Boll should have his say in the *Gospel Advocate,* R. H. Boll and H. Leo Boles carried on a lengthy correspondence to lay down the guide lines for the written discussion. In one of his letters to Boles, the Louisville preacher stated he wished to be addressed as Boles' "respondent" not "opponent." After all arrangements were completed, the debate between the two men got under way in the *Advocate.* While no unpleasantries marred their discussions, both men quickly warmed up to their task.

H. Leo Boles was precipitated into a controversy destined to have deep and unhappy repercussions for the brotherhood. Each man counted the other his friend when the debate began and after it ended. The debate began after some delay, May 19, 1927, and concluded with the issue, November 3, 1927.

The debate was hardly under way when R. H. Boll objected to Boles' statement that R. H. Boll should now express his most "radical views and that he keep nothing back that he teaches and believes on the subject." R. H. Boll took exception by saying that Boles' statement suggested that he held and taught "some dark hidden doctrine" that he might breathe only in secret.

Boles was quick to clear up any misunderstanding on that score—"I did not intend to intimate that Brother Boll might not be frank and fair in expressing himself on the subject." But Boles added that a "tense situation has arisen among church members over the question."

What H. Leo Boles and R. H. Boll said in their classic debate is a matter of record. The propositions they discussed are namely: (1) The Scriptures teach that Israel (fleshly descendants of Abraham through Jacob) shall be nationally restored; R. H. Boll affirms and H. Leo Boles denies. (2) The Scriptures teach that the event signified by the smiting and destruction of the image in Daniel 2: 35-44 began to take place on the Day of Pentecost; H. Leo Boles affirms and R. H. Boll denies. (3) The Scriptures teach that after his coming Christ will be with his saints and reign over all the earth; R. H. Boll affirms and H. Leo Boles denies. (4) The Scriptures teach that Christ is now on David's throne H. Leo Boles affirms and R. H. Boll denies. (5) The Scriptures teach that the coming of Christ is premillennial and imminent; R. H. Boll affirms and H. Leo Boles denies.

At the conclusion of the debate neither Boles nor Boll was willing to disfellowship the other, and had only the highest praise for one another. Later when R. H. Boll visited in Nashville he was invited to speak in chapel and H. Leo Boles sat on the platform with him. In a faculty meeting when the advisability of inviting R. H. Boll to speak in chapel was discussed, A. G. Freed showed no enthusiasm for the proposal because R. H. Boll did not believe the kingdom of Daniel 2 to be a prophecy of the reign of Christ.

Unfortunately the premillennial controversy rumbled on after the conclusion of the debate; and for more than three decades troubled the church as no other issue had since the music and society problem. In the late 1930's any preacher who failed to take a stand was branded as a "premillennialist or a sympathizer." And in the 1940's the doctrine became a testing point of fellowship among the "loyal brethren" as they chose to describe themselves. The grave implications of the doctrine is pointed up in a plea made by L. L. Brigance, late beloved teacher of Freed-Hardeman College, who urged the presidents of the Christian colleges to declare themselves on the issue, and

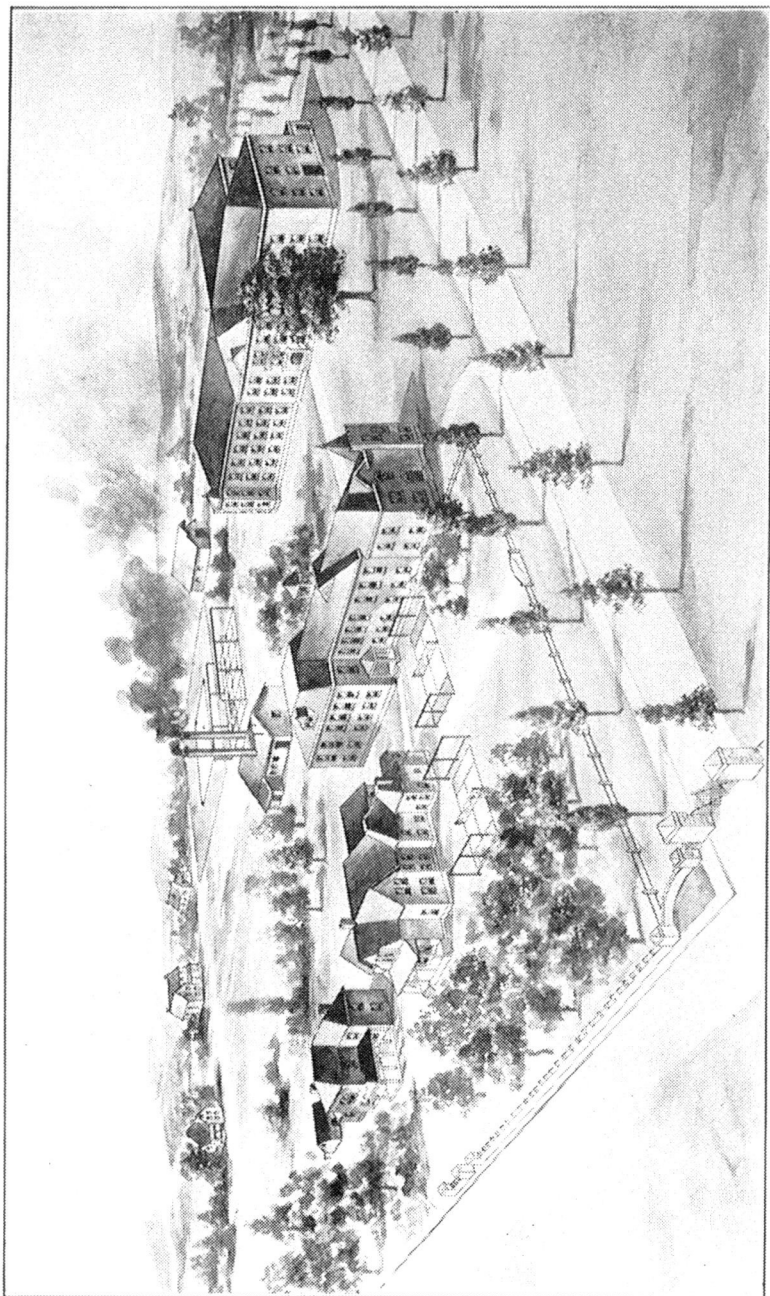

BIRD'S EYE VIEW OF NASHVILLE BIBLE SCHOOL

one by one each did in the *Gospel Advocate*. Preachers throughout the brotherhood likewise followed suit. There were those indeed who were persuaded that it was a question of Christian liberty to believe in premillennialism. Others who had no sympathy with the doctrine defended the right to believe it as a matter of conscience.

The church weathered the storm none the better for the experience. Some today believe the whole transaction was handled poorly from beginning to end. Premillennialism is now a dead issue; but remaining scars continue as painful reminders of a church controversy that came to a head in 1915 and slowly built up until its painful erruption in the 1940's. While no man can set up himself as an authority on what the Bible teaches, the brethren of H. Leo Boles regard his written debate with R. H. Boll as the classic statement on the subject. And no evangelist stood more adamant than H. Leo Boles against the doctrine when it threatened to divide the church.

A long chapter could be written in church history about the numerous and futile attempts to bring about universal Christian unity. Hopes were entertained in the late 1930's and early 1940's that the Disciples of Christ and the churches of Christ could close the breach separating the two groups. The brethren of H. Leo Boles somehow managed to stir up one controversy after another, and sooner or later called in Boles to say what he thought about the issue.

The leaders of the unity movement in the Disciples of Christ church were Edwin R. Errett and James De Forest Murch who were associated with the *Christian Standard*, the leading paper among the Disciples. Claude E. Witty, minister of the West Side-Central church of Christ in Detroit took the lead among the members of the church. A warm friendship developed between Witty and Murch following an arranged meeting. Together they launched the movement for unity among the Disciples members and the churches of Christ. The first formal meeting was called the National Unity Meeting and was held in the Detroit church of Christ building, May 3, 1938. More than a thou-

183

sand people attended. J. N. Armstrong and George Benson were among those who spoke.

The Unity Movement generated considerable interest among the members of the churches of Christ. Murch and Witty published the Christian Unity *Quarterly* as a medium to freely discuss the proposal. The Unity Movement climaxed in Indianapolis, May 3, 1939, in a highly publicized meeting. B. C. Goodpasture had been invited to speak on that occasion; instead he recommended H. Leo Boles for the task. W. L. Totty described what happened when it came Boles' time to speak:

> The meeting reached its zenith in the afternoon of the second day, when H. Leo Boles spoke for an hour and thirty minutes. He told them in no uncertain terms what had caused the division and what it would take to bring about unity—that if they expected a compromise they were mistaken. Perhaps no greater address had been given since the Restoration.

Witty also said that speech meant that the Unity Movement would fail; and he added as an afterthought that H. Leo Boles resembled his great grandfather in one respect —he spoke about as long!

James De Forest Murch said in his book, *Christian's Only* that there were many incidents that deserve a place in history. He singled out H. Leo Boles and the *Gospel Advocate;* and Edwin R. Errett, editor of the *Christian Standard* and their discussions of the issue. The movement died with the passing of Edwin R. Errett in 1944; and Murch was removed as editorial secretary of the Standard Publishing Company. In recent years the Disciples of Christ continue to move into the liberal ranks of Protestantism and the old battle-crys of the Restoration slowly die away among them.

Along about this same period, H. Leo Boles was engaged in another transaction about which very few knew. F. L. Rowe was no longer able to continue publishing the *Christian Leader.* Some well known members of the church formed a corporation associated with Clinton Davidson of Bernardsville, New Jersey, to take over the management of the paper. A widespread poll was taken to learn what the majority of the members wanted in our papers. As a result of this plebiscite by mail, the paper proposed to say what the public wanted. These men proposed to copyright the paper and protect the contents by federal law. Any article had to be quoted in full or be subject to prosecution. What concerned H. Leo Boles and others was the fact that Clinton Davidson was unknown to the church.

H. Leo Boles made it his business to protect the church whenever its integrity was threatened in any fashion. He needs a defense against some of his old friends who say that if he were alive today, he would oppose the support of Christian education and orphan homes if the funds came from the churches. This is best settled by allowing Boles to speak for himself. He wrote in the *Gospel Advocate* on page one hundred and seventy in 1937: "Christians have a right to contribute of their means to Christian colleges, orphan homes, old people's homes, and other good works. Churches have a right to contribute to these if they so desire."

H. Leo Boles served as an elder of the Reid Avenue church for many years. It was the practice of Reid Avenue church of Christ to support by contribution from the church the Nashville Christian Institute and the Tennessee Orphan Home. The collection of one Sunday for each of the two institutions was made annually. According to I. C. Finley this was the church practice while Boles served the church as elder; and the practice is continued by the Reid Avenue church.

H. Leo Boles engaged in his last public debate in late December of 1944 and most of January. The debate was with J. M. Hoffman, a Seventh Day Adventist, who at first for reasons best known to himself did not disclose his church affiliation. Hoffman moved into Nashville and spent thousands of dollars in full-page advertisements to publicize himself and his sermon topics. It was apparent that he was a promoter of the Seventh Day Adventist Church because of his sermon topics such as "The Mark of the Beast."

J. M. Hoffman was a colorful speaker and attracted

many to hear him in the War Memorial Auditorium. Quite a few of the Nashville protestant churches were alarmed because he was making inroads into their ranks. Some went so far as to say that Hoffman should be answered and that the church of Christ was in the best position to give a Bible answer to his sensational lecture topics.

Some interested members of the church in Nashville met to lay plans to engage Hoffman in a debate. They chose H. Leo Boles for the job. J. M. Hoffman indicated at first that he would meet one of the preachers in the church of Christ in a public discussion of the religious issues but changed his mind. This was a unique debate in that neither man faced the other. How the whole transaction came out is best told by Boles in his black ledger:

J. M. Hoffman, a Seventh Day Adventist, had begun lecturing in the War Memorial Building in October, 1944, and continued his lectures for many weeks. Brother H. M. Phillips challenged him to debate but he was ignored; then S. H. Hall challenged him. He told Hall to get churches of Christ to agree upon a man and he would let them know in twenty-four hours whether he would debate. Some of the brethren met and selected me to debate with him. He refused to debate and then the churches of Christ in Nashville asked me to lecture at the War Memorial Building on the main points of the Seventh Day Advent Doctrine. The first lecture December 17 was on "Founders of Seventh Day Adventism—False Prophets." This was Sunday afternoon at 2:45; the building was filled to its capacity. The second lecture was on "The Two Covenants," December 18; the third, December 19, on "The Sabbath"; and the fourth on December 21, on "The Lord's Day." An ediphone was used and the speeches were recorded, transcribed and printed in pamphlet form—50,000 of each one were printed and distributed. Then on December 31 my subject was "Dangerous Errors Exposed," and January 7, 1945, "Second Advent of Christ."

J. M. Hoffman then replied to the first four lectures and his speeches were taken down in shorthand by Howard Fish as Hoffman refused to let the ediphone be used. The Chapel Avenue Church sponsored the lectures and the other churches with "few" exceptions cooperated. After six addresses had been made J. M. Hoffman attempted to make reply to the four addresses on the main topics that I had discussed. I was furnished copies of Hoffman's addresses and then the Auditorium was rented for two Sunday afternoons at 2:45, January 21 and 28, 1945. These two addresses covered the replies that Hoffman had made to my addresses. These addresses also were put in printed form for free distribution. The lectures were enjoyed but were hard work.

The sands of time were running fast for the redoubtable old warrior. He had a few days more than a year to live, and this year was like all the rest—full to the brim and running over. On the day he took to his sick bed he was "chomping at the bits" to be on his way to the Freed-Hardeman lectures. In his seventy-two years on earth H. Leo Boles obeyed the laws of Caesar and respected the rulers of the land, but first he had lived a dauntless life of faith and service in loyalty to Christ.

Chapter XVIII

A COLLEGE GROWS IN ATHENS

In late May, 1920, the *Gospel Advocate* carried the statement that A. B. Lipscomb, the nephew of David Lipscomb, had been selected by the Board of Trustees and would be the next president of David Lipscomb College. H. Leo Boles had tendered his formal resignation to the Board earlier to become editor of the *Gospel Advocate* and to devote more time to evangelism.

During the graduation ceremonies H. Leo Boles was tendered a rising vote of appreciation for his fourteen years of faithful service to David Lipscomb College. A. B. Lipscomb was complimented by the outgoing president who enumerated his splendid qualifications. A. B. Lipscomb was a graduate of the University of Kentucky and Vanderbilt University with the earned B.A. and M.A. degrees from the two institutions. Before coming to Nashville to preach for the Tenth Street church (now Russell Street church), A. B. Lipscomb had been the regular minister of the Highland church in Louisville. He served as the first page editor of the *Advocate;* and after David Lipscomb's death, he was elected the Chairman of the Board of Directors of the college.

In several important respects the Lipscomb administration laid the groundwork for the second tenure of H. Leo Boles. As stated in another place, the school had changed little since its founding. The schooling of H. Leo Boles was such as Burritt College and the Nashville Bible School had been able to provide. This meant that Boles lacked the knowledge about modern education that was undergoing radical changes in that period. H. S. Lipscomb was the school's first dean—an office that was created by the Board of Directors. Horace Lipscomb was a well educated man holding the M.S. degree from Vanderbilt University. He was a very successful teacher and administrator in the Nashville, Tennessee, public schools. The reorganizing of the institution to the junior college level was a realistic move on the part of the Lipscombs. David Lipscomb College was already a member of the Tennessee College Association. The change in the school's organization ended the practice of awarding degrees which had been the custom since J. A. Harding's time; however, the class that had done four years of work received degrees at the close of the school year 1920-1921.

In addition to departmentalizing the institution, the regular school year was changed from the semester to the quarter sessions. Another memorable event was the issuing of the *Haviland Acts*, the first college paper. The name of the new publication was a composite word suggesting the activities centering around Harding Hall, Avalon Home, and Lindsay Hall. This was a student publication, and its editor was chosen by the four literary societies; the purpose of the paper was to inform the public and the widely separated alumni of the school's progress.

The Lipscomb era was marked by another event of both interest and historical importance. N. B. Chenault of Wichita Falls, Texas, offered the college $50,000 to endow a Bible chair to be called the "E. A. Elam Bible Chair." The conditions of the gift were that Elam should occupy the chair as long as he could do the work, with the interest on the principle going for Elam's personal use. At Elam's death the fund would revert to the college to be used unreservedly for the teaching of the Bible. The Board of Directors accepted the gift on the condition that Elam would be subject to the constitution and by-laws of the college. While Boles was not a party to this transaction, he would be in its final disposition.

A. B. Lipscomb did not finish out the school year 1920-1921, and H. S. Lipscomb served as president for the next two years. One significant fact emerged from H. S. Lipscomb's administration. Although he was a good schoolman with the best interests of the school in his heart, he was not a preacher. Without an exception the outstanding leaders in Christian education were colorful and capable preachers in addition to their leadership talents in education.

A tradition that has continued since was inaugurated

in H. S. Lipscomb's last year as president. This was the custom of honoring David Lipscomb as the founder of the institution on his birthday, January 21, 1923.

The exercises consisted that first year, as they have since, in original orations delivered by the young men of the college.

Three years had now gone since H. Leo Boles left the college. Then in the *Gospel Advocate* issue of June 7, 1923, the terse announcement was carried: "At the close of the present school year, H. Leo Boles, who served seven years as president of the college, has been re-elected and will take charge of the management at the close of the present school year." At a meeting of the Board of Directors, April 23, 1923, A. M. Burton nominated H. Leo Boles for the presidency and this was seconded by C. C. Chenault; whereupon, the Board made it a unanimous decision.

H. Leo Boles years later stated that he had not sought a return to the college and accepted the earnest solicitations of the Board of Directors to return to his former position; but there can be no doubt that he was pleased and elated. He was also better educated having been awarded the M.A. degree from Vanderbilt University in philosophy, sociology, and Christian Doctrine, June 9, 1920. Like so many who have taught in David Lipscomb College, H. Leo Boles finished his education between classes. He would dash over to Vanderbilt for a class in the graduate department and hurry back down Granny White Pike to teach a class of his own or perform some other chore connected with the school.

H. Leo Boles was not only familiar with the ideals and goals of David Lipscomb College after seventeen years of service with the school, he had not, as a matter of fact, lost interest in the school a single day since he had been gone from it. What happened to David Lipscomb College was ever one of his deepest concerns. He was joined in his new work by one of the grand old men of the church, A. G. Freed. Freed had long been identified with Christian education in Kentucky and Tennessee, and was the senior co-founder of Freed-Hardeman College. H. Leo Boles honored the new vice-president of the college and principal of the high school saying that "no man who had not been trained in David Lipscomb ever brought more to the college than A. G. Freed."

President Boles entered upon the duties of his second administration with his usual characteristic energy and foresight. The summer of 1923 found him working hard in the field laying the groundwork for the September opening of the college. On September 23, the tolling of the big chapel bell summoned the students, faculty, and patrons to another opening year of David Lipscomb College. Whatever may have been Boles' emotions on this day, his stern and immobile face did not display. But he must have been pleased with the old and new friends and the largest number of students ever to assemble in the halls of Lipscomb. The audience sang "Stand Up for Jesus," President Boles read from the Bible and E. A. Elam delivered the main address. By the first week in October some two hundred and thirty students from thirteen states had enrolled.

In the three years that Boles had been away from the school sweeping changes had been made but not all were academic. During the first tenure of Boles a separate dining hall had been maintained for the students. Not until Horace Lipscomb had the practice changed and the common dining hall was established for the students. Boles, a stern disciplinarian and authoritarian, intended to take up where he had left off with the students. The Nashville Bible School had begun as a co-educational institution, and properly supervised communication between the sexes had been deemed proper. H. Leo Boles learned that times changed even on the college campus. While the supervision was as strict as ever, the movement of the students on the campus was relaxed and the change was probably for the better.

H. Leo Boles witnessed and frequently was the leading party to many changes in the school. Student participation in athletics had been a concern of David Lipscomb, and he persuaded himself that athletics could serve no useful purpose in the Nashville Bible School. Tennis and basketball had for a long time been a popular diversion of the students. A survey of college catalogs year by year reflects the growing awareness of collegiate sports by

President Boles as he made his decisions to meet the growing needs of the school. At least one good thing came out of World War I, and that was the realization of the American people of the importance of physical fitness. President Boles announced the school's new policy; athletics would not be stressed, but that a proper value would be placed upon physical development.

At the beginning of his second administration, Boles called the Board's attention to the urgent need for a new gymnasium; a contract was soon thereafter let for the building. The official opening of Burton Gym was set for February 1, 1923. C. M. Pullias representing the Board of Directors presented the new gymnasium to the school on the afternoon preceding the society games. President Boles in his responding acceptance speech said, "When I asked Brother Pullias and the Board if we might have a good gymnasium, their unanimous reply was 'You may have anything that is necessary to make David Lipscomb College a bigger and better school.'"

The college president acted in other areas of enduring importance to the college. The institution was already operating on the quarter system. Since Lipscomb students were penalized in other colleges of higher learning, the credit system was revised from the unit to the hour credit basis. Ninety-six hours were the required minimum for the junior college academic program; but counting the Bible courses David Lipscomb College required one hundred and twenty hours to graduate.

H. Leo Boles for several years envisioned David Lipscomb College as a four year standard college. President Boles moved resolutely to make that dream come true. J. Ridley Stroop said that H. Leo Boles had a way of making things work out the way he meant for them to. So President Boles declared his purpose to make the school a standard four year college. By then the persons most closely associated and responsible for the college were beginning to sense the importance of the school and its relation to the phenomenal growth of the church. The boast was then being made that Nashville had now become the radiating center of the New Testament church in the world as

Jerusalem had been in the Old World. The announcement was made in the school paper, the *Babbler*, that four years of college work would be offered in the college beginning in the year 1924-1925.

The old Nashville Bible School days were the infant and adolescent years of the school's growth, and H. Leo Boles guided the institution into its youthful college years. At the close of the school year 1923-1924, the college reached other mile posts in several respects. The high school conducted its first graduating exercises; Leo Lipscomb Boles finished in that class. President Boles boasted that the school had its best trained faculty that year in its history; six of the faculty held M.A. degrees. The location of the Nashville Bible School in the Athens of the South was a blessing in many guises. The splendid schools, beautiful rolling hills, historic sites, descendents of famous pioneer families—all of this presented Lipscomb students with unparalleled opportunities.

H. Leo Boles was loyal to the ideals of the school's founders in that he honored in word and practice the primary position given the Bible in the curriculum. There was a continuous offering of religious services for the students. In addition to the chapel devotions, prayer meeting services were largely conducted by college students each Thursday evening. The students never left the campus except by special permission and most of them worshipped Sundays in the college Chapel with the neighbors. Faculty members usually spoke in those services when their turns came. An occasional preacher who dropped by would be invited to speak, and others came by special invitation. S. P. Pittman, J. Ridley Stroop, R. P. Cuff were among the preachers who spoke frequently during the Sunday worship services. B. C. Goodpasture was slated to hold the meeting for the college church in this year of Boles' return. Due to illness, however, he could not and the meeting was begun by H. Leo Boles and continued by A. G. Freed.

A pressing problem always plaguing the school was a matter of money to operate the school. No friend of the college stood so faithfully by David Lipscomb College over the years that were both good and bad as A. M. Burton. He initiated in June, 1923, the "Bible Education Fund" to help young men who desired to preach the Bible and subscribed a generous amount to that purpose. By October of the same year the sum had grown to $26,000—mostly in pledges never collected. The plan called for a return of the money to the college so as to create a revolving fund. President Boles said that the money gradually disappeared because unfortunately some who made their pledges forgot them.

The first year of Boles' second return to the college was an exciting one; life on the campus was moving at a swifter pace. The college was now growing up in a hurry and Boles was growing with it. The busy schedule of Boles changed little; he conducted four meetings all in easy driving distance of the school. He resumed his customary practice of traveling during the summer months soliciting funds and students for the school and using the college as his headquarters. He preached somewhere every Sunday.

The thirty-fourth year of the college began September 17, 1924. E. A. Elam was one of the featured speakers for the occasion. A reading of the *Babbler* issues for that school year leaves the impression that it was a good and full year with the spirit and morale of the student body never higher. Nothing of unusual interest occurred during the school session with one exception. About 11 o'clock on a Friday night, February 27, 1925, a fire broke out in Lindsay Hall; a boys' bucket brigade was formed which put out a fire that for a while threatened to be a disaster.

When school opened the following September in 1925, the largest body of students in the college's history assembled in Chapel Hall. This year turned out to be a historic one in several respects. The *Babbler* said in one of the December issues that David Lipscomb College is now an accredited college with students in all four years of work. It was further declared that since the college had only recently been made a four-year college that the junior college would still be maintained. At the close of the school

194

year the picture of C. J. Garner was carried in the *Babbler* with the caption that he was the first senior graduate of the college.

The incident that moved the student body most deeply was the death of Margaret Lipscomb, who passed away on March 5, 1926. For more than forty years she had lived on the Lipscomb campus in the ivy covered red brick home. She was affectionately known by the students as "Aunt Mag." To honor her memory the big chapel bell was silenced and a memorial service was conducted in Chapel Hall for her on Saturday. Margaret Lipscomb's funeral was conducted in the Lindsey Avenue Church of Christ with C. A. Moore, E. A. Elam, and H. Leo Boles officiating, and she was buried by the side of her husband in Mt. Olivet cemetery.

H. Leo Boles had stopped his last time at the Lipscomb home to chat with "Aunt Mag," and in her passing Ida Boles lost her next door neighbor and one of her best friends.

Back in those years, Bill Brown, a negro handy man, was a colorful campus character. He had been the personal servant of David Lipscomb and constantly attended the old gentleman. After David Lipscomb suffered a stroke, his ability to walk was impaired. Bill Brown's services to the Lipscombs were devoted and indispensable. After Lipscomb's death he remained to serve Margaret Lipscomb; however, she required his services for only part of the day. He thus became the school handy man and his salary was paid by the college. He was known as "Faculty Bill" and some of his statements became classics in his day. "Faculty Bill" referred to the stage platform as the "flatform," and broad grins were forthcoming from the students when they asked Bill who were the oldest members on the college faculty. He would invariably reply, "Me and Brother Pittman."

Other events crowding the year were important and others less so. The college made arrangements with the city to tie into the city water main coming down Granny White Pike for $3500. During the school year, thirty-five acres of the David Lipscomb farm were sold for $25,000. It

195

was recognized later that the transaction was a mistake, but no willing scapegoat turned up who was willing to take the blame. The senior class inaugurated a plan so the college could meet the Southern Association's requirement for $300,000 permanent endowment for college accreditation. The class made payable to the college $60,000 worth of insurance which they had taken out on themselves to be payable to the school and to become a part of the permanent endowment.

When the thirty-sixth session of the school opened in September, 1926, President Boles stated in the opening exercise words that are so typical of the man: "The session will begin as it closed last year and it is hoped that we will read and study God's word." Other than being a busy year, it differed little from the others. The senior class's plan to help provide the college with a permanent fund paved the way for another plan. At the close of the school year, the Board of Directors, faculty, and school patrons met in the Andrew Jackson Hotel banquet room, June, 1927. Their purpose was to open a drive to raise one million dollars to provide new and needed equipment for the college and build upon the endowment fund. C. M. Pullias presided over the meeting and A. G. Freed was elected to head up the money raising campaign.

The years were clocking right along; the institution was growing older. The thirty-seventh session began on a high key of hope. S. P. Pittman who had been on a leave of absence to earn a degree at the University of Tennessee came back to resume teaching. A. G. Freed was busy in the field raising funds for the college.

H. Leo Boles had never been assured of tenure in the college. At a meeting of the Board of Directors, December 14, 1927, President Boles recommended to the Board that the president of the college be given a five year tenure since the president was in constant attendance to his duties, and that he have the authority to organize the college faculty, to maintain the highest educational standards, and to select a dean of the college to relieve the president of the smaller details of administration. The Board of Directors took the recommendation under advisement and appointed President Boles to a five year term with the provision that if the Board or president deemed it necessary to make a change that it should be declared in the January Quarterly Meeting.

Though he had laid his plans for a senior college at the beginning of his second administration, the words, "A Senior College" were omitted from the college catalog for 1927-1928. The college had begun conferring degrees in 1903, and by 1928 had graduated 350 young men and women. More than 5,000 students had attended the college who were not counted among the graduates. Near the close of his second administration Boles would again raise the "four year college" idea. Once more the matter was discussed and then shelved. H. Leo Boles died in the year his dream became a reality!

Since the Nashville Bible School period David Lipscomb College has been a leader in Christian education. H. Leo Boles was no timid man; responsibilities and new ideas never frightened him. He was the first to keep the old and unafraid to try the new. Boles was responsible for the first formal lectureship in the college that was calendared for February 20-25, 1928. The outstanding preachers of the day were invited to appear on the program. This became an annual affair in the college and other Christian schools have adopted the practice.

When the President entered into the thirty-eighth year of the school's history, he would be faced with a fact he already knew—that the clouds with silver linings have other sides. A. G. Freed who had gone out to raise a million dollars collected about enough money to cover his expenses. E. A. Elam, then in his sunset days, pointed out the responsibility of the Board of Directors to maintain a president "who can lead both the faculty and school in both the knowledge of the Bible and true spirituality and righteousness." And Elam continued to say: "I am glad to repeat that we think in our best judgment, that Brother Boles is an all-around man in these qualifications, and in his practical ability is unsurpassed in the entire brotherhood."

Another signal honor came to H. Leo Boles in the fall

of 1928. C. M. Pullias who was secretary of the Board of Directors resigned his position to go to Texas, and Boles was elected to his position on the Board. By now H. Leo Boles had held every position and claimed every honor the college was able to bestow! He at one time or another had become all things to the college.

This thirty-eighth year of the college was a crucial one for H. Leo Boles. E. A. Elam died March 14, 1929. This was a great personal loss for Boles. The younger man had sailed through many stormy seas; and had it not been for the steadying hand of Elam on the helm, the life of Boles may well have turned in another direction. When the hand of David Lipscomb grew feeble, the reassuring and powerful hand of Elam guided Boles. As counsellor and friend, Elam supported Boles as long as he lived.

No man had done more for David Lipscomb College than E. A. Elam other than David Lipscomb; nor had travelled further or raised more money. At the time of his death, he had written for the *Gospel Advocate* for more than forty years; and for thirty years, Elam had written Sunday school literature. He had been on the Board of Directors for twenty-eight years and president of the Board since 1922. E. A. Elam not only knew the ideals of David Lipscomb, he cherished them. He was always anxious that the college fulfill its mission and remain loyal to the ideals of Christian education. His name was a household word in thousands of Christian homes which knew of him through the *Gospel Advocate*. He preached extensively in the United States and Canada. H. Leo Boles and S. P. Pittman preached his funeral in his home near Lebanon, Tennessee.

The fall of 1929 differed little from all the other school openings. Another banner enrollment was recorded. There was not even a cloud on the horizon to suggest that this year would be one of major recurring crises. The school year was marred by two tragic fires and the passing of Ed Darnell, a young business administration teacher and popular basketball coach. The prelude to the sorrows happened with shocking suddenness on October 24, 1929. This was the day that the "death knell" of the "Roaring Twenties" was tolled. This was the "Black Thursday" when the Wall Street House of paper tape came streaming down. A slow economic paralysis gradually seized the great nations of the earth. There were people in those days who said Boles was not a good business man—a remark that hardly makes good sense now.

On the night of December 24, 1929, a fire was discovered in Lindsay Hall about 3 o'clock in the morning. Smoke from the fire aroused one of six young men asleep in the dormitory. So fiercely was the fire raging they barely had time to escape. Ten minutes after the alarm was sounded a fire engine joined by two others waged a hopeless battle against the raging flames. The morning was bitter cold with the thermometer standing at ten above adding to the misery of those who stood helplessly by.

The burning of Lindsay Hall removed a famous landmark from the campus. The Board of Directors met at once to plan a new dormitory; and plans were soon made to build a fine new dormitory. A. M. Burton led the Board of Directors by stepping forward to give $25,000 toward the new structure. The naming of the dormitory resulted from the request made by C. C. Chenault, a member of the Board of Directors, to divert the "Elam Bible Chair" fund to be applied to the cost of the building. Upon the death of E. A. Elam, his widow turned over intact the full amount of the original $50,000 Chenault gift. The new dormitory would be called Elam Hall as an enduring monument to the memory of one of the school's greatest benefactors.

The day school reconvened after Christmas holidays. Chapel Hall was full but this was no longer unusual. More than ninety-five per cent of the student body came back. But even before the college recovered from the shock of the Lindsay Hall holocaust, another blow fell with devastating suddenness. In the early morning of March 28, 1930, the matron was awakened to discover a fire raging in the elevator shaft of Avalon Home. Seventy-five girls were living there. A small number of girls were blocked from the stairway and the fire escape exit by fiercely raging flames. A few girls jumped from the third floor onto quilts held by young men. Only five girls were hurt, but two of them were seriously injured.

With both dormitories gone the doomsters predicted that the school had perished forever in her ashes. The next Monday morning classes began as usual. But the halcyon days of H. Leo Boles were done. The heart breaking years of a heavy indebtedness would plague the school in the years ahead. But H. Leo Boles was not the sort of man to crumble under the heavy blows of events. What best describes him is what one of his students said about him—"His gaunt face reminded me of his middle name." Indeed he had the heart of a lion.

That the school continued with hardly a loss of momentum may be likewsie credited—not only to the faith, courage, and sagacity of Boles—but to the school's greatest single benefactor, A. M. Burton. These two strong men knew how to win in the highly competitive struggle of life. The name of A. M. Burton was beginning to loom in growing importance to the school in the early twenties. A. M. Burton stepped forward again after the burning of Avalon Home to pledge another $25,000 toward a girls' dormitory. Another good friend of the college came forward at this time to subscribe $25,000 for the second building. She was Mrs. Helena Johnson, one of the founders with A. M. Burton, of the Life and Casualty Insurance Company. Mrs. Johnson recommended that the dormitory be called Sewell Hall in memory of E. G. Sewell, a co-editor of the *Gospel Advocate* with David Lipscomb for fifty years.

Perhaps no other member of the church in modern times has contributed so generously to the support of the church as A. M. Burton. He has preached the gospel and supported numerous gospel preachers. Few men of such prestige and great wealth have so unselfishly supported the cause of Christ as this good and great man. At the most crucial points in the school's history, Brother Burton lent his influence and gave his financial support to save the school. When the history of David Lipscomb College is written in this century, A. M. Burton will take his place alongside of David Lipscomb, H. Leo Boles, and E. A.

Elam in dedication and service to the classic ideals of Christian education.

Spanning the years from David Lipscomb to the present, no other person has served David Lipscomb College so many years as A. M. Burton. Burton has been acquainted firsthand with the ideals of Lipscomb and Lipscomb's successors. A. M. Burton was not only a financial saviour of David Lipscomb College; he has lent his support only to those who were true to the Bible. History will credit this unusual man as one who used his personal power and great wealth to advance the cause of Christian education in the efforts of David Lipscomb College and numerous other activities. He has been true to the Book and dedicated to the principles of the founders of the Nashville Bible School. What David Lipscomb College may have become without H. Leo Boles and A. M. Burton gives food for thought. That it has remained founded on "the rock" may in a very large measure be attributed to them.

In the May 15 issue of the *Advocate,* following the burning of the two dormitories, toward the school's close, the Board of Directors complimented the president and his staff:

> At our last meeting we were constrained to extend a vote of thanks to President Boles and his faculty and the people of the community for the splendid way they have overcome all difficulties occasioned by the fires and have kept practically all the pupils, having them well cared for and the regular work of the college carried on without interruption. We did not believe it could be done, but it has been, and we extend our heartiest congratulations.

The fortieth session opened September 16, 1930. The old part of the campus had begun to take on its present appearance. Students were living in the new dormitories. Six college presidents spoke during the dedication ceremonies of the new structures. Among those were N. B. Hardeman, Batsell Baxter, and J. N. Armstrong. In its new setting the school year ran as all the others had under the Boles administration.

The forty-first year of the college was Boles' last to head the school. He operated that school year successfully and the year was good like all the others. The Depression

201

Years seized not only the college but the whole world. When the Board of Directors met October 9, 1931, President Boles submitted his letter of resignation saying in part: "I am conscious that I have made many mistakes. I have had many problems and difficulties with which to deal. I am human but I have done by best." President Boles at this time served as a member of the Executive Committee of the Tennessee College Association.

H. Leo Boles upon resigning said that he had given the best years of his life to the school. But Boles was dead wrong here. Every year as long as he lived would be a better year, and no man stood higher in the esteem of his brethren during his lifetime nor has any surpassed him since death.

H. Leo Boles continued on as a Bible teacher for two additional years. Batsell Baxter came from Abilene to act as college president following Boles' resignation. H. Leo Boles was honored by the Nashville press upon his resignation which said: "The loss of H. Leo Boles as president of David Lipscomb College will be keenly felt. But the institution will continue to have the advantage of his wise counsel for he is to remain as the Secretary of the Board of Directors, after his resignation becomes effective at the end of the year."

When Batsell Baxter resigned to go to Abilene Christian College to become head of the Bible Department, Boles resigned as a member of the Bible faculty, but continued to serve on the Board of Directors. He always liked to tell that David Lipscomb had selected him as the school's head five years before Lipscomb died. There was no blot or stain upon his character, and he was recognized by his brethren as a superior educator, writer, and preacher of the gospel. He was without question one of the best educated Christian leaders of his era. At the time of his resignation, he was in the prime of his life in good health and with strong mental powers. He had financed the college making every year pay its current expenses with no supporting endowment.

At the time of his resignation there was really no need for a change in presidents, but the school had made many such changes. The patrons of the college were behind him. Max Hamrick said that no man in his memory was better suited to the ideals and purposes of the founders of the college than H. Leo Boles. Each year he served as president a large student body was in attendance standing as a monument to his ability as president to maintain a good school.

One of "his boys," D. Ellis Walker, sums up perhaps what the best contribution of H. Leo Boles was to the college: "I firmly believe that if David Lipscomb is the founder of David Lipscomb College, that H. Leo Boles is the preserver of the school. I dare say that he came nearer to preserving the ideals of Lipscomb and Harding." Boles was the last of the great pioneer preachers and educators bred and born on the high Cumberland Plateau. H. Leo Boles had been associated with the Restoration giants of yesteryear and among them he was by no means the least.

In the words of Shakespeare:

His life was gentle; and the elements
So mixed in him, that nature might stand up
And say to all the world, *This was a man!*

Chapter XIX
JOB'S CHILDREN

"There was a man in the land of Uz, whose name was Job; and that man was perfect and upright, and one that feared God and eschewed evil. And there were born unto him seven sons and three daughters." This is the story of H. Leo Boles and "his children" and two were his flesh and blood and the others were his children in the faith.

Whatever memories have lingered longest with the students of the old Nashville Bible School, one must be that the school campus was a complete little world all to itself. When the school was moved to the northeast corner of David Lipscomb's farm, it became the radiating center of the social, cultural, and spiritual life of the students. Without special permission, the young men were allowed to go downtown on Saturday afternoons and the young women on Monday mornings with their chaperones. The campus was as isolated otherwise from downtown Nashville as New York City. In those days no boy dared meander across the driveway that separated the two campuses, and promenading up and down that drive would have been foolhardy. Constant vigilance was the price paid by the faculty and neighborhood dames to insure in all seasons the Christian deportment of the students. And there were eyes everywhere; on the street cars and even the corners downtown.

David Lipscomb and James A. Harding were indeed educational innovators for their day. They realized the necessity of a liberal education for both young men and women. An early school catalog contended that "girls should by all means be well trained in the best and noblest learning." Until the turn of this century, this country was a man's world and a woman's world, and the twain met almost exclusively in the home.

Although the school was intended to be co-educational from its inception, until the school was moved to David Lipscomb's farm it was not popular with young women;

most of the young men who came in the early years planned to preach. Afterwards the beautiful and spacious campus in its setting of great natural beauty became appealing to young women. There has seldom since been enough room for girls wishing to attend the institution.

When H. Leo Boles retired from the college in 1934, no person had a longer continuous association with the college. No college President had lived closer to the students, and as he grew older he fondly referred to them as "my boys" and "my girls." The pattern of the campus life changed slowly and almost imperceptibly. President Boles steered the school in much the same channel as first chartered by David Lipscomb.

There was little about the Nashville Bible School that resembled a college. As a matter of fact, the school changed little until the Lipscomb administrations of the 1920's gave the college a typical collegiate character. Whatever the Nashville Bible School said was its purpose in the early years, the college catalogs reflected its aspirations to train preachers. In 1897, there were thirteen churches and seven missions in and around Nashville. By the turn of the century more than a hundred preachers had been trained by the school faculty and some were preaching in the faraway places of Persia and Japan. In the few years following the school's beginning, thousands had been baptized by students trained in the school. H. Leo Boles fostered this service of the school as long as he was associated with it, and hundreds of "his boys" were numbered among the finest evangelists of this century.

No suzerain ever reigned over his subjects with more complete control than the school heads and faculty of the Nashville Bible School, but the spirit of their rule was love and devotion. Strict regulation controlled the social life on the campus. Young ladies were not allowed to receive calls from young gentlemen, and no associations between the two sexes were permitted outside of the classroom except in the company of the faculty. It was not until the years after World War I that the young women were allowed to wear such clothes as they brought from home. The girls of the Nashville Bible School were required to wear simple dresses made out of blue or black materials. Other girls' schools in Nashville also had their own distinct uniform, and a girl from the Bible School could be easily singled out by her distinct dress.

The founders of the college intended to train young Christians, and the school catalog served fair notice that the institution was not a "reform school." It also warned that unruly students would not be tolerated. It was against this background that H. Leo Boles came as a student and served as President.

Students early and late in the life of Boles found him to be a blunt man indeed, and whenever he made a decision no student felt at liberty to question that decision. Neither student nor faculty member questioned the authority of President Boles; he controlled everything and delegated authority to no one. When he wanted something done, he wanted it done right and right then. The staff who worked under him performed the chores. Faculty as well as students remember that Boles had a temper. One student said that while the President was sternly lecturing a student, if his emotions were aroused, "the whites of his eyes turned red." Once students learned Boles' walk, they could recognize him from afar off. As Sarah Cawthon Garner said, "He walked as if he wore 'seven league boots' and especially when he was taking those long strides down to Lindsay Hall to check on some of the young 'heathens' living there."

What no student ever forgot about H. Leo Boles as E. A. Emmons put it was "the most expressive pair of hands I ever saw on a man." But it was that right index finger they remember best of all; for with it, he punctuated everything he said be it a statement, a question, or an exclamation point. C. J. Garner said that finger "looked a mile long when it was pointed in your direction." Frank Pack remembered some of the boys used to say that "they feared at times that Brother Boles' finger would go off like a Colt revolver and that if that finger were pointed in your direction, you felt like you had been shot."

David Lipscomb and his associates took their responsibilities seriously and they said in the school bulletin: "Pu-

206

pils are accepted for mental and moral improvement—*for study*—nothing else." Their strictness is reflected in a statement in the school bulletin for the school year 1896-1897: "There is scarcely a home in the land where girls are so well guarded as with us. It is almost impossible for a boy and a girl to speak to one another except in plain view of a number of others. When it has been attempted (and it has been in two or three cases in five years) it has been immediately discovered and the guilty parties dealt with." This kind of severity was gradually relaxed but never the strict supervision of campus life.

There were discipline problems under President Boles and he moved with dispatch to handle them. Though Boles was fiery and abrupt, the students soon learned he moved slowly and expelled a student when no other recourse was left. J. Ridley Stroop remembered the college under Boles as well managed and the student body rather strictly disciplined. Students who were afraid to approach President Boles found himself considerate once they got up enough courage to approach him.

The classic student misdemeanor happened during Boles' first administration. On Friday morning, and it happaned to be on Criticism Morning, some boys anointed the chairs on the stage where all the male faculty members sat with oil of mustard. E. G. Sewell was up talking. Pretty soon the students observed President Boles sliding out of his chair getting "madder and madder" and his face "redder and redder," and students said that on such occasions his face would turn a "cherry red." President Boles aimed his right index finger at the students and cocked his right foot back on the heel and began to rock it. When he did these two things simultaneously, it was an ill-informed student who did not know things were picking up right then. The President started down each row asking each boy if he were a party to the act, or if he knew who did it. When one boy said he knew who did it, a student down front spoke out, "Brother Boles, I want to change my story; I had a hand in it." The students were punished for their thoughtfulness and allowed to stay in school.

For many years the school conducted a farming operation on a part of the farm. There was the usual barn with its mules and tools, and a hog pen to dispose of the kitchen garbage. In those days smoking was strictly forbidden on the campus with one exception. A boy who would have his smoke had to go off down behind the hog pen for his pleasure. Emps Fussell was attending the school session (1915-1916), and he obtained permission from Lacy Elrod to go to a dentist downtown. Emps was suffering with a terrible toothache. Clarence Nicks, his roommate, sent a gasoline iron by Fussell to be repaired. By the time he arrived downtown, the toothache was gone and just as promptly forgotten. On his way to the shop with the pressing iron in his right hand and a long cigar in his left, he turned a corner right into the path of Brother Boles who reached down and took Emps' left hand with the cigar, and exploded, "Emps, what are you doing in town?" He stuttered saying that he had brought the pressing iron to be repaired; Emps rarely at wit's end was taken off base so completely he could not think of the real reason why he was in town. But in such cases a student had nothing at all to fear from Boles.

H. Leo Boles had a fine sense of humor but business was business and fun was fun. Sometimes they were joined in a happy way.

Cornelius Abbott, a student befriended by President Boles, appeared on the campus penniless after being robbed in Cincinnati, Ohio. True to the tradition of Tolbert Fanning, the school's policy had been not to turn away a student because he could not pay his tuition. H. Leo Boles told young Abbott on that occasion: "If you want an education, and you are willing to work for it, there will be a place for you." Sometimes afterwards the young man attended a meeting where Boles was preaching and memorized one of his sermons. A few weeks later Abbott was preaching one Sunday at the Green Street Church of Christ when he spied Boles in the audience and he exclaimed in dismay: "Brother Boles, I did not see you in the audience, and if I had I would not be here delivering your sermon." Whereupon Boles arose slowly from his seat and said, "That's all right; the fellow I got it from said you could preach it too."

Among Boles' many splendid talents, he was preeminently a Bible teacher. His keen and accurate memory of the Scriptures was such that he was often able to teach an entire chapter verse by verse without referring to the Bible a single time. A boy coming out of his Bible class once said, "He can make those Old Testament characters walk." Batsell Baxter who was a student in the Bible School soon after Boles came there said of his old friend after the death of H. Leo Boles: "His Bible classes were full of information, free of speculation, true to the book."

He was then above all other things a master teacher whether in the pulpit, the classroom, or in the pages of the *Gospel Advocate*. He was a thorough teacher and his students were required to prepare their lessons strictly according to the classroom assignment. When he entered a classroom there was absolute quiet. He would point a finger at an unruly student in such a way that each student in the classroom felt that the reprimand had been intended for him. Students had to look Boles squarely in the eyes while he taught; and if one dared sneak a look at his watch, the teacher would say, "What time is it?" He always stood up to teach a class and was never late. Always a quick spoken man, but never crude, he insisted on gentle manners and good morals on the part of his students.

Though students were accepted in the Bible School for study and nothing else, there were other activities to enrich their lives. The societies played an important part in the lives of the students in both of Boles' administrations. The societies were created to provide such training the classrooms could not provide. It would be hard today to imagine the keen interests that students in those days had in their respective societies. The Babylonian Society was so named because it included all the male members of the school, and it continued for a while after Lewis and Boles organized the Lipscomb and Calliopean Societies in 1904.

At this same time the young women of the school organized their own society with the imposing name, Puellarum Sodalitas. There were twenty-four young women in that first group. Their first programs were infrequent and

209

it was only by special permission of the faculty that they were rendered. At the end of the school year the name was changed to Sigma Rho. This was the only girl's society until Boles became president the first time. Then the society had so many members it was thought necessary to change it. On March 10, 1914, a group of girls met in the living room of the Boles home to organize the Kappa Nu Society. Paralee Cowan was elected President, Mary Creath Cato, Secretary, and Sybil Lillie the Editor. In their first meeting the girls decided to have an open program the first vacant Saturday and to plan for an annual program beginning the following year. They proposed to request the faculty for the Tuesday evening during commencement week. The purpose of the society, they said, would be to develop its members in literary work and parliamentary procedures.

The other girls of the Bible School were divided into the Sapphonean Society. Eulalia Holland was chosen President of the new society. The original minutes of the organization of the meeting are not available. The two societies were eventually dubbed the *Sappho* and the K-Nu. S. P. Pittman said that the rivalries became pretty heated at times but there was never any hair pulling. Their programs largely consisted of readings, piano recitals, and such that delight the hearts of young girls. Each society strove to present the best chapel program; and for the more hardy among them, the tennis court settled many a duel.

The young men were the emulators of the great orators and public figures of their day. Their enthusiasm, if not their oratory, would have vied with that of the Tennessee brothers, Bob and Alf Taylor, who as rival candidates sought the governor's mansion by way of the golden tongue. Occasionally one of the societies called a "kangaroo court" into session to try a boy who had absented himself from a regular meeting. They were forever debating with the best two out of three falls going to the winner. In the early years the societies were strictly literary, but in time they became something different.

On Saturday evenings the doors of Chapel Hall were

opened to the friends and patrons of the Nashville Bible School for the society programs. Each society presented its program when their time rolled around. One of the all-time favorite student socials grew out of the programs; this was the "after-meeting" which was a kind of social get-together between the courting couples. Howard Stubblefield described the "after-meeting" as a period when the students stood around or sat together talking. If a boy and a girl began whispering or if a boy sat a little too close to a girl, President Boles angled in their direction. The "after-meetings" lasted about thirty minutes if Boles was in fine humor; but if he was "sleepy" the session soon ended. Some infraction of the school's rules resulted in the cancelling of the "after-meeting," or it would last just for a few minutes.

There was another side to the stern schoolmaster that students fondly remember. The office of President Boles was always open as a meeting place for a boy and girl in love provided the President was sitting at his desk. Many a lovers' quarrel was patched up while Boles worked away on his roll-top desk with a prominent ear cocked in their direction. Another practice he allowed was the passing of "love notes"; the letter had to be left in his office and unsealed. This is how this "gruff man" played the role of both cupid and messenger. And he always delivered the mail on time; the rain, the snow, and clouds of many a stormy courtship sailed peacefully away under his watchful care.

Irma Lee Batey, longtime Lipscomb music teacher, said every Sunday afternoon each student retired to his room between two-thirty and four o'clock. A student once in his room could study, meditate, write a letter home, or just sleep. No one wandered in and out of rooms; and once a student who thought he could, was caught, found himself better persuaded the next time he felt the urge. This practice known as the "Quiet Hour" ended soon after the close of World War I.

Chapel time in the old Nashville Bible School was the high-light of the day. President Boles conducted the chappel hour along with other male faculty members regularly

211

at ten o'clock. Boles, according to S. P. Pittman, was the best chapel man the college ever had. The students looked forward to the occasions, and often they had the pleasure of hearing some famous person speak in chapel. S. Comer Sadler remembered President Boles with his "Abner speech" which would turn up at regular intervals. The Old Testament Abner was Brother Boles' favorite "whipping boy." He would often chastise him in chapel—"to all of you there comes a time when you are not mindful of your direction; you are apt to be headed down the wrong road. Stop and think; take inventory of yourself; just reach up and grab the hair on the top of your head and say, 'Now look here, Abner, where do you think you are going?' " The students often referred to President Boles as "Abner", but they were careful that he was well out of ear shot.

During the early years of the school, roll call was made in chapel by Dr. J. S. Ward. The number of students was never great and all the students knew each other by name. The chapel devotion generally consisted of a Bible reading, prayer, and hymn singing; often the chapel would run over into the next class period. No one seemed to care. It was the practice for all the faculty men to sit on the stage and most of them knelt during prayer. It was not uncommon for each faculty member on the stage to comment on the subject after the speaker was seated. H. Leo Boles was thoughtful of other peoples' feeling; though there were those who felt otherwise. He often advised the students in chapel: "Don't write a letter home if you are disturbed. By the time your letter gets home you will have forgotten your problem and it will be just beginning for your parents."

A high light in chapel came on Fridays; this was "Criticism Morning" which was a practice for many years. The sessions were conducted by the faculty men. S. P. Pittman and John T. Glenn were the most popular leaders among the faculty in this. All sorts of criticism would be voiced on good manners, student deportment, and bad grammar. This was a two way street and both faculty and students came up for criticism. In later years the practice got out of hand, and a student could only voice criticism through a student representative. Finally the practice became a nuisance and was abolished.

Since the days of J. A. Harding, the "Topic Class" had been a favorite meeting with the young preachers; E. A. Elam was one of the most popular leaders of the Monday night meeting. But H. Leo Boles was considered by the students to be without an equal. None who came before or after Boles ever quite measured up to him here. He would write a sermon outline on the board and carefully work through the mechanics of the sermon presentation. Often students presented their own sermon outlines to the class, and many of the church's finest evangelists received their first training in this setting.

Prayer Meeting service were conducted each Thursday evening in the Chapel Hall for the students and neighbors who worshipped there. The meetings were pervaded with a strong spiritual atmosphere and Boles' unfailing presence and demeanor served as a sure anchor. Generally one or two students spoke and frequently H. Leo Boles would have a few words to say after they concluded. He often told the students that not one of them stood to speak but that he prayed for him. President Boles always sat on the front seat and often corrected the mistakes the students made. On some occasions he would call a young aspiring preacher from the audience to make a speech. During one of the prayer meeting services, Brother Boles called on J. M. Powell to come down front for a devotional talk. The class was studying Mark 14 that tells of Mary's anointing the feet of Jesus. Powell read: "She hath done what she could." Whereupon he said, "So have I," and promptly sat down.

The college annual was introduced into the college after H. Leo Boles began teaching in the Bible School. Only one annual, the *Ark,* was printed before Boles became President the first time. Batsell Baxter who got out the *Ark* told the story many years later; he said that he was not only the Editor but the whole staff. Baxter said he had a lot of problems with the school annual: "Yes, we put out the first annual and we had our troubles. We had a time explaining to the students what an annual was. One

213

boy got up in chapel and asked how many times a year it came out." The McQuiddy Publishing Company did the printing. Each student purchased his copy for three dollars. Baxter said, "We called it the *Ark* because everything went into it." The school published three annuals during Boles' first tenure called the *Zenith*. The annual was renamed the *Backlog* in 1922 during the Lipscomb administration and has continued to wear the name.

When H. Leo Boles returned to the college in 1923 he meant for little to change of what had gone on before. But there were changes and he was not the man to block whatever promised both progress and excellency. One of the first steps Boles made after he took over the college reins in 1923 was to change the name of the college paper, *Haviland Acts*—a composite word suggesting Harding Hall, Avalon Home, and Lindsay Hall. President Boles wanted the name changed because it meant nothing until it was explained.

J. C. Greene, Editor-in-Chief of the first *Babbler,* tells the story. While working on the campus in the summer of 1923, Boles called Greene into his office and said that he wanted the name of the college paper to be changed. The President wanted a new name to suggest the religious character of the institution, and he told the young editor-to-be to go to work and select one. Boles was always ready to help young people, but first they had "to hatch" their own ideas. Greene thought of such namse as *Tattler, Lipscomb Voice*—titles too obvious to be catching. Greene kept coming back to the *Babel* as a possible masthead. While talking the matter over with the President, Boles said, "Son, you are on the right track, but you haven't read your Bible carefully. The word you are groping for is 'babbler' "; then he read from the book of Acts the Scripture—"What will this babbler say." Green was jubilant for he knew the paper had been named. After the first publication, congratulations were received from numerous colleges with one lament—"Why didn't we think of that?"

The last chapter of the old literary societies closed in Boles' second administration. For a quarter of a century

DAVID LIPSCOMB E. A. ELAM

A. G. FREED B. C. GOODPASTURE

they had been the focus point of the students' social life. When Boles came back, the societies were more active than ever. The students recall that their homesickness and the little things that worried them passed away in those hours when the societies were meeting. President Boles was always accused of favoring the Callios and he never bothered to deny the charge. Both Elam and Boles had been Callios in Burrett College. A short time before his death the venerable old gentleman was seen to halt at the stairway leading to Lipscomb Hall to exclaim to himself: "Ho, I can't go up that way." The spirit of the Callios never seemed to die or even to fade away!

What eventually happened to the literary societies is tied in with athletics. The college catalog first began to take notice of college athletics about the time of World War I. Both the young men and women were encouraged after the school was moved to the farm to play tennis, basketball, and take hikes; but they were advised to play at such sports as befitting ladies and gentlemen. Professional as well as inter-collegiate sports were condemned; and if a student slipped away to watch a Vanderbilt football game, he was subject to dismissal or at least being campused. Only one football game was played during Boles' first tenure. The faculty sounded the death knell of the sport since several of the young men were painfully injured. The Lipscomb students became avid baseball and basketball fans, and with the building of a new gymnasium, basketball became the rage. The spirit of Patrick Henry and Demosthenes no longer dominated the literary societies; even the girls were forsaking Shakespeare and Paderewski to play basketball in Burton Gymnasium. Once the boys had orated their way to victory; now they settled those contests of prowess on the playing fields of Lipscomb. And publish it not in Gath—occasionally, a fist was seen!

Rivalries between the two societies became so intense and heated over athletics and other contests, it was believed by the school officials that the usefulness of the literary societies had been served and they were dissolved by the Board of Directors. Though four new societies were organized—the Tawassan and Estrellita for college stu-

215

dents and the Zenith and Excelsior for high school students—the students showed little enthusiasm for the new groups. The new societies were described in the college catalogs with the school year (1930-1931). They disappeared after the school year (1931-1932), and this ended one of the most colorful chapters in the school's history. School rivalries afterwards centered in the junior and senior classes of the college.

Debating that had once occupied a major interest in the societies was moving into the arena of inter-collegiate forensics. The contests at first were with sister Christian colleges. The traditional annual Thanksgiving and Valentine celebrations began to lose their charm. The young men and women entertained one another on these colorful occasions around World War I days; but after a common dining hall during the Lipscomb period served all of the students, the traditions gradually disappeared. A student organization was attempted beginning in 1924, but it was never more than a disciplinary body. The constitution included such admonitions as: Be sure to read the *Babbler;* throwing food in the dining room is forbidden; be very quiet while taking a bath during study hours.

H. Leo Boles never forgot the early years of his life nor the hardships he endured. He never experienced poverty, but he had known what it meant to be poor. In his young manhood he had signed notes for money that he had borrowed for as little as $3.00; those notes now in B. C. Goodpasture's possession carry the words—"Paid in full." Any student who came to David Lipscomb who was willing to make an up hill struggle foot by foot found President Boles on his side. Boles said that while he was President the school was spending from $6000 to $10,000 to help boys and girls get an education that would have otherwise been denied.

Adolphus Rollins repeated the words of H. Leo Boles at the outset of the Depression Years: "So long as I am president of David Lipscomb College the school will never close its doors to a young man who wants to preach the gospel of Christ." Many of the young men worked their way through college; and others partly did so and signed a note for the remainder. Some never honored that obligation; most of them did.

No other contemporary of H. Leo Boles knew more gospel preachers living and dead than he, nor had a deeper sympathy for the preacher and his problems. In the last years of his life he met preachers from widely scattered places during the Freed-Hardeman lectures, but the hundreds of young men who passed through Lipscomb had special places in his heart. He referred to them as "my boys" and their wives as "my girls" if they too attended David Lipscomb College. When H. Leo Boles was at home on Granny White Pike between meetings, the neighbors said that hardly a day passed without a former student pulling into his yard to spend two or three hours discussing two subjects—the Bible and the state of the church. When they came to his meetings in the mellow years of his life, he called them "my children" from the pulpit and addressed them by name.

H. Leo Boles had a way of inspiring "preacher boys" as they were often called. In the school year 1930-1931, Boles commented while teaching the Bible that man, not God, had divided the Bible into chapters and verses— "There is a beauty and unity in the New Testament. If one should read it at one sitting then the beauty would become more apparent." Some of the young bloods took him up on the proposition and proposed to begin a reading of the New Testament on Friday until it was completed. The reading was done in the chapel auditorium. Forty-one students met May 15, 1931, at 7:05 in the evening; dawn came and day wore on until they finished the last verse twenty hours and fifteen minutes later. Thirty-two of the original group were still around for the reading of the last verse.

Batsell Baxter came to the Nashville Bible School as a young student in 1908 when Boles was the youngest teacher on the faculty. He said:

> It was my privilege to be in his classes in college mathematics, solid geometry, trigonometry and surveying; and also in psychology, logic, and debating. He was good in all these subjects. Boles knew his subjects but he knew the poor beginner did not. His

class standards were rigid, but he had that quality of human sympathy and understanding that made students work for him. Though he was a busy man working for the college and preaching on Sundays, he always had time for the students. He helped the boys in Lindsay Hall build their first tennis court and became one of the best players.

Baxter commented further:

The 'preacher boys' especially looked on him as I think Timothy must have looked upon Paul—as counsellor, friend, and helper.

Perhaps a letter to Boles from the young evangelist, B. C. Goodpasture, that was dated November 11, 1920, sums up how young preachers felt about their teacher and friend: "I shall not count letters. I regard you, in many respects, as a father rather than a friend; in recounting the influences which you have exercised over me and the lessons I have learned from you. I can think of nothing that affected me except for the good."

About six months later his young friend wrote Boles another letter: "No living man has helped me as a preacher as much as you. Whatever shall be the reward of my toils in the day of final reckoning—you will have labored through me."

As long as Boles lived, "his boys" came by his home to seek his advice. The passing of H. Leo Boles left a broad breach in the ranks of his fellow evangelists, but a host of gospel preachers to whom he referred as "my boy" rallied to fill the gap. "So the Lord blessed the latter end of Job more than his beginning."

Chapter XX
WHITE UNTO HARVEST

Whoever saw the richly endowed H. Leo Boles in the prime years of his life and heard him speak would hardly forget the occasion. His brethren generously acknowledged him to be among the outstanding evangelists in the first forty years of this century. The number of gospel meetings that he conducted and the sermons he preached over forty-three years beggar numbering or description. He could never accept all of the invitations to preach that were proffered him, but he accepted all that time allowed.

There was nothing particularly comely about Boles that attracted people to him. He was a little above the average height and weighed one hundred sixty-five pounds, give or take a few pounds. Forty years later Boles could still put on his wedding suit. With the exception of a severe case of typhoid fever, he enjoyed excellent health until his final illness in his seventy-second year. His features were rugged and his eyes were a clear blue. When a person saw Boles he wanted to hear him, and he was easy to look at and hear.

Jennie Pittie Brown, of the Lipscomb English faculty who heard him in a meeting at the Creswell Street church in Shreveport remembers the evangelist standing on the pulpit platform with a flexible New Testament rolled up in his left hand saying with intense earnestness: "I want to go to heaven when I leave this earth and I want you to go with me." The lectern had been removed and not once during the sermon did he refer to his outline or his New Testament which he read with perfect accuracy from memory. His stance in the pulpit was dignified and his manner was calm. Boles was no shouting preacher. He was slow and deliberate in delivering his sermon. H. Leo Boles was what his brethren called a "strong preacher." A listener hearing Boles preach for the first time would settle down for a long tedious sermon; spell-bound an hour

219

later, he wondered how the time had passed so rapidly. He was not the glib-tongued, flowery-orator type. H. Leo Boles was a master pulpiteer because he could tell clearly in his firm and resonant voice what the Bible taught on the subject of the hour. His rich background of experience and knowledge of the Bible coupled with a splendid education enabled him to relate the Bible to the religious needs of man.

It was not his practice to play upon the fears or other emotions of those who heard him preach. Instead he appealed to the deep needs a person had to establish a right relationship with God. He loved people and through his stern demeanor there shined a genuine warmth and sympathy. B. C. Goodpasture said this powerful and humble preacher was like a spiritual tonic for a church when he came to hold a meeting. He inspired the members to greater devotion and service and awakened in the hearts of those who were not Christians the realization that man is at his best still a sinner. H. Leo Boles was baptizing more people with each passing year of his ministry, and his later years were the grandest in this respect.

His sermons were plainly biblical and they were fashioned word by word through his clear and powerful logic. A person felt no great need of a formal education to understand his lessons. His brethren liked him because he was a thinker. Indeed H. Leo Boles in his preaching was calm, and severely logical; but in his last years there was a noticeable relaxing of his stern ways and severe manners. John T. Lewis said of his old friend—"In his wide acquaintance with school mates, students and gospel preachers, if he had lived to be as old as Methuselah, he would have always had calls for gospel meetings."

The personal qualities of the man were singular and outstanding. He was known as "Brother Boles" by most everyone who knew him which included his friends and acquaintances of different religious beliefs. Some people have a way of growing on you, and H. Leo Boles was such a man. His memory still lives in the minds of thousands who knew and honored him in his lifetime. In his later years he went into the rural areas of Jackson County,

Tennessee, and similar places to hold meetings. He endeared himself to these people by his friendliness and pleasing personality. His custom was to hold a second and third meeting and refuse the fourth because he did not think it served the best interest of the church. But he would promise to return at some later date. On such returns he would make a great hit with the folk as he passed among them calling each by his name. Many a boy and girl got their inspirations in those revivals to attend David Lipscomb College.

It was his custom while in a meeting to make up his own bed and tidy his room, and even to help busy hostess hang out the family washing. While in a meeting at Kettle Mills, Tennessee, not a long while before his death, he was staying in the home of Dr. H. G. Kennedy. The family tells that during the day he would take a brisk walk, read some, and spend a while in pleasant conversation; and after the evening service he would wait up for the ten o'clock news. H. Leo Boles was a family man and loved his home. If someone in the family would promise to drive him to his meeting appointment, he would stay home that Saturday night just to be with the members of the household.

H. Leo Boles is remembered as having great personal pride. Though he was not considered a fashion plate, Boles was always immaculately dressed. He was as careful about the suits he chose for a meeting as the sermon outlines he selected. He was not a creature of habit but a man of sensible behavior. While he never adopted any rituals, what he would do could always be predicted by "Ma" as their young friends addressed Sister Boles. When the time came for him to go away for a meeting as Violet DeVaney tells that he would carefully select two suits with "Ma" and Violet sitting close by. After making a careful selection, "Ma" and Violet would discuss which ties and what color of socks with the lapel handkerchief would go best with his suits. This would be done the night before his departure.

Then H. Leo would take out seven or eight notebooks filled with sermon outlines and select three. After hiding a $20.00 bill in one of the notebooks, he would put them with two or three books in his brief case. Once he had his brief case stolen while he was in a meeting in Kentucky, and later returned with the $20.00 bill still tucked away in the hiding place. He read the books for one reason or another; sometimes he reviewed a new book for the *Gospel Advocate*.

H. Leo Boles was an expert on preachers, and no contemporary of his knew as many preachers or as much about them. He categorized preachers and said there were "good ones" and "bad ones." Some he wrote preached their "pet theories." Others he labelled as wise "who knew and heard all in the brotherhood and became religious peddlers of every mistake and scandal heard about preachers and leaders in the church."

Like Benjamin Franklin who was good at giving advice, Boles was equally adept. Some of his dictums designed for peachers are worth quoting:

(1) Preach the gospel and live in harmony with its teaching, and you need not defend your character.

(2) Heat up the people, but keep your hammer wet and cool. It takes a cold hammer to bend hot iron.

(3) A preacher should not scream and bawl out his sentences. "Powder is not shot, and thunder is harmless. It is lightning that kills. If you have lightning, you can afford to thunder."

(4) Put thought in your sermon. "It is true that a pound of feathers is as heavy as a pound of lead, but will not sink as quickly."

(5) A preacher should make a few promises and live up to the ones he makes.

(6) Keep out of debt, and do not lend more than you are able to lose.

(7) Be patient with all men; make friends with children as well as parents.

(8) Remember that each sermon may be the last one you will preach, or the last one that some of your hearers will ever hear.

(9) Preach in view of the judgment and seek to please God.

(10) Let others praise you and refrain from boasting.

While there is no complete record of the life and preachings of H. Leo Boles, a wealth of material exists. His red-trimmed black ledger tells the most crucial part of the story. He faithfully transcribed between 1904 and 1912 all the meetings he held. He closed the ledger when he became president of the Bible School in 1913. But in 1918, 1919, 1920, 1921, he made other inclusions in the ledger. In 1920 the evangelist conducted fourteen meetings and seventeen in the following year. The "earthy" nature of the preacher is best appreciated in some of his statements made in his journal during the big meeting time.

The evangelist described a meeting with the Greenwood church in Wilson County, Tennessee. The World War had ended with its bitter aftermath, and Boles' reflections about the war show up in his commenting that the church was somewhat indifferent to the meeting and still disturbed over the war." Almost a year to the day he returned for another meeting, and he again said—the church "was very indifferent—still disturbed over the war." Though he rarely ever mentioned a member of his family in his journal, he commented that Leo Lipscomb, Cleo and Lemma drove down for services one day.

H. Leo Boles was no longer connected with the college in the summer months of 1920 which freed him to hold gospel meetings. He began his first meeting with one of Nashville's historic churches—the North Spruce Church (now Eighth Avenue). David Lipscomb wrote—"In May 1867, I began preaching in the old army barracks in North Nashville. A few brethren of the working people lived in that neighborhood and began to worship . . . . The present North Spruce Church grew out of this." Of this meeting Boles said: "The church is very weak and but little zeal—it is 'lukewarm.' " In later years Boles wrote in his "History of the Nashville Churches" that the cause of Christ in North Nashville stemmed out of the North Spruce church. The establishment of the church in West Nashville later grew out of Lipscomb's original preaching efforts in the Civil War barracks building.

Later on that summer he held a meeting in Mackville, Kentucky, where he had "farmer trouble." Most preachers who go into rural areas have the same trouble. Only night services were held because the farmers "were very busy working in tobacco." During two nights of the meeting he preached in the "Baptist house on account of a corpse next door to our house." His next stop was Bunker Hill, Tennessee. He said that the "church is weak and nearly dead." One thing is certain, when H. Leo Boles cocked that right index finger in the direction of his listeners, they had little choice but to show him the "white of their eyes." He would wake up a sleeping student in his class with a sharp clap of his hands, and he had also been known to single out a favorite brother in church who would have his "forty winks."

Among the seventeen meetings Boles conducted in the Summer of 1921 the "F" Street Church of Christ meeting in Louisville, Kentucky, was an especially memorable one for Boles. From Louisville he made a trip to Lexington, Kentucky, in the company of M. C. Kurfees. The journey was occasioned by his desire to visit the tomb of his great grandfather, "Raccoon" John Smith; and while there he saw also the grave of William McGarvey and Robert Milligan.

Although H. Leo Boles closes his journal in 1921 not to be re-opened until 1944, he adopted a new practice that traces his movements exactly year after year. He kept all of his sermons' outlines on small notebook paper enclosed in a binder. When one notebook was filled another was begun. At the time of his death a large briefcase would hardly hold all of his jammed notebooks. On the back of each sermon outline he would write the date and place it was preached with no additional comment. He preached one of his old-time favorite sermons "The Christian Home" at the St. Elmo church in Chattanooga, Tennessee, March 20, 1921. The same sermon was preached at Obion, Tennessee, twenty-four years later. In the meantime the sermon had been delivered forty-two times. One of his all-time favorite sermons was "God's Circles." It is recorded he preached the sermon first at the Reid Avenue Church,

February 15, 1925 and finally on December 9, 1945, making a total of fifty-four times he preached this sermon.

Boles kept no kind of descriptions of his meetings during these years, but what they were like may be judged by those that had preceded. Then in 1944, he resumed recording his meeting work which included sixteen protracted meetings, three college lectureships and one church lectureship at Paragould, Arkansas. The evangelist preached in meetings ranging from Akron, Ohio, to New Orleans, Louisiana.

While few preachers would like to admit it, preachers are often jealous of one another. There were few jealous bones, if any, in H. Leo Boles' body. H. Leo Boles had a great personal interest in worthy preachers, especially the young men, and promoted them one by one in the *Gospel Advocate* with a picture and a brief biographical sketch of each. And with his death they keenly missed him. A preacher felt free to drive into his yard or write him a letter for counsel and it was forthcoming. He was alert to discovering new plans to preach the gospel to even larger numbers.

A review of the *Gospel Advocate* in April of 1937 reveals that H. Leo Boles was busy encouraging a city-wide evangelical effort with all forty-five churches in the Nashville area conducting gospel meetings simultaneously. He paid his respects once again to N. B. Hardeman in this connection by writing—"The auditorium meetings a few years ago brought the churches into public notice as they had never been before." He was looking ahead and he suggested sometime in 1938 for the efforts.

One meeting especially merits attention which he conducted in Moundsville, West Virginia. This was his second time there and he wrote in his journal—"I visited Bethany College and Alexander Campbell's home. This was my fourth visit to the home of Alexander Campbell, but I enjoyed it." H. Leo Boles was seldom given to making personal comments about his life or accomplishments. But there were occasions when his pride shined through such as a meeting he held with the Moreland Avenue church in Atlanta, Georgia—"There was held a fellowship

225

dinner in my honor at the Henry Grady Hotel. There were about 147 tickets sold at $1.50 each. I spoke on co-operation."

His last meeting for the season was with the Charlotte Avenue church of Christ. He conducted services twice daily, spoke in three sessions to the young people, and spoke the two Sunday afternoons on the "Eldership" and the "Teaching Function of the Church." He said of that meeting—"Brother A. C. Pullias was the local minister at that time and co-operated in a fine way to make the meeting a success. At some of the Sunday services there was estimated 1200 people to be present. There were six additions. Received $300." This was next to the largest amount a church paid the evangelist for his labors of love; only the Old Hickory church awarded him a larger sum.

In 1945, Boles scheduled his usual seventeen gospel meetings. His first meeting was with the Central Church in Miami, Florida, his fourth with that Church. His wife and Violet DeVaney went down with him on that occasion. His son, Dr. Leo L. Boles, then teaching in the Miami Beach School, was with his parents daily. Boles' work that season carried him to Seminole, Oklahoma, where a Seminole Indian was baptized. He was in St. Louis, Missouri, and finally in Dallas, Texas. This would be his last gospel meeting. He commented in his journal—"It was pronounced a mighty good meeting. The entertainment of the preacher was most excellent. The sisters kept flowers at the church house and in my room at the hotel. There were ten baptisms. Received $275." He suffered a swollen foot while in the meeting and it never got any better.

During these last two years, Boles baptized 319 people and received a total of $7,465 for the two years which included the lectureship programs. One thing is certain H. Leo Boles was never over-paid for his work. His salaries over his whole life were moderate and the amount of work he did was prodigious. He was a good manager and knew the worth of a dollar. Never a tight-fisted man, he was neither extravagant. The best word to describe him is generous. B. C. Goodpasture tells the story that the evangelist was about to purchase a good, but inexpensive suit at Burk's, a downtown Nashville Store. The clerk remonstrated with the advice—"Brother Boles, a man of your position and prestige cannot afford to wear this suit; you should buy this one (the expensive suit)." Brother Boles took his advice and purchased the better suit. Then the clerk brought out the neck ties for Boles to select one as a gift. And he said, "Brother Boles, these are the one dollar ties, these, the two dollar ones, and here are the three dollar ties." This was tailor-made for Boles and he said— "Well a man of my prestige and position can't afford to be seen wearing a cheap tie." There is no need to guess which he selected.

Just how many persons Boles baptized in more than forty years of preaching can never be known. But such incomplete records as he left, he baptized 160 on the average each year during his meetings. If he baptized forty more in his regular work each year, the total would run around 8000 persons over forty-three years. Add to this the total baptisms of the "boys" he trained to preach the gospel and the number would be formidable.

To describe H. Leo Boles, the preacher, is a hopeless undertaking. Not one of his contemporaries was as versatile and all recognized his incomparable genius. N. B. Hardeman wrote at the time of his death:

> He was one of the best Bible teachers of all that have gone before. There was a magnetism about him that attracted men to hear him. He filled his audience with a love for the truth and with courage to defend it. He spoke with confidence and knowledge that carried convictions. Weak and ailing people were heartened by what he had to say. Eternity alone can give him proper reward for his untiring efforts and devotion to God's word.

And in a letter dated May 26, 1945, N. B. Hardeman never left any question in the mind of H. Leo Boles when he wrote to the Nashville evangelist of his regard for Boles' work with the Henderson college—"I doubt if you know how much I appreciate your influence in our behalf. You are in a position to be more effective than almost anyone else."

Batsell Baxter who had a way of seeing history in its true perspective made his evaluation of H. Leo Boles:

Brother Boles took good care of himself. He did not even have the general preacher habit of drinking coffee. I can hear him say: 'No, I'll take a glass of milk, please.' Brother Boles always met his appointments and always seemed physically fit. Many of us who had been acquainted with him for years felt that in his last year he was doing the best preaching of his life. He studied diligently to the last, and this showed in the freshness and the interesting quality of his sermons.

George S. Benson, president of Harding College, wrote generously that—

perhaps no man in the brotherhood has exercised a more general and wholesome influence over the church in the last generation than did H. Leo Boles. Brother Boles was favorably known from coast to coast and from the Gulf of Mexico to the borders of Canada. People relied upon his judgment and sought his advice.

The illustrious roll call of his fellow preachers honoring H. Leo Boles is contained in the Memorial Issue of the *Gospel Advocate,* March 28, 1946. On the fortieth anniversary of his preaching years, Boles drew back the curtains to let us look for a moment into his heart. Under the title—"Forty Years as a Gospel Preacher," H. Leo Boles penned the following words:

With my father, whom I still honor, I drove from his home in horse and buggy to Stony Point, De-Kalb County, Tennessee, Saturday afternoon, June 6, 1903. The next morning at 11 the people assembled to hear my father preach. After he had read a portion of Deuteronomy 28 and commented on it, he led the people in prayer. Praying for "the speaker that he might speak so as to please God," my father then announced: "My son, H. Leo Boles, who has just returned from Texas, where he has been engaged in teaching, will now preach for us." I had prepared to speak on "The Human Side of Salvation." I spoke rapidly. I knew what I was going to say, and I said it.

It now has been forty years since I preached that sermon! When my father prayed for me that I "might speak so as to please God" on that occasion, I said, "Amen!" in my heart and vowed that I would always so speak. During these forty years I have preached thousands of sermons, and I have not preached a sermon that I did not so pray. I am not so sure that I have always pleased him in preaching—I am sure that I have not knowingly preached any error.

As I now write these thoughts on the fortieth anniversary of my first sermon, I cannot recall any other petition of my father's prayer, but this one, "that the speaker speak so as to please God," has lingered with me and has been a rich blessing through these forty years. In the secrecy of my own soul I continue to pray as I step into the pulpit to preach that I may "speak so as to please God," and so may I ever speak to please God and not man.

It would be safe to say that the passing of no other preacher has been so deeply missed by the church in this century as H. Leo Boles. When he was alive, Boles was taken for granted. He never joined anything or anybody which would compromise one "iota" his loyalty to Christ and the church. H. Leo Boles was "indeed a man in whom there was no guile."

Chapter XXI

CLARION PEN

Job said, "Oh that my words were now written! Oh, that they were printed in a book!" The same spirit that moved the Patriarch inspired H. Leo Boles "to take a pen and write." He was clear in his thinking that a man is known by what he writes and that a good book outlasts the eroding rocks of the everlasting hills. Seven books bearing his name on the title page issued from his fertile mind, a very great number of pamphlets, and his popular "Correspondence Bible Course." In several important respects the books of H. Leo Boles occupy a minor place among his numerous accomplishments. H. Leo Boles did not write books to gain the honor of being an author, nor had he the least desire to go into the book publishing business. He wrote for the same reason he preached—to enlarge the kingdom of God. Such books that he penned came primarily out of his contributions to the *Gospel Advocate.*

To make up a definitive bibliography of his contributions to the *Advocate* would be a formidable task. The least known of Boles' labors undoubtedly is his work for the Gospel Advocate Company in the field of Sunday School literature. Jesse P. Sewell did as much as any member of the church to popularize Christian education among the churches of Christ. Sewell and Henry E. Speck, Sr., wrote perhaps the first work, *The Church and Her Ideal Educational Situation,* discussig the organization, teaching materials, techniques of the Sunday school organization largely adopted by most local congregations. The book was first published in 1933 and has since been completely revised by Henry E. Speck, Sr. But it was H. Leo Boles who did the spade work after David Lipscomb and E. A. Elam pioneered the Sunday School Movement among the churches.

It is almost fifty years since David Lipscomb died and only now is the impact of his life upon the efforts to restore

New Testament Christianity being recognized for its full value. The proof of this is a matter of simple statistics which show that the Disciples of Christ have a smaller membership numbering now 1,779,046; while the churches of Christ have a larger membership in the last counting with a total of 2,250,000. David Lipscomb made the *Gospel Advocate* a powerful instrument in stemming the tide of "creeping liberalism," and the fact becomes daily more apparent.

Whatever threatened the integrity of the church in the time of David Lipscomb was of immediate concern to him. "To contend earnestly for the faith" meant also for Lipscomb the support of the Sunday school movement. There were those who said it was an organization just like the missionary society. On January 22, 1880, Lipscomb took his stand and wrote in the *Gospel Advocate*—"There is just the same authority for teaching old and young the Bible in classes or in a school on Sunday morning at church, that there is for preaching sermons, God requires the Bible to be taught to the old and young."

David Lipscomb wrote and published seven volumes on *Notes on the Sunday School Lessons* as a part of the answer to his critics. His *Commentary on the Acts of the Apostles* resulted from his comments on the Uniform Sunday School Lessons for 1897, though he had not originally intended to make it into a book. As is true in almost every case, H. Leo Boles followed in the steps of David Lipscomb in this respect.

The immediate successor of David Lipscomb, however, was E. A. Elam who continued the preparation of Sunday school literature. There can be little argument that H. Leo Boles brought their efforts to win approval for the Sunday School into widespread approval. And the amount of material that H. Leo Boles produced in this area staggers the imagination.

The efforts of Boles to advance the program of religious education is little known, and hence slightly regarded. No other activity of his full life was so demanding of his time and best thought as his ceaseless labor with teaching materials for the church. To fully appreciate the

231

work of Boles in this respect, it is necessary to turn again to David Lipscomb and his accomplishments. When Lipscomb directed his thinking to the Sunday school movement, it was already a going concern and had been for a long while.

The expression "Sunday school" is so common now that only the religious extremist objects to its phraseology. Because the term "gospel meeting" does not appear in the New Testament, however, has not eliminated its popularity with the same church members. "Religious Education" is indeed of ancient vintage dating back to the "synagogue schools of the Jews and even to the schools for the young prophets in pre-exilic Israel." Ezra was one of the great teachers of his time; and he was honored as great scholars are in every age.

The Sunday school movement resulted from the concern that Robert Raikes, an English philanthropist and reformer, had for the poor children of England. Public schools were unknown in nineteenth century England and only the children of the well-to-do received a secular and religious education. Raikes had a large and warm place in his heart for poor people. In nineteenth century England both mothers and children had to work for their daily bread. Raikes became first interested when a resident of Gloucester complained of the disorderly conduct of the children in the slum district. Raikes was moved to do something about it since he was convinced that bad conduct resulted from idleness and ignorance. So he set up a school first in Gloucester which he financed out of his own pocket to provide instruction in reading, writing, and moral training. The schools met on Sundays when the people enjoyed a brief respite from their toils.

Robert Raikes was little encouraged by his friends who dubbed him "Bobby Wild Goose." Nevertheless, the plan worked; so in 1874, Raikes announced in the *Gentleman's Magazine* a program to provide religious and moral training for the poor. The program was organized under the Sunday School Society of London. When Robert Raikes died in 1811, the Sunday school was widely established throughout England with an attendance of 400,-

000. But the movement achieved its greatest growth and development in the United States. Two years before this country was granted its independence the first Sunday school was established on this side of the Atlantic.

In 1791, Dr. Benjamin Rush, world famous physician, William White, Episcopal Bishop of Pennsylvania, and Matthen Carey, all of Pennsylvania, formed the first Sunday School Society. The nineteenth century were epoch making years in the development of the Sunday school, especially in the last half. In 1872 the movement was international and was called the International Sunday School Convention.

New interest and impetus were added as a result of the rapidly growing graded public schools. The success of the graded classes so impressed the religious leaders that modified practices were borrowed from the public schools. The international Uniform Lesson plan came in on a tremendous wave of enthusiasm. Within three years the plan had gone into nineteen nations, and by 1890 there were no less than eleven million members.

The International Lesson Committee, whose business it was to prepare the lessons, were challenged to do their best from the start. A major problem not even now solved was the advisability of using the same lesson texts for all age groups. The Committee was realistic and prepared a new set of lessons known as the International Graded Series of 1910; and by 1914, all the lessons were complete. The lessons were undergoing continual improvement and by 1918 were called the International Improved Uniform Lessons which were adapted to four different groups—Primary, Junior, Intermediate and Senior, and Young People and Adults. And there were later adaptations and changes which is another story.

In 1922 the Sunday school organization was first officially known as the International Council of Religious Education. H. Leo Boles was a member of the International Council and served for nineteen years as the representative for the Gospel Advocate Company. At the time of his death, H. Leo Boles was the only member of the church to have served in that capacity. The Gospel Advocate Company paid $1600 annually for the privilege of using the lessons. The Council met each year at Chicago in the Stevens Hotel. The Gospel Advocate Company prepared lessons for a great number of churches and the *Firm Foundation* which had an arrangement with the Advocate Company did likewise.

That H. Leo Boles was such a knowledgeable man should cause little wonder when it is revealed that for nineteen years he met and matched wits with the great and near-great leaders of most of the major Protestant groups. He served as a member of the Committee of Uniform Lessons, which meant that he could speak with authority on the best that was being thought and said on the subject. This is part of the answer which explains why the brethren of H. Leo Boles looked no further than this man to discover what "religious straws" were blowing in the wind.

Such contributions that H. Leo Boles made to the Sunday school movement among the churches of Christ have been invaluable and lasting. He was continually faced with multiple responsibilities. He not only defended the concept of the Sunday school, but also the purpose and quality of the *Gospel Advocate* teaching materials. He wrote to explain what was meant by the "uniform lesson" and the "non-uniform lesson" plans and the "grading" of the lessons to fit the needs of the various age groups. He solved many thorny problems and his successors are wrestling with problems that he passed on to them.

In 1923, H. Leo Boles was writing extensively in the *Gospel Advocate* to the use of the "Uniform Lessons" among the membership of the church. And in 1927 the names of James E. Chessor, S. H. Hall, H. Leo Boles, F. W. Smith, F. B. Syrgley and Hall C. Calhoun were listed as the writers who were preparing the graded lesson materials. Boles by then held membership on the International Council. This year marked another solid advance in the teaching program of the local churches. The firm hand and confident voice of H. Leo Boles provided safe steerage for the church in this period.

The announcement was carried in the *Gospel Advo-*

234

cate that Boles would serve as a co-editor of the *Elam's Notes*. After the death of Elam in early 1929, Boles became sole editor of the *Notes* through 1931, after which the lessons were written for awhile under the title of *Annual Lesson Commentary*.

Perhaps the least appreciated of the labors of H. Leo Boles was his work in the field of religious education at the bequest of the Gospel Advocate Company. Other than his work with the college, he is owed in this the greatest debt and recognition by his brethren. Year after year he tirelessly promoted the teaching program among the churches. He carried on a determined writing campaign in the *Gospel Advocate* contributing about ten articles in 1934 to instruct the readers of the *Gospel Advocate* about the Sunday morning Bible school—its organization, materials, methods, and procedures. However one may look at Boles' leaving the college in 1934, his usefulness in exploring the teaching program of the churches through literature is of inestimable importance.

The fertile mind of H. Leo Boles was continually creating down to the very end. He added another popular feature to the teaching program of the *Gospel Advocate* in 1931. He started writing a brief study of the International Lessons for teachers, elders, and others. In 1939 the announcement was carried that a guest writer would supply the weekly comments. The lessons were planned to appear in the *Gospel Advocate* a week early to give teachers and students time to make lesson preparation. Boone L. Douthitt was slated to write the first article and W. Claude Hall the next one, and the practice has continued to the present.

A change in the thinking of H. Leo Boles toward the International Council of Religious Education began to shape up in 1939. The International Council appointed a Committee on Lesson Policy, with three other groups—the Committee on the Uniform Series, Committee on the Graded Series, and a Committee on the Curriculum Guide. Boles continued his membership on the Committee on the Uniform Series. The Committee on Lesson Policy was composed of sixty-five persons representing twenty-six denominations in Canada and the United States. The Committee adopted new policies and principles which Boles immediately recognized as being permeated with the spirit and form of contemporary modernism.

On returning to Nashville, he voiced his objections to Leon McQuiddy and recommended that the Gospel Advocate Company make a clean break with the International Council of Religious Education. Such moves were characteristic of the stout-hearted Boles; it was not his practice to be in the rearguard saying "me too." The Gospel Advocate Company had already acted in severing connections with the International Council when twelve major groups objected on the identical grounds voiced by Boles that the lessons failed to provide a unified knowledge of the Bible and that the new lessons were leaning toward certain schools of liberal interpretation.

This is a good place to say that H. Leo Boles filled another unique niche in the church in this century. He was the leader of the Vanguard who first warned against a new form of liberalism cut out of the same cloth and spirit of the society and music issues of another day. H. Leo Boles stood a towering figure between two eras joining his own fading generation with the upsurging religious leaders who were to shortly follow. That long-index finger of H. Leo Boles went up like a weather vane pointing to the signs of the times. He pointed to the future of the churches of Christ with their present-day massive programs of religious education and their splendid facilities. He pointed to the threat of a new form of "modernism" posed for the church—"neo-orthodoxy" that has occupied the center of the stage among the religious liberals since World War I.

When Boles could no longer serve as a member of the International Council, he had to convince Leon McQuiddy that the members of the church were competent to prepare their own lessons. In 1944, Leon McQuiddy accepted the recommendation and commissioned Boles to work up the first series of lessons which were soon due. Lesser men would have shuddered at the responsibilities. The churches had been accustomed to the International Lessons for so

236

many years that it would be no small job to explain why the change was being made.

The Editor of the *Firm Foundation,* G. H. P. Showalter, was invited to go along with the program free of charge. Showalter at first favored the proposal but later declined. The original plan of H. Leo Boles had been to incorporate the best writers of the *Gospel Advocate* and *Firm Foundation* into a Uniform Lesson Committee to prepare outlines for use among the churches of Christ.

H. Leo Boles faced formidable problems such as the objections from church members who would not understand the reasoning that lay behind the change. To inform his brethren and to prepare good lessons, as Boles knew, would be his best lines of defense. It would not be easy and all the other objections against the International Lessons would now be directed against Boles and his new program. He took to the pages of the *Advocate* to outline and to defend the program for the next two years. Boles never intended to vie with the International Lessons for popularity; but rather to teach and strengthen the church. The master outline of lessons covered a seven-year cycle that included both the Old and the New Testament. The lessons were designed to fit the spiritual and instructional needs of the church.

H. Leo Boles lived just long enough to see his visions crystallize into a going program. He wore the official title —Editor-in-Chief of the Gospel Advocate Series of Lesson Literature. The lessons for 1945 planned by H. Leo Boles were on the "Pre-fleshly State of Christ," "The Fleshly State of Christ," and the "Glorified State of Christ." After the death of H. Leo Boles in early 1946, the responsibilities were turned over to B. C. Goodpasture who served as the new Editor of the Lesson Literature. Twenty years have now gone since Boles engineered the shift and his achievements have proved solid and lasting.

Somewhere along the way H. Leo Boles was associated intimately with every major concern of the church and was invariably drawn into situations where clear thinking was needed. He was the spokesman for his brethren not because he solicited the role, but because they always wanted to hear what he thought about a matter. On the eve of the translation of the Revised Standard Version of the Bible, Boles was listed as one of the fifty members on the Advisory Committee, and he attended their first meeting. The entire transaction was utter boredom to him. He was aware that he had been so honored as a means of promoting the sale of the new Bible among the churches of Christ because of his great popularity with his brethren. The group making up the Advisory Committee could make recommendations to the scholars actually responsible for the translation, but the translators were in no fashion dependent upon the wishes of the advisory group. The same spirit and form of modernism controlling the New International lesson materials also controlled the thinking of scholars translating the Revised Standard Version of the Bible. Boles ignored the next notice of a meeting of the committee.

It is said that only David Lipscomb wrote longer and more for the *Gospel Advocate* than Boles. But since no one has gone to the trouble to accumulate the voluminous writings of each man; the matter who wrote more remains a moot question. There is no doubt that their writing habits were similar and their concerns about the same. David Lipscomb authored books incidentally and so did Boles. Such books that each wrote grew out of something else. One of the major concerns of the Restoration leaders was to write good books for the churches. Among such great works, Robert Millingan's *Commentary on the Hebrew Letter* and the *Scheme of Redemption* are counted among the literary mounuments of the period. It was only natural that David Lipscomb should have an equal concern.

In July of 1928, H. Leo Boles began writing a series of biographical sketches of pioneer preachers for the *Advocate*. He worked up ninety-four brief biographies each telling the story of a deeply earnest and greatly capable man who preached the gospel. Alexander Campbell's sketch naturally came first and Boles included his own father along with "Raccoon" John Smith. These were the men in whose religious endeavors that religious polemics reached their highest estate in America. The series of

238

sketches were published in 1932 under *Biographical Sketches of Gospel Preachers.*

Two other volumes preceded this one. Boles' debate with M. D. Clubb was published in 1927, and his debate with R. H. Boll was published in 1928 and reprinted in 1954.

Perhaps his most appreciated books were the three commentaries and his work on the *Holy Spirit.* In 1936 his Commentary on the *Gospel According to Matthew* was issued. Only J. W. McGarvey had done a similar work among members of the church. He said in connection with the commentary—"No effort is made to display any deep piety or rare learning; the book is written in a style that meets popular demand." He added another statement true to his nature—"Those who claim a high degree of erudition may read it with profit, yet those who may be among the 'common people' who heard Jesus gladly will find that it is easily understood and may be comprehended without any great effort." A reader of the Commentary discovers that Boles makes numerous references to David Lipscomb's thought.

In 1940 his *Commentary on the Gospel of Luke* came out; only J. S. Lamar of the *Christian Standard* had written a commentary on Luke which had been published in 1877. In writing this commentary he said that he had been careful not to lift out the parallel readings in Matthew. What he said was that the contents would not differ in context and that he had taken the trouble to re-phrase each comment in a new and fresh way.

J. W. McGarvey brought out a popular commentary on the Acts of the Apostles in 1863 which was revised in 1892. David Lipscomb also wrote a commentary on Luke's work which was drawn from his comments on the Uni-from Sunday School Lessons for 1897, which he modified and enlarged in preparing his commentary. When the Boles' *Commentary on Acts of the Apostles* was published in 1941, he said that he had worked two years on it, and had gone to a very extensive bibliograpny for his information.

. As so often is the story, the writing of a book is the

239

lonely task of a solitary man. One of the rare gifts of H. Leo Boles was his ability to think and compose in dictation. The prodigious amount of work H. Leo Boles accomplished was made possible by this fact. L. L. Brigance expressed his wonder at the amount of work Boles produced:

"The volume of work he did was amazing. It would seem physically impossible to do all of this writing with one's own hand. However, I presume he dictated most or all of it to a stenographer. I once expressed to him my astonishment at the amount of his writing, and he very modestly replied that he had a very efficient secretary who was of great help to him." He worked right on to the end, writing his last article the day before he died.

H. Leo Boles was speaking of Violet DeVaney. While holding a meeting in Russellville, Alabama, the evangelist met the DeVaneys, a prominent family in Russellville. He needed some letters typed and Violet took the dictations and typed on that occasion some of his endless correspondence. In the fall of 1937, Violet DeVaney came to live with the Boles family. She worked for Boles in the afternoons and attended David Lipscomb College for a time in the mornings. She lived in the Boles home until the deaths of H. Leo Boles and Ida Meiser Boles. Over the years she came to live more as a daughter to the elderly couple, and an only child could not have been more devoted and loyal to both.

Violet lived in the "golden years" of Boles' declining life and took down all of his dictations. She then typed them into beautiful manuscript forms. This is how the *Holy Spirit* finally came to be a book. At the close of the Freed-Hardeman lectures, N. B. Hardeman, L. L. Brigance and C. P. Roland urged Boles to put his lectures on the Holy Spirit in book form. Boles began his research on the work in earnest with the assistance of B. C. Goodpasture. Boles collected every book he could find on the Holy Spirit until a whole shelf was filled. When he went away for a meeting, he carried two or three along to read. He would mark statements in each book with a large question mark, or he would write "little or no good," or "author cannot prove his point," "too much speculation," and so on.

Boles was up for a working day at 4:30 or 5:00 a.m., he would dress neatly for the day and any visitor who might drop by. He would retire to his library to pray for judgment for the day's labor. He would read quietly until 7:00 o'clock when it was rising time for other members of the household. After breakfast the work began. He would prepare a chapter outline "to see where he could go." He checked every scripture reference to the Holy Spirit with the best commentaries. On a particularly troublesome point, he would drive down to the Advocate office to discuss it with B. C. Goodpasture. However, the trip downtown to visit with the editor was a daily ritual when Boles was at home.

Boles would not turn loose until he traveled every avenue of approach to the problem. He would continue studying until he was certain he had the correct solution. B. C. Goodpasture said that Boles would defend his position until it was clear that he was on the losing end of the logic. They said up in DeKalb County that the Boles family were just naturally argumentative. Some even said that if a Boles were to drown that he would be so contrary they would look for his body upstream! This is how Boles used his logic to check his thinking against a possible error. Those who best knew Boles were not surprised to find him dogmatically supporting their point of view that he had so recently opposed.

Boles dictated very slowly, and his secretaries learned through his gentle rebukes never to interrupt nor to interfere with his slow deliberate pace. Violet said to him on one occasion—"Come on Brother Boles, get your brain to working." He turned and chided her with a little lecture. When tears welled up in her eyes, he said, "I am sorry I had to be cross." However, he would welcome teasing while working on Sunday school materials just to break the monotony. In writing the Holy Spirit manuscript, some whole days would be spent in re-doing the labors of the previous day. He had the patience of Job in clearing up a point in the Scriptures. Violet sould say, "Can't you leave that comment out and let's go on." Such a comment would be answered with "that is the trouble with most authors" (pointing to the commentaries on the shelf) ; "they either didn't know or were too lazy to find out."

The typing desk was set at an angle so he could read the copy being typed, and no amount of audible sighs increased his deliberate pace which included just which punctuation mark to put in. Each of his secretaries had to adjust to his reading over her shoulders. Some days he would write a chapter, and when his energy flagged, the day was ended. He never pushed his work and rarely himself. There are some people who stoutly maintain that H. Leo Boles would never have been the success he came to be had it not been for that right index finger. Even in dictation he would be pointing that finger as if he were in the pulpit. Finally the manuscript was carried to the Gospel Advocate office. When it was published in 1942, he came home with a copy of it under his arm "grinning like a school boy." He sat down and read the book as if he had never seen it before!

The picture of H. Leo Boles at work on the Adult Quarterly was much the same. His practice was to dictate one lesson a day; or if the lessons posed no difficult problem, two finished lessons resulted. Sometimes when he was pressed to meet a deadline he would work an hour or so at night. A day like this meant eight tedious hours of continual dictation. Such days were draining on Boles' energy in his later years, and he had to rest a day or two to regain his strength.

While he was writing a lesson he would look into space or stare at a book shelf in deep meditation in what seemed endless minutes of silence finally to be broken with such a comment, "Don't write this down but listen carefully." Boles was testing for clarity and simplicity. Then he would say—"Let's see if I can clear that point up a little." Woe be to the secretary who pretended to understand just to get on with the work, and a short lecture generally followed. H. Leo Boles was not a religious charlatan or a pious "four flusher." Boles spent a lifetime turning that "last stone" for each iota of information.

There is another facet to the personality of H. Leo Boles about which few know. He was a poet with the soul of a poet. Though H. Leo Boles never published his poetry, several poems including religious hymns which he composed and signed his name are extant. The poetry includes a light poem about his "school marm" sweetheart, Ida Meiser, or a poem he wrote while President of David Lipscomb College inviting the boys and girls to the annual Valentine party. The poetry from a stylistic evaluation is little better than good "doggerel verse." But had he concentrated forty-three years mastering the art of the poet another dramatic story could well be told about his life. The importance of this little known fact in his life is that Boles was an exact master of the English sentence in both verse and prose form.

Shortly after H. Leo Boles came to the Nashville School, he wrote a hymn with a purple-lead indelible pencil which is typical of his religious verse:

"The Fadeless Crown of Glory"
By
H. Leo Boles

Toil not for things that soon will cease,
But labor hard for Christ, the King,
Not for the wealth of fame, but peace,
And love, and joy of Him, we sing.

The verdant fields and faultless flower,
Of every clime and age will fade,
But the crown of glory must each hour,
Become more bright than all that's made.

To God be loyal, consecrated, true,
Make garlands for the faithful here,
And heaven hath a halo for you,
Which fadeth not but cast out fear.

Refrain

Oh, the fadeless crown of glory by
   and by we'll wear
When robed in righteousness with
   angels bright and fair
When the waving ripples run along
   the river of life,
In heaven's home of happiness free
   from care and strife,
Never fading crown of glory decked
   with jewels of love
Shall we wear eternally with the
   saints of God above.

243

The statement is made is another place that Boles was a knowledgeable man, and the statement may be enlarged to say—and in just about everything related to the church. In 1930 he wrote an article, "Early History of the Church of Christ in Nashville"; and this was followed by another the next year, "History of the Churches in Nashville." And in 1939 another important article came out in the *Gospel Advocate*, "General History of the Church in Nashville." If he had lived to be as old as Methuselah, H. Leo Boles would still be reading, thinking, writing and saying things both old and new.

Mention has been made that H. Leo Boles was a writer of letters, and he dictated thirty-five letters on the eve of his death. The amount of letters he wrote over a life time was of gargantuan proportions. In the possession of B. C. Goodpasture are seemingly endless files of his correspondence arranged in alphabetical and chronological order. H. Leo Boles wrote like he spoke for all to see and hear. Boles was not the small-souled man who engaged in petty "personal vendettas" with some of his brethren against others. There were endless efforts to draw him one way or another into some controversy. He criticized the extremist who swung as the pendulum from one extreme to the other and advised—"keep the golden mean between saying too much and too little." And he said that a "well balanced mind and life may be difficult to find, but it is to be coveted." Boles would freely discuss a position in which he possessed a competence. He respected other men and knew that a person could be better informed than he on a subject. His personal correspondence reveals that he was not a willful enemy of any man. H. Leo Boles was a magnanimous and great-souled man and "may his tribe increase." If there is a reason why his friends have not honored Boles in their life time, it may be he was just as quick to chide them for their mistakes as he was to honor them when they were deserving.

Chapter XXII
GOLDEN YEARS

When H. Leo Boles appeared on the Freed-Hardeman lectureship in January of 1937, it was not evident that he was entering a grand new era of his life. The final curtain was due to fall in the nine scant years left in his life. His worth had been often recognized and his services gratefully acknowledged. But somehow his full stature as one of the outstanding religious personalities of his time had been overlooked. Now in his fading years the honors he deserved were like the "bread upon the water" returning many fold. H. Leo Boles was a giant among the leaders of the churches of Christ which was listed in the 1940's as one of the ten largest religious groups in the United States. Furthermore, at the time of his death, Boles had been listed in *Who's Who In America* for thirty-nine years. About fifteen hundred active preachers had received a part of their training under his teaching and guidance.

In October of 1931, H. Leo Boles resigned the presidency of David Lipscomb College to become effective at the end of the school year. The responsibilities of the job had grown until it rested like a mountain on his shoulders. The Depression Years were on and the times were hard. The Board of Directors faced the task of finding someone equal to the demands of the position. With Boles soon to be gone from the college, the David Lipscomb College faculty expressed their concern in a letter which they signed and sent to the Board of Directors:

TO THE BOARD OF DIRECTORS
DAVID LIPSCOMB COLLEGE

Gentlemen:

We, the undersigned members of the faculty for the school year 1931-32, wish to make a humble suggestion. We most certainly do not desire to dictate to the board nor to hamper either it or any president of the faculty that might be selected. Nor does any selfish motive underlie what we herein say.

Inasmuch, however, as President Boles's resignation as head of the faculty has several times been published, it is reasonable to suppose that some plans concerning the administration of the college for next year will soon be made. Our suggestion must, therefore, be offered now, or even should it be judged of value it would be given too late.

For several years we have observed Brother Boles's teaching of the Bible in his classroom. As a teacher of that blessed Book his reputation is deservedly high. Comments on his ability in imparting Biblical truths to the students have often been made and by a large number of persons.

During the present year fifty-two young men are attending the college to prepare themselves as gospel preachers. We think that shows that the institution has provided a service for them—has offered instruction for which there is a demand.

Further, we wish to mention that Brother Boles was a student of the Bible under the teaching of the lamented David Lipscomb. It seems evident to us that there has been a wholesome continuity of thought and purpose flowing through the Biblical instruction which has been provided in the institution from the beginning until now. We think it would be well if the continuity were not broken in whatever plans may soon be laid.

We humbly suggest that the board consider taking whatever steps are wisest to retain Brother Boles in the chair of the Bible after his term as president shall have expired, provided his consent could be obtained. We base this suggestion on our firm conviction that Brother Boles's ability in teaching the Bible is of high order indeed and on our belief that his continuance in that work would help to further the noble ideals to which Brother Lipscomb clung and would be a blessing to the college.
October 30, 1931

Respectfully,

P. M. Walker	Margaret Davis
Jno. L. Rainey	S. C. Boyce
Max Hamrick	Ora Crabtree
R. P. Cuff	Mrs. R. S. Owen
Mrs. Otto Prater	J. D. Fenn
S. P. Pittman	Mrs. Ida C. Noble
J. Ridley Stroop	Leonidas T. Holland, Mus. Div.
Mrs. Max Hamrick	

The high regard in which the college faculty held H. Leo

Boles was justly deserved, and the reasons they gave were well anchored in the mainstream of Restoration history.

Batsell Baxter who came to the college to serve as president stayed two years. Boles continued to teach Bible in the college. Batsell Baxter found his responsibilities a heart-breaking job. The first thing he did was to cut the salary of each teacher half-in-two. At the end of two years he resigned to return to Abilene Christian College as head of the Bible Department, and the Board of Directors elected E. H. Ijams to the presidency. H. Leo Boles quit the college for his last time with Baxter's departure. He continued to serve as Secretary of the Board of Directors; his name finally disappears from the college catalog after the regular school year 1938-1939. Boles' leaving the college, however, was not regarded with any great degree of apprehension. He was a good worker with other chores to do. H. Leo Boles stood as one among many of his gifted contemporaries; no one regarded him as indispensable and Boles himself would have been the first to agree.

Boles was often seen on the Lipscomb campus in the following years, and he attended the January lectureships when he was in town. His home on Granny White Pike was just across the street from the campus. Whatever happened to David Lipscomb College mattered to him. David Lipscomb, the man, was described before the turn of the twentieth century by Isaac Errett of the *Christian Standard* as the "balance wheel of the Restoration." In much the same way H. Leo Boles can be described in his relation to the college as long as he lived, and what he said and thought is still respected.

The unique qualities of H. Leo Boles may not have been recognized had it not been for his association with N. B. Hardeman in the Freed-Hardeman lectureships. Hardeman was perhaps the most colorful leader among the churches of Christ in the first half of this century. His influence among the members of the churches of Christ was widespread. The fame of Freed-Hardeman College as a good place where gospel preachers were taught the Bible spread everywhere the church was known. Hardeman would tell his students that the churches would not question their loyalty to the Bible unless their conduct proved them unworthy of confidence. Although the Freed-Hardeman students who went out to preach the gospel were easily singled out as the preachers who had received their training in the Henderson college, their willingness to stand up for the faith was generally acknowledged.

N. B. Hardeman wrote Boles a letter in the summer of 1936 saying that he was thinking about a lectureship program for preachers to run for four weeks. The lectureship would be planned to suit the needs of preachers who had been denied the opportunity to receive the benefits of college education. The tuition would be free and such practical courses as church history, spoken English, vocal music, Bible geography, and preparation and delivery of sermons were to be offered. H. Leo Boles was invited as a special teacher to assist the Freed-Hardeman faculty.

The first series of such lectureships were conducted in January of 1937. Some sixty-five preachers from seventeen states attended the school and this did not include the thirty preaching students who were enrolled in the college. The featured speakers for the lectureship were N. B. Hardeman and H. Leo Boles. Other well known preachers appearing on the program included F. B. Syrgley, Foy E. Wallace, Jr., B. C. Goodpasture, Batsell Baxter, E. H. Ijams, C. R. Nichol, John T. Lewis, J. F. Cox, J. T. Hinds, E. R. Harper, J. N. Armstrong, and I. A. Douthitt. At the conclusion of the January lectures, N. B. Hardeman celebrated with his guests at a banquet the burning of the last mortgage against Freed-Hardeman College.

The lectureship proved to be successful and L. L. Brigance said that Boles was an able and popular teacher. Plans were laid for a similar program the next year, and the Nashville evangelist was invited to return the following year and every year as long as he lived. N. B. Hardeman summed up his feelings for H. Leo Boles when he spoke at the funeral of his friend:

I think I first knew Brother Boles about twenty-five years ago. I have ever been impressed with his scholarly attainments, his love for the cause, and his devotion to the church of our Lord. The regard that

I have had for him during these years was evidenced most concretely nine years ago, when I selected him to come to Henderson and have the leading part in our special courses designed to instruct rather than simply to entertain those who came to attend.

For nine years he came and taught these courses. Every time he delivered himself to the satisfaction and the admiration of those who assembled. He stayed in my home for two weeks at a time, or eighteen weeks in all. During these years we learned to appreciate him as a man and we counted him as a member of the family. I had occasion to observe his untiring efforts, and many times suggested to him that he ought to let up and take time out day by day, but he had so many obligations upon him that he felt it of necessity to continue to accomplish that which he had in mind.

The lectureship at Freed-Hardeman College the following January was equally an outstanding success. N. B. Hardeman was a most powerful individual among the leaders of the church in the thirties and early forties. It was perhaps as a yoke-fellow with Hardeman that Boles was seen at his best. The two men, who were not now rivals in any respect, complemented the splendid talents of each other as they went about their teaching duties. At the conclusion of the 1938 session the preachers who were present drew up the following resolution:

Be it resolved that we render Brethren N. B. Hardeman, H. Leo Boles, L. L. Brigance, and co-laborers our heartfelt thanks, our warmest love, and our highest esteem for service so faithfully rendered, assuring them our support, our influence, and our prayers so long as they are loyal to the plain revealed will of the Lord. *Be it resolved* that we hold them in the highest honor, the most lofty esteem, and deserved appreciation.

The Freed-Hardeman January lectures had in a brief time become one of the most popular features among the preachers of the church. The time was shortened to three weeks for the 1939 lectureship. This was an especially memorable lectureship. Daniel Sommer—that ancient foe of the Christian colleges—spoke at Freed-Hardeman College. He had been invited to come and express his views. N. B. Hardeman in a fine humor declared he was delighted to have Brother Sommer to teach in his college.

249

Claude F. Witty was invited to come and explain the Unity Movement. It was during that occasion that H. Leo Boles engaged Witty in a "question and answer" session about the movement; the auditorium was filled and many were visiting preachers who sat in rapt attention while Boles fired ten questions to Witty which were typical of the way he went about his work. Some of Boles' questions were:

(1) Are you not a self-appointed representative of the churches of Christ?

(2) Have you told Murch and his brethren there can be no unity until he puts the organ aside and gives up the missionary societies?

(3) For union you say that both sides must move. Now what will the churches of Christ have to give up?

(4) What will they have to begin teaching that they are not now teaching?

(5) What will they have to begin practicing that they are not now practicing? What will they have to quit teaching and practicing in order to effect this union?

(6) The Christian Church has gone off. It has organized measures to "perpetuate the cause of division." How can it come back without abandoning these things? How can we "go to them till they abandon the things which cause the division?"

This is how H. Leo Boles lived out his life. He would not only draw the line, but he would hew it right down to the end. Whoever had some new idea or plan to promote among his brethren sooner or later had to come by Boles to explain his position. For friend or stranger, the Scriptural test was always the same. H. Leo Boles learned this lesson well from David Lipscomb, and he was equally as good a teacher.

When the Freed-Hardeman lectures began in the first month of 1940, Boles was there and starring downstage center. Someone has said that comparisons are odious. Anyhow the human race is addicted to the practice. Ira A. Douthitt once commented that if forty men who were total strangers came together in a company that in a short time N. B. Hardeman would be singled out as their natural

250

leader. For the first time Hardeman and Boles stood side by side and comparisons had to be made. It was apparent that N. B. Hardeman had developed a great fondness for H. Leo Boles. Hardeman always found it a little awkward to acknowledge that the other sister colleges could be quite the equal of his own school. This is to say that N. B. Hardeman was an unabashed partisan for his own school, and those who attended there came away with much the same spirit. H. Leo Boles, once a competitor, was now playing on his team; and Boles' popularity soon made him know that he had picked a winner. The preachers who knew and heard Hardeman and Boles in those years sensed that N. B. Hardeman had accepted Boles into a full and equal partnership. The Henderson educator generously recognized that H. Leo Boles came as close as any one man could in being a spokesman for his brethren; at least, they invariably called upon Boles when they wanted a man who could say with confidence what the Bible taught on a subject. L. L. Brigance phrased the point:

> Brother Boles had grown in the confidence of the brethren until he was probably regarded as the best 'authority' in the church on what the Bible teaches on any and all subjects. When it came to a statement of facts, in the Bible or out, one could depend on what he said. When there was doubt as to the teachings of the Scriptures on any matter, his opinion or judgment was as good as the best.

Like the clicking of a counter the last years of Boles' life were checking off. Each was a good year and better than the preceding, and it goes without saying that Boles was excited and pleased that he stood so highly in the esteem of his brethren. He was little given to patting himself on the back; if they came, he waited for the plaudits from others. It would be almost impossible now to trace his busy life in any one year. Fortunately he told in the *Advocate* what his work in 1943 had been. During that year he preached in eighteen gospel meetings in nine states. This year was an exception since he preached in more meetings than was his general practice. He baptized two hundred and eleven persons. This did not include the number of restorations to the church. He conducted fourteen funerals, and performed five marriages. On eighteen occasions he spoke to as many colleges and schools. During some of his revivals, he conducted special classes for elders, deacons, Bible teachers, and young people. In most of the meetings he spoke twice daily, and he added: "Not a single service has been missed; neither was the writer tardy at any service."

Each January he travelled to Henderson to teach his classes and each year found a sizeable and enthusiastic audience largely of preachers eager to hear him. No one lecture was especially marked above the others; but the January session in 1945, as well as the preceding year, was noted in his journal. He was busy morning and evening and commented that "there were more than three hundred preachers present. Made my home with N. B. Hardeman. In fact, I have made my home with him each of the nine years. We planned a program for 1946. Received $100.00."

Though Boles never complained, there may be no doubt he missed being away from David Lipscomb College. Not until 1940 was he invited back to have a part on the Lipscomb lectureship. A. C. Pullias was serving as director of the lectureship. Boles spoke on ten different occasions in three scheduled sessions during the third week in January of 1945.

During the last session, the assembled group considered the topic, "Keeping the Church Pure." Boles wrote in his journal that "the entire hour was given to the discussion of the question—'Can a church choose to make contributions to colleges, orphan homes, and old folks' homes?'—the discussion was confined to contribution to colleges." Boles at this time just one year before his death, as he had on other occasions, made his thinking clear and unequivocal on this issue. He had written for the *Advocate* in 1935 that there are " 'old peoples' homes,' 'orphan homes,' 'Bible colleges,' 'missionaries,' both home and foreign, and the building of church houses in destitute places. All of these make earnest appeals for help."

Boles two years later in the *Advocate* wrote that Christians are under obligation to support these good works. He singled out the Christian colleges and clearly said "that churches have a right to contribute to these if

252

they so desire." H. Leo Boles was not the sort of man who endeavored to re-arrange the thinking of others. He simply tried his best to understand and interpret what the Bible taught.

The Lipscomb lecture in 1945 provided a highlight in the life of Boles. He wrote in his journal—"nearly all the speakers were 'my boys.' " And he added—"The auditorium was filled—many compliments were received. A. C. Pullias said that I had kept the lecture week from being a failure." An annual dinner honoring preachers of forty and more years of service was especially marked this year. When the name of H. Leo Boles was called the applause was warm and lasting.

With the opening of the school year in the fall of 1944, Athens Clay Pullias and Willard Collins were spearheading a massive expansion program for David Lipscomb College. The announcement as carried in the *Nashville Banner*, October 16, 1944, from the office of President Batsell Baxter, that a group of business leaders had pledged to give $300,000 to the school on the condition that the school raise a similar amount. A. C. Pullias who was serving as Vice-President of the college was appointed chairman of the campaign to raise the matching amount. Willard Collins, the preacher of the Old Hickory congregation at that time and now Vice-President of the college, was named as Pullias' assistant. President Baxter further outlined the program that the plans included making the school a standard four year college with full recognition by the highest accrediting agencies. This was one of Boles' early dreams for the school, and it came true in the year of his death.

H. Leo Boles never had any trouble making up his mind about how the college should be run while he served as president, and there was never a day he was not concerned with how others ran the school. He was wrong many times but he was always right in one respect. That was his unfailing loyalty to the school and its original purpose. He was among the first to respond to the plea of the Lipscomb Expansion Program. A. C. Pullias wrote him a letter dated February 15, 1945, which said:

May we express our appreciation for your generous contribution of $50 to the Lipscomb Expansion Program. Every dollar given means two dollars invested in our young people. You will be pleased to know at the first report made February 2, 1945, a total of $86,636.20 had been raised in money. This does not include promises or pledges. We feel that this amount is substantial and that by hard work the goal will certainly be achieved. Any encouragement which you may give others to make contributions to this worthy work will be sincerely appreciated.

Just one full year of Boles' life remained at the writing of the letter.

H. Leo Boles made his plans to be with both David Lipscomb and Freed-Hardeman colleges in January of 1946; and in a letter dated December 11, 1945, he wrote to A. C. Pullias:

Your kind letter of December 6 has been received. I appreciate the invitation to have a part on your Annual Lecture Week Program. It will give me pleasure to be present and do my best to make the program a success.

He was also laying his plans to go to Henderson for the 1946 lectureship which always preceded the David Lipscomb College program. G. E. Woods and his wife who were going to Freed-Hardeman College called by Boles' home for him since he had made arrangements with the Woods to ride down with them. When they arrived, Boles was in the doctor's office downtown; and he phoned back to tell them to go on since the doctor had ordered him home to bed. From his deathbed H. Leo Boles dictated to Violet this letter to N. B. Hardeman dated January 8, 1946:

I regretted to hear that you are in bed and I hope that you are now up, and that you have a good enrollment at the Special Courses.

Most of all I regret not being with you. I want you to express to the group my great disappointment in not being able to come. I have been preaching a little more than forty-two years, and this is the first time that I have had to cancel an engagement for a meeting or lectures. You must know that it is a sore disappointment to me. Express my love to all and say that I am praying that the greatest good may be accomplished.

My trouble is a swollen limb caused by a blocking of the large vein in the left leg. The trouble began in my ankle last September, but I continued my work. I have been examined by five doctors, but they seem not to find the trouble (I doubt if they have found it yet). The swelling is extended from the ankle to the calf of the leg and is now in the thigh. The doctor wanted me to go to the hospital, but I told him that I had a better bed at home and as good a nurse as could be found. I am in bed with my leg elevated to give nature a chance to correct the trouble without an operation; but if it does not clear up within a reasonable time I will have to submit to the operation. Fortunately I am not suffering very much except when I am on the limb.

Again, I express my regrets at not being with you. Ask the brethren to pray for me.

H. Leo Boles stayed busy every day during the closing weeks of his life. He answered letters, kept up his work with the *Gospel Advocate,* and visited with his many friends who came to see him. One letter is of significant interest. David Lipscomb College was undergoing other sweeping changes. The Board of Directors had decided to make David Lipscomb College a senior Liberal Arts College. In 1944 while Boles had been in a meeting with what is now the Druid Hill congregation in Atlanta, where J. M. Powell was preaching; he received a long distance telephone call from S. H. Hall feeling him out on the possibility of his taking over as president of David Lipscomb College when E. H. Ijams resigned. Batsell Baxter came instead to serve as president for the next two years. When Baxter resigned the presidency of the college, the Board of Directors elected Athens Clay Pullias to the position. H. Leo Boles wrote a letter just before his death to the president-elect who had been a student when Boles was president of the college:

I read with interest the announcement of your being elected president of David Lipscomb College, and hasten to congratulate you on this elevation. I know of no one better qualified for the position than you; you have worked in the institution as a student, teacher, official and manager until you know thoroughly every detail of the work required of the president. You know the ideals of it and its mission among educational institutions. You know the dire

255

need of giving to the young people of this generation a Christian education.

I need not remind you that with the honor conferred upon you by the Board of Directors that there is a corresponding responsibility. You have a responsibility now in the brotherhood of making David Lipscomb College the faithful servant of the brotherhood. With the Expansion program by which David Lipscomb College is to become a Senior College the field of service for the institution is enlarged; this adds greater weight to your responsibilities. I am interested in the college; I have had a close connection with it for 32 years; I could not lose interest in it after having given the best years of my life to it. I pray that you may measure up to the full responsibility that rests upon you and that you may guide the institution in filling its mission. Feel free to demand me when I can serve you.

On the eve of his death his interests were the same of forty years ago—he was writing for the *Advocate,* and watching the course of David Lipscomb College. He was assured that his spell of illness was changing for the better.

H. Leo Boles had been remarkably healthy through his whole life. His eating habits were as strictly disciplined as his other habits of sleeping, work, or his diversions for pleasure. He never used tooth paste because he did not believe in its value; not that he had any scruples, he simply thought that natural salt was best. At the age of seventy-one not a tooth was missing. For over forty years he weighed 165 pounds unless strenuous revivals reduced him; even then he never weighed less than 160 pounds or more than 166.

After his return from Dallas in November, he had been in constant pain. While he worked at his desk, a drawer had been pulled out where he could rest his foot upon a pillow placed on the drawer. The doctors at first were unable to learn the nature of his illness and attributed the swelling to his constant standing. Later his illness was diagnosed as phlebitis. He was put to bed January 7, on the eve of his proposed trip to the Freed-Hardeman lectures. This day was planned to be like just another work day in his life. Though he had the patience to experience physical pain, he was too busy to be sick.

It was in the early morning of February 7, 1946, his wife and Violet were awakened to hear his cry of pain. Dr. S. T. Ross who was Boles' physician was urgently summoned to come to the residence. Margaret Howell, the school nurse and friend of H. Leo Boles, came over immediately to wait on him, and she was joined by a close neighbor of the Boles family, Mrs. F. B. Owen. An attack of pneumonia had complicated his phlebitis, but Boles was over the pneumonia and recovering from the other. B. C. Goodpasture and his wife, Cleveland, came over to be with their friend in his dying hours. On Thursday morning of that same day at 10:30 a.m., the soul of Henry Leo Boles took wings.

The funeral services of H. Leo Boles were conducted at the Grace Avenue Church in Nashville, on February 9, at 10:30. He had preached his last sermon at the Grace Avenue Church just one month before his death on the subject—"The Unfinished Prayer." For thirty years he had preached at Grace Avenue the first Sunday of every month when he was in the city. He had left a sealed request that his funeral services were to be conducted by N. B. Hardeman, S. H. Hall, and B. C. Goodpasture. The congregational singing was led by Mack Wayne Craig who was then preacher for the Reid Avenue church and is now Dean of David Lipscomb College. H. Leo Boles was buried in Woodlawn Memorial Park in Nashville. The simple words "At Home" mark his last earthly resting place.

Ida Meiser Boles outlived her husband nine years. She continued to live in their home on Granny White Pike; and during the last years of her life, she attended worship services at the Reid Avenue church. She was ill several months prior to her passing and was confined to her bed for several weeks before her death. Violet DeVaney who became secretary to B. C. Goodpasture after the death of Boles continued to live in the Boles' home and attended the widow of H. Leo Boles to the moment she passed away. Death came to Ida Meiser Boles on Monday evening, October 17, 1955. Her funeral services were preached in the Reid Avenue church auditorium on Wednesday by B. C. Goodpasture and J. E. Choate, then minister of the church. They were assisted by I. C. Finley who served for many

257

years as an elder of the congregation with H. Leo Boles. She was buried by the side of her husband. The words over her grave site read "With God."

What was this man, H. Leo Boles, like? In the memorial issue of the *Gospel Advocate* for March 28, 1946, special tribute was paid to him. Some of the statements are especially pertinent. Gus Nichols of Jasper, Alabama, one of the beloved evangelists of the church for many years wrote: "I reached the conclusion some years ago that Brother Boles was the greatest man known to me in all the brotherhood."

H. Leo Boles was not a perfect man and none knew this better than his friends. T. Q. Martin, a famed evangelist of his day, said he had known Boles for a long long time; and he said that "Brother Boles was somewhat in a class to himself. He could be, and was, 'brutally' frank with friend and foe, and still retained the respect of both."

There is another side to the picture that needs to be told. Not everyone admired H. Leo Boles without reservation and some said so. One of his former students writes perhaps the best thumb nail sketch of the man:

> I often benefitted by his counsel and friendship. As I gained maturity, I learned to evaluate Brother Boles with somewhat more objectivity. To me, he is still a complete enigma. He would reason most logically, one should never rely on insurance, and entertain Brother A. M. Burton and his wife in the girls' dining hall. He would insist that higher education was a handicap to a Christian and then he would race over to Vanderbilt to meet his next class as a graduate student. . . . These seeming inconsistencies never tell all the story of H. Leo Boles. The more you study his achievements alongside his shortcomings, and the more you realize that God has to depend on mortal men like Brother Boles, the more you feel like shouting: "How Great Thou Art.'

If a "foolish consistency is the hobgoblin of little minds," then H. Leo Boles would not qualify in this respect. For that matter, he took out a $5000 insurance policy not long before his death.

The grand symphony of Boles' life was played out to the very end. The themes were clear and distinct. With the poised pen or the lifted Bible on the pulpit platform, the performance was as good as the best. Indeed there were sour notes along the sweep of the grand movements of his life.

One of his favorite poems was, "Crossing the Bar," that had been set to music and often sung by the Lipscomb quartet. The last lines somehow express in a simple fashion what should be said about the passing of Henry Leo Boles:

Sunset and evening star and one clear call for me!
And may there be no moaning of the bar
When I put to sea.
But such a tide as moving seems asleep,
Too full for sound and foam,
When that which drew from out the boundless deep
Turns again home.

Perhaps the finest footnote to the life of H. Leo Boles was added the day after his death in an editorial that appeared in the *Nashville Banner*:

In the death of H. Leo Boles the church of Christ has sustained a keenly-felt loss in its preaching-teaching ranks, and a genuine sorrow in his passing is shared by all who knew him.

His was pioneer Southern stock in the religious field to which early in life he set his hand. The call he heard and heeded as a young man led him through long and active years into fields that were "white unto harvest," and to the labor of his calling he dedicated every effort of a talented service. Evangelist, educator, writer, his was the forthright address of faith and courage. An able speaker and gifted writer, it was in these fields that Middle Tennessee knew him best, but it was in the educational field that his work will linger in the years yet to come.

He helped build David Lipscomb College into its present stature, with administrative service that continues to bear fruit. In the classroom his life touched many lives. On those lives his own is indelibly impressed—its vision, its energies. They were close to his heart. They are among the thousands who will long remember him. He was a good and faithful servant, and would prefer to be remembered as that.

Like the Apostle Paul, H. Leo Boles would have said

259

that he was "the least" among the pioneer restorers of New Testament Christianity. But church historians can do no less than to honor H. Leo Boles by placing him in the ranks of Alexander Campbell, Barton W. Stone, Tolbert Fanning, and David Lipscomb, whose names are immortalized in the pioneer days of the Restoration Movement.

INDEX

261

262

263

www.ingramcontent.com/pod-product-compliance
Lightning Source LLC
Chambersburg PA
CBHW031945080426
42735CB00007B/272